"Ollie"

The Autobiography of
IAN HOLLOWAY

With David Clayton

Green Umbrella Publishing

This edition first published in the UK in 2007
By Green Umbrella Publishing

© Green Umbrella Publishing 2007

www.ollieontour.co.uk

Publishers: Jules Gammond and Vanessa Gardner

Creative Director: Kevin Gardner

Picture Credits: Getty Images and PA Photos
Special thanks to Jean Holloway for providing family albums
"Ollie" caricature John Ireland

Robert Segal Representation

Printed and bound by J. H. Haynes & Co. Ltd., Sparkford

ISBN: 978-1-906229-17-7

For Mum and Dad

Contents

Acknowledgements

First off, I'd like to thank my wife Kim for all her love and support over the years, and for giving me my beautiful children, William, Chloe, Eve and Harriet.

To my mother and father-in-law, Wendy and Terry, for creating Kim in the first place – I didn't know you had it in you Ter!

To my brother John, whom I love very much.

To my sister Sue and her husband Phil, for their unbelievable love and support and outstanding baby-sitting service that's still going strong today.

For Becky, my niece, and her husband Vaughan and their baby daughter Iris. Becky is the world's most natural signer.

For Luke, the best nephew I could have wished for, and one cool customer.

To Kim's sister Trudi and her husband Dave. We love you both very much. We definitely prefer the new you, Trude, make sure you save us a basket of runner-beans.

To the scout who first found me, Joe Davis. To coaches Bobby Campbell, Bobby Jones, Colin Dobson and Bill Dodgin Sr, for my early grounding at Bristol Rovers.

For Gordon Bennett, my first mentor – thanks for being right in your advice and guidance that I still tap into today. It's fantastic to have you at Argyle and I hope we can work together for many more years to come.

Thanks to Sheila Marson for all her help during my time as QPR manager – I couldn't have done what I did without her and I'm happy to say she remains a close family friend to this day.

To David Clayton, my ghost-writer, for helping turn hours of taped interviews into the book you are now holding. Thanks also to his wife Sarah and their children Harry, Jaime and Chrissie for allowing me to 'borrow' him for several days at a time.

To Robert Segal – my agent and trusted friend – and his lovely family. I've enjoyed our long conversations over the years and look forward to many more, and I thank him for the excellent team of people he assigns to look after me.

To Gerry Francis, for rescuing me and showing great belief, and helping me through difficult times and teaching me to love the game again. Your knowledge and guidance I will never forget.

To all the friends I've met or played alongside during my career – you all know who you are – thanks for everything. My dad told me I'd meet some wonderful people in football, and he was right.

Finally, I've left this bit until last on purpose because without these two I wouldn't be here in the first place. To my mum, Jean – short legs, big heart – you're lovely Short One. Dad, you're my inspiration, then and now.

Ollie, Plymouth, Summer 2007

Foreword

By Gerry Francis

Ian Holloway – 'Ollie' – remains the only player I've ever paid for out of my own pocket, so if that isn't an indication of how much I thought of him as a player and a person, I don't know what else is.

I was well aware at the time how highly regarded he was by Bristol Rovers fans (and still is) and I thought he would be the ideal person to build my team around.

I had to loan the club the money to bring him back to Bristol, which was a major risk for me because Rovers were in a very bad state financially, but it ended up being the best £10,000 I ever spent.

Ollie had been struggling at Brentford, mainly due to the effects of a nasty dose of glandular fever, and I could see when I went to watch him play for their reserves at Aldershot that his confidence was at rock bottom.

After speaking with Brentford, I called Ollie and I think he found it hard to believe that anybody would be interested in signing him at that point and actually said as much to me. I told him I wanted to bring him back to Bristol, his home city, because I could get him playing again and also make him a better player. That was enough to convince him and I think it was the ideal move for him at that time in his career, and he never looked back afterwards.

It's hard to express my admiration for him because he was such an influential figure in my team, both on and off the pitch. He had a heart as big as a lion and wasn't afraid to speak out if he felt someone wasn't pulling their weight, regardless of reputation. I don't think either of us imagined just how long our working relationship would stretch to when he first started playing for me, but I think it was in the region of 10 years, all told.

I recall the day Ollie's dad died and the way he handled himself, deciding he wanted to play for Rovers later that same day. It was a massive game for us and I told him that if he wanted to play, it was fine by me. I knew he'd want to go and play for his dad and he was magnificent on the night, helping us win 4-0, though afterwards in the dressing room the emotion and grief hit him hard, which I'd thought would happen.

Ollie was a terrific trainer, too, and he never gave less than 100 per cent, either when he trained or when he played, and you can never have enough players like that in your squad.

When I left to manage QPR, I felt that a few players at Rovers were good enough to play in the Premiership and Ollie was one of them.

I got the impression after he arrived that, because of all the big name players we had at Loftus Road back then, initially he felt as though maybe he was a little out of place. The truth was that he'd earned the right to play at the highest level as much as anybody on my playing staff, and he served the club with distinction during his time at Rangers.

I also brought Gary Penrice to QPR around the same time. 'Pen' had been with me before at Rovers before being sold to Watford. Pen and Ollie were an amazing double act and they were the heart and soul of the dressing room at Rovers and they carried that on at QPR. They could have you in fits of laughter all day long, but on the other hand the pair of them together could drive you nuts.

I always felt Ollie was someone who could handle responsibility, which is important if you want to be a leader or manager. He used to take the penalties at Rovers, which is a very individual responsibility, and he converted some really high-pressure spot kicks on our way to Wembley and winning the championship in 1989/90. As somebody who used to take penalties myself, I know what a burden that can sometimes be and only a few will take on that type of responsibility throughout the season. It's the only time football is not a team game and becomes an individual situation.

I was very pleased to see Ollie go on to become manager of Bristol Rovers, where he did a fantastic job for the club he loved.

When I made the decision to step down as manager at QPR, Ollie was the man I recommended to the chairman and I'm happy to say they took my advice, because he went on to do an excellent job in tremendously difficult circumstances.

I think he's gone on to prove what a good young manager he really is and if anyone can take Plymouth Argyle into the Premiership, it's Ollie.

As a man, I admire his passion, loyalty and commitment, not just in football, but to his family. Having to raise four kids aged four and under, plus deal with the fact that his three daughters were all born profoundly deaf AND play Premiership football must have been all but impossible at times, but Kim and Ollie managed it somehow and I know how proud he is of his wife and children, and rightly so – they are a credit to him.

I feel honoured that Ollie thought of me to open his autobiography and I'm sure there will be another book in the pipeline – talking was never a problem for Ollie, and I wish him every success in the future because, boy, he's earned it.

Gerry Francis, August 2007

Chapter 1

Believe

I must confess I had to have my arm twisted to write this book because my initial reaction was, 'who'd want to read about the life story of Ian Holloway?' I'm still not convinced this won't end up in the bargain baskets of book shops around the country because let's face it, I've not got the track record of Sir Alex Ferguson or Jose Mourinho – at the moment – even if I am better looking than both of them.

Maybe a few Argyle fans will be curious enough to pick it up and I'm sure there'll be one or two Bristol Rovers supporters who might bother, too. Throw in the odd QPR fan, my mum and Tim and Helen off Soccer AM and we might creep into double figures. Who knows what life will throw at you next? I've learned to take each day as it comes in both my professional and personal life over the past 44 years, as you'll discover in the next 200 or so pages, and if you've not shed at least one tear or had a couple of good belly laughs by the time you finish, then I've not done my job. Lovely jubbly!

So, like all good yarns, which I hope this is, I'll start at the beginning. My mum and dad gave me a wonderful home life and we were a family in every sense of the word. My dad, Bill Holloway, was an only child whose mother died when he was just a toddler but he was fortunate enough to be put in a loving home and adopted within a year by a relative on his mother's side. Sadly, he was never actually told that until he was 13 and then it was only because of circumstances that left no other choice. The man he'd thought was his natural father was blown up during the Second World War. He'd been serving in the Home Guard when a German bomb landed just 500 yards from the family home with the poor bugger right underneath it.

Not long after, a life insurance man brought a cheque to my dad's house and when he answered the door, the bloke looked at his documentation and asked, "Is your step-mum in, son?"

Understandably confused, dad said, "What are you on about? You've got that wrong, I think…", but the bloke insisted he was right, tapping his documentation that suggested exactly that, just as the woman dad had thought of as his natural mother ran down the stairs screaming, "Oh my God, no!"

It was a hell of way to find out he'd been adopted and, hardly surprisingly, it took him a long time to come to terms with it, but he did eventually. Rather than developing into some kind of insecure, untrusting adult, however, that shocking revelation moulded him into the most wonderful husband and father anyone could wish for. His loss would be our gain, because whatever emotions might have been stirred within him by his own experiences, they only served to make him protect and love his own children all the more. He sheltered us under his protective wings and all he ever really cared about was his family and doing right by us. Whatever we wanted was more important to him than anything else in the world, and he'd go about trying to get us it in his own, old fashioned way.

Christened William Holloway, he was born in 1928 – old school stock, as they say. He'd open the door for ladies, pick up their hanky, and was always a perfect gentleman in their company. He never swore in front of my mother – though he'd make up for it when he was with his mates at the match because he was a man's man, too. He loved football and he was a fair player – much better than he'd ever let on, and if he allowed himself one passion outside of his devotion for his family, it was football, something I would happily inherit from him.

He was dark-haired and fairly dark-skinned for a Bristolian so he'd often got mistaken for an Italian, which used to annoy him a hell of a lot. "You from the old country?" he'd occasionally get asked from some olive-skinned stranger. "No, I'm bloody not! I'm English and proud of it," he'd bark back.

My mum was christened Jean Malcolm Young – her dad had given her the middle name of Malcolm and she absolutely hated it! Her parents were both Scottish, but she was brought up in Saltash in Devon and attended a local grammar school there. She had two elder brothers, Bert and Tom, and she was five years younger than my dad.

My parents first met on a train coming over the River Tamar. They started chatting politely about the weather and both felt comfortable in each other's company. She liked him and he liked her and that journey turned out not just to be a means to get from A to B, but the meeting of two hearts and minds that had been destined to join since the day they were born – if you believe in that kind of thing, of course, like I do! Mum was wary of this handsome stranger, though, if for no reason other than because he was a sailor. Her father had been a chief petty officer in the Royal Navy and that had left her with a lasting impression of men who went to sea for months on end, travelling the world with a different girl at every port, so the legend would have us believe. She didn't see her dad much as she was growing up, or care for some of his antics when he did come home. He'd drink too much and would shout a lot when he returned on shore leave and it was obvious his real life was on the ship, not in a home built from bricks and mortar. She knew from an early age that she didn't want to be a sailor's wife and if the good-looking, personable William Holloway intended on continuing his adventures at sea, this would be one port he would have to sail on past. After he plucked up enough courage to ask whether or not they might meet again at some point, she told him straight – if he was serious about courting her, he'd have to leave the Navy. Wham! No messing, no ifs or buts – those were her conditions and, of course, her test of how serious he really was – but that's exactly what he did, no doubt already love-struck! It suited dad, in all honesty, because he'd never really wanted a life at sea, anyway. His heart had been elsewhere when he'd joined up – Eastville, to be precise – then home of Bristol Rovers Football Club, where he had once had a trial. He would have been offered a contract, too, had he been patient enough, but he got fed up waiting (another trait I'd inherit) and went to sea instead, probably wanting to be as far away from his boyhood dreams as possible. He wasn't the first man to sail into the horizon leaving a shattered dream behind and he won't be the last.

So Jean and William met, fell in love, got married and moved up to Bristol to live with dad's side of the family, and soon after their first son was born – my brother, John. Life wasn't easy, but they were blissfully happy together and when mum fell pregnant for the second time with my sister, Sue, dad managed to get a brand new council house in the small Bristol suburb of Cadbury Heath.

The grass in the garden hadn't even had time to grow yet, but my dad was as chuffed as a badger when he first got the keys. He even managed to keep it from mum until it was all signed and sealed, so it was a complete surprise when he eventually told her they had a new home in which to raise their young family. Fantastic!

I was conceived and born at that house – 175 Earlstone Crescent – making my way into the world on March 12, 1963. The house has only ever had the Holloway family living in it because it had just been built and was part of a new housing estate, and mum's still there to this day.

They were a perfect match in every way. Mum is a very kind-hearted, warm and wonderful person – a motherly mum, if that makes any sense – whom my dad loved very much. He was a gregarious character, very out-going and very much a people person. He gave everyone a lot of love and was very generous, all of which, I believe, came back to him. He was a man of statements and he liked to say things that influenced me, picked up from here, there and everywhere. He wanted to be a rock in our lives having not had his own father around from the age of 13 onwards, but he was, in actual fact, more of a mountain. He was very independent, strong-minded and stubborn. The stuff dad said was so clear and concise that I remember everything as if he'd said it yesterday and I'll be forever in his debt for that.

My brother John is nine years older than I am and is very well-read and intelligent. He found school very easy and ended up going to Kingsfield Grammar in Bristol. My sister is six years older than me and is one of the kindest people you'll ever meet in your life – an embodiment of our parents' nature and beliefs.

John had it tough because dad would be harder on him simply because he was the first child. "You're the oldest, you should know better…" he'd tell him, even if it had been Sue or me that had done something wrong. He was very strict and very hard on John in that respect, but he handled it well. Dad was very much a boys-don't-cry sort and I think he favoured my sister slightly, because she could get away with things John and I would land in hot water for.

Being the youngest, though, I got a lot of mum's attention and thinking back I was very astute at getting it – I was playing the game and playing it bloody well, too. Whenever mum popped out, I'd side up against John because, bluntly, I preferred my sister to him back then. There was a lot of arguing in my early years, usually caused by me or over me. I'd cry on tap when mum got home from shopping or tending an elderly relative and it worked most of the time. Even if she thought I'd been bad, if she gave me a slap on the leg I swear she'd pull back a bit just before she hit me! I was a bit of a grass on John and I'd squeal on him because I knew how to manipulate the situation to my advantage and I can't say I was a particularly nice kid, in all honesty. I'd rather go out and play with my sister and her friends rather than stay with John because all he wanted to do was sit and read, which I couldn't relate to. I just wanted to be outside kicking a ball around and if that meant hanging on to Sue's coat-tails to get out, no problem.

I always had a keen sense of fairness and if I felt something wasn't right, I couldn't let it go. Being the youngest, the pocket money I got was less than John's and Sue's, which I didn't think was right and obviously my curfew time in the evening was earlier, too, which of course was right, though I didn't think so at the time. I always seemed to get the wrong end of the stick. I was so easy to punish it was a joke, because all dad had to do was stop me playing football – end of story. He'd just send me to bed if I'd done anything wrong and I daren't answer him back – once he'd spoken, that was it. Seething at the injustice of my world, I'd seek retribution in some form or another, albeit on a minor scale in the grand scheme of things. I used to have posters of Tottenham Hotspur on my bedroom wall because I liked their kit and wanted to be Steve Perryman or Peter Taylor, and I'd lift them up and gouge out holes behind them, taking my anger out on the walls in frustration. The Shawshank Redemption had nothing on me at that age.

I was a terrible loser too, and if dad and I had a knockabout in the garden, I was never allowed to score a goal against him – I had to try and beat him fairly and squarely. He'd tell me that I'd get a lot more satisfaction when I actually did rather than him pretend I was better than I was. "You might not have beaten me today, son," he'd say, "but one day you will and then you'll know what it feels like."

He was good at most things and would never let me win anything – even draughts or darts – but he'd always play with a sense of humour, telling me, "I'm the south-west champion of England at this," no matter what we played. Sometimes I'd lose my rag completely, even if only because he'd taken three or four of my draughts in one move, and I throw the board up in the air in a fit of pique. "Right, get to bed," he'd say. I think that's where I got my competitive edge from, though there were other influences, too. I'd even throw a strop playing pitch and putt with my mates if I didn't win and I'd throw my clubs a mile in anger if I lost. They hated me for being like that, though I had no idea they felt that way at the time because I honestly couldn't help myself.

Our house was always open to other families during the school holidays and because mum didn't work, she'd end up looking after kids whose parents did. This was my mum, with other kids getting the attention I thought should be reserved for me, so something was going to give. My mum's best friends, (Auntie) Vera and (Uncle) Gordon had three kids, Gary, Mark and Colin Thomas, all around the same age as me, give or take a couple of years, and I'd resent them being there, especially when I got sent to bed for reacting to any winding up I was on the end of. They could play the game too, and you're always going to come across as nice and polite in somebody else's house aren't you?

I think a lot of my frustration stemmed from a time my mum went into hospital to have a bunion removed. Nobody told me where she'd gone and I hadn't a clue where she was. She was missing for a week but her whereabouts were kept from me because she thought it would upset me, but by the time she came home, I just turned evil. Keeping things from me had worked exactly the opposite and I suppose I rebelled for a while.

Mum was always busy running the family, a full-time job in itself, and dad was the breadwinner. He'd leave home at the crack of dawn, not returning till early evening, and he'd come home and expect his dinner to be ready by a certain time, as most men would in those days. Sometimes he'd joke to us as he ate, "God, I wish I hadn't said I liked this…" because if he enjoyed a particular meal, mum would make sure it was a regular on the menu to the point of overkill, and you could almost tell what day it was just by what we ate for our tea.

It was hard to make ends meet, but they did it somehow and dad would come home on pay-day, hand over his wallet to mum and say "Right, there it is, all yours." He gave her complete financial responsibility for food and bills and just let her get on with it – a foolproof policy for any husband! She'd put the wallet back in a sideboard drawer when she'd accounted for everything and if there was anything left by the end of the week, he'd go up to the local working men's club and have a drink with his mates. Some weeks there'd be hardly anything left and he'd say, "Well, I suppose I won't be going out tonight, then, my love," but he'd always do it with a wry smile and a wink. He'd never deprive us for his own gain and I can remember him almost bursting with pride every time he talked about us, which I thought was a bit strange back then because we'd be in the room with him. I now know that he was just speaking his thoughts out loud.

He was very opinionated and strong, but he stood up for all that was right and good. He wouldn't be talked down to and he drummed that into all of us. "If you see someone being bullied, you step in and do something about it," he'd instil in us. He wouldn't stand for anything like that and he wouldn't allow us to, either. He was fair, in a life where most things aren't fair, and he and mum – who was unbelievably fair and the closest thing to an angel I've ever known – brought us up knowing that we came first by a million miles. They showed us how to love ourselves and how to love others, and for that, I feel very privileged.

"Come here, love, and give us a cuddle," he'd say to mum. "You're a cracker, absolutely beautiful," he'd say lifting her off the ground. He always tried to make her feel special, though it wasn't all sugar and sweet. There was jealousy on occasions because he was quite a good-looking fella and attracted glances from other women from time to time, and they'd argue like any other couple.

I'd class it as a normal family home where what we had, we had to work for and, come Christmas and birthdays, it could be tough, but we always got something because they did their best for us. I remember being asked what I wanted the most in the world prior to one birthday and I said a snooker table and dad just laughed and said, "Well there's no chance of that, try again." A week later, though, they'd somehow managed to get me it and it was a belter, too. Proper balls with a lovely green baize surface and I absolutely cherished that table and after I'd mastered it, I even beat dad and he was right, it did feel good. I still get goose pimples thinking of the first time I saw it.

During the late Sixties and early Seventies, we didn't have a car or a phone for many years and our telly was black and white, but we appreciated the things we did have rather than mope about the things we hadn't got. That was all material stuff anyway, and in terms of love and security we were one of the wealthiest families in the south-west and it was the perfect foundation for any kid to have.

Chapter 2

Gordon Bennett!

Dad had numerous jobs over the years. One of them was working in a local shop as a deliveryman and he got to know an awful lot of people during that time, driving round in his delivery van, long before the days of Tesco home delivery. He would try his hand at anything so long as he was able to collect a wage and provide for us all and he put his heart and soul into whatever he did.

I didn't care where I went so long as I could spend time with him, though our mutual love of football was the basis of our special bond. I remember being aged around six and Dad saying to me, "I hope you like football, son, because if you do, you'll meet some wonderful people through being involved." He never forced me to play, though he'd tried to get my brother interested, but John wasn't having any of it. "It doesn't matter if you don't like football, though" he added, "because whatever you do, I'll be there to support you."

He needn't have worried. I loved playing and I knew that it also meant I got to spend a lot of quality time with him. I'd go along with him when he played for his team and I'd join in the warm-ups and various training sessions. His mates would all call me 'Little Ian' and I loved it because I felt like part of the squad – plus I was there, right by my dad's side and for a young lad who worshipped his old man, there was no better feeling. He was always very protective of me and if any of his mates kicked me or went in a little harder than they perhaps should have, he didn't like it one bit and he'd dish out his own brand of justice. He actually had a bit of a nasty streak, though it would only rear its head on very rare occasions, leaving his foot in every now and then as a 'back off my boy' warning. I think they got the message!

It was a very special time for us both and by the time I'd started playing regularly, dad was working as a milkman and I'd help him on his round each Saturday morning to make sure he finished in time to come and watch me play. He'd run from his cart delivering milk and was fit as a butcher's dog – you had to be. That job made him constantly tired and uncharacteristically bad tempered because he couldn't sleep during the day, no matter how hard he tried and eventually he got fed up with it and moved on to employment with more sociable hours.

Dad was a central midfielder with two great feet, though physically, he was a much stockier build than I am now. We both stood at five feet, seven inches, but he was a couple of stones heavier due to a full chest and broad shoulders, none of which was fat. I watched him play whenever I could, though I didn't appreciate what a good player he was at the time. It was just my old fella playing football, but a lot of people have told me since just how good he was. He was well-respected throughout the amateur game, playing for Radstock & Paulton among others around the West Country and Bristol – even playing a game at the age of 52, which I'll come back to later.

He adored football and on any given night he'd go out with a mate and watch a match somewhere, taking in as much local football as he could. He almost got a job working for Bristol Rovers on one occasion and in later years would help out some of their younger age groups in any capacity that was asked of him, just to be involved.

He took me to watch Bristol Rovers and Bristol City as a kid and though I think he did have a preference, he never tried to influence me either way. There was a bloke who was the son of dad's boss when he worked for a company called Pomeroy's, and he regularly had tickets for Ashton Gate. Dad would go along just to watch a match, taking me with him whenever possible because he wanted me to see the best that there was in our area at that time. When City made it to the top flight in the Seventies, I must have gone along to watch them five or six times during one season, always in a Pomeroy's van with six or seven work-mates of dad's crammed in the back.

All the while, my own game was coming along and I was playing for my primary school team, and aged nine, I was invited to trials for the area team, even though the age group was a couple of years older than I was. Dad borrowed his gaffer's car and took me along and, as usual, he was encouraging me all the way, no doubt picking up on my self-doubt which was obvious even back then. He told me: "Just try your best, son, that's all you've got to do. Work hard and give it everything you've got and if you don't make it, don't let it be through lack of effort." He never put one ounce of pressure or expectation on me and that made things much easier, especially in my junior years. I wasn't trying to perform just to make him happy; I was just playing football and enjoying myself.

Even at that age I felt the need to organise everyone around me and I think that probably came from dad buying me a proper leather football for my birthday. It was a cracker, much better than anyone else had on our estate and I was never short of mates to have a kick-around with. As a family, we didn't have much materially, but when we wanted or needed something important, mum and dad would do everything they could to get us the best available. All the local kids wanted to play with my ball, putting me in a position of power. I could kick that ball a country mile with my right boot – not so much with my left – though I'd be sent out into the garden on occasion with a 'dap' (plimsoll to non-Bristolians!) on my right foot and a boot on my left to try and balance things out.

Despite all the coaching and endless practice sessions, I got taken off during the area trials and I thought that was it and that I'd blown my big chance. Joe Davies, a scout for Bristol Rovers, had obviously seen something though, and came up as I sauntered off, head down, and he said, "You'll be alright, son. You'll end up being captain."

I told him not to be stupid, but my dad, knowing who Joe was, just said, "You see? Who knows if you're good enough, eh son? Who knows?" Dad would never tell me I was great or went over the top, he just tried to build up my confidence steadily, and not long after Joe had spoken to me, a scout from Bristol City asked dad if he could arrange a time to speak to me. He invited both the City and the Rovers scouts round to our house, both at different times on the same evening, to see what they had to say.

City have always been the more fashionable of the Bristol clubs, with more money, a better ground and players with exotic names – at least to a nine-year-old Ian Holloway – like Chris Garland, Tom Ritchie and Gerry Gow – unusual names for the era. Rovers had Frankie Prince and Brian Godfrey who sounded like old blokes to me, plus they played at Eastville, with a dog track running round the outside of the pitch for Christ's sake – hardly the Theatre of Dreams. The fact was that it was much easier to support City at primary school, not that it bothered me. Rovers were my team because I liked the fact they did their own thing and were a good, honest club.

There were two blokes from City who came round to see me and after a general chat, they offered me schoolboy forms and a professional contract until I was 21, adding I'd never have to buy another pair of boots – quite an offer for a kid who hadn't even turned 10 yet! They told me what a big club City were and were willing to guarantee me this, that and the other because they were going places and they wanted me to buy into it all.

All dad said after they went was, "What do you think?" and I shrugged my shoulders and said, "Well how do they know how good I'm gonna be?" It was a simple enough question from a kid my age and he replied, "Well, the answer is they don't know." I asked how they possibly promise all that, then? He told me they'd done it because they obviously wanted me to join their club, but added it was up to me and I could do whatever I liked.

Then, the aptly-named Gordon Bennett, a youth coach from Rovers arrived shortly after. He sat down with a cup of tea mum had made him and said, "I've heard that you're fair, average maybe – how bad do you want to be a player?" That was it – no promises of long contracts or free boots, no dangling carrots – nothing in fact. Yet Gordon said all the right things as far as I was concerned and told me it was all about hard work and how much I really wanted it.

After he'd left, I looked at dad and he made me choose which club I wanted to join, and I admire him for that. He gave me responsibility, which could have turned out to be a bit risky, thinking about it, but it actually worked out a treat. I opted for Bristol Rovers, happy in the knowledge I'd have to work hard for whatever I got, just as dad had taught me. Things were pretty much black and white in Ian Holloway world, even at that age, and if something came in fancy wrapping, I'd wonder why they hadn't used brown paper and string instead.

There were other clubs interested, too and for three Christmases running I got a card from a scout at Birmingham City who were in the top-flight, inviting me to have a trial at St Andrew's. Dad said, "They obviously want you. You've not signed anything with Rovers so do you want to go and have a look?" I asked if it would mean living away from home if I liked what I saw and he told me it would. I said I wasn't interested, though I think he wanted me to go and at least have a look.

I'd been playing up to three games on a Saturday for various teams, but Rovers stopped me doing that eventually because I was playing far too much football in their eyes. I'd never miss a training session or game for the school, county or Rovers because I couldn't get enough. Dad was there with me every time I played, wind, rain or shine and seeing we didn't have a car, I often wondered how he managed to get me around as well as he did, but he'd find a way and never once let me down.

I began training with Rovers twice a week and we'd go to various schools around the area, not having a proper base of our own. Gordon Bennett would organise some first-team coaches to take some of the sessions, which was fantastic for us all because we knew we were learning some of the same techniques as the Rovers players were. Wayne Jones, Tom Stanton and Bobby Jones were excellent coaches, full of enthusiasm and bursting with knowledge and advice on how to make you a better player, and I was soaking it all in.

During the school holidays we were taken by Colin Dobson, Bill Dodgin Senior and former Chelsea player Bobby Campbell. We were always under the wing of a good, solid pro and I consider myself to have been very fortunate to have had such quality coaching as a young kid. One thing they all drummed into us was football was a simple game and the main thing was being in position to receive the ball if you weren't in possession, and that grounding would serve me fantastically well throughout my career.

Choosing Rovers over City had been the right choice. From the ages of 9 to 16, the management hardly changed at all so there was a familiarity and consistency that felt comfortable to be around. Not dissimilar to Liverpool's way, Rovers would promote from within and always had a very strong backroom staff that focused on having an excellent youth set-up. They needed a stream of local talent coming through to the senior side because they didn't have the money City did to bring in players for big fees. We were tested often, too, against a Rovers nursery side from South Wales, run by another terrific coach called Stan Montgomery. He'd bring various age groups across once a month and we'd play them at a neutral venue, just to make it feel a little more important. I played in those games once a month for seven years and we knew they were, in effect, trial matches, so nobody could ever rest on their laurels. Any one of us could have been thrown out at the end of any of those seasons, but thinking back, I needed that fear to progress.

Away from football, I wasn't a big lover of school, especially my first school, Parkwall County Primary which I absolutely hated. I didn't like having to do things, especially things I had no interest in and I rebelled in my own way, growing my hair fairly long and generally dragging my heels when it came to anything academically related. It was football or nothing as far I was concerned and when my reading wasn't up to scratch, the school suggested to my parents that they buy football annuals for me so I'd at least read something from cover to cover. They said that it was alright me being good at football, but what if I didn't make it? What was I going to do then? I didn't care at the time because I knew I'd be giving everything to be a footballer and I carried that attitude through to my secondary school, Sir Bernard Lovell Secondary, which was about a mile from our house in Cadbury Heath.

I'd walk there with a couple of mates each morning and in truth, I didn't mind it as much as I had my primary school. I knew a lot of the lads in my year and they had a bit of respect for me because they knew I wasn't a bad player and was on Rovers' books. My work was acceptable, though I probably aimed for the minimum level Bristol Rovers would be happy with. They were always impressing on us the importance of education and regularly checking with the schools to make sure we were attending and doing what was being asked of us.

They weren't after scholars with high school degrees, but they did want some assurances in place in case they released us at any stage, otherwise kids would be leaving the club with shattered dreams and no chance of getting a decent job.

I'd become good mates with a kid called Gary Penrice who was also training with Rovers, although he was a year younger than me. 'Pen' as I came to know him, was from a more affluent family and lived across town in Mangotsfield, but we soon hit it off. He was a lad you either loved or you hated because he never shut up, not that it ever bothered me – I wonder why?! When he stopped, I started, so I suppose we were always destined to be good pals. I found him to be a fascinating character, totally hyper, but funny and honest as the day was long. He was small for his age, but he had incredible skill once he played and could do things you could only hope or dream of doing and even at that age, he was a precocious talent.

Pen was also part of a local amateur side that a mate's dad had started, called Longwell Green Juniors. It was made up mostly of youngsters I'd grown up with and we had a fair old side, too. Rovers allowed me to play for them because they were well-organised and played at a good standard. The team flourished and there was even one occasion when a trip to America was arranged. We were to take part in the Bolingbrook Tournament with teams from all over the place and we had to do all kinds of sponsored events over a period of a year to get the necessary funds to pay for our travel and accommodation. It was an exciting trip to be a part of and five adults travelled over with us, each taking charge of one group of five lads – my dad's group included both Pen and me, poor sod. Pen was all over the place and never kept still for a minute from the moment we picked him up to the moment we dropped him back at his house. Dad grabbed me after we'd landed in the States and said, "If he steps out of your sight I'm going to kill you first and him second. Make sure he doesn't get into trouble."

We were based in Washington DC and to be honest, Pen was a complete nightmare. "What's this over here? What's that? Jesus Oll, look at that." If he'd had a tail it would have been wagging furiously 24 hours a day.

"Come on Pen, we've got to catch everyone up."

"No, no, look it's the White House... look at those over there."

There were huge water sprinklers operating in the grounds near the White House and Pen booted one, causing it to fall over and spray water into a row of parked cars, many of them convertibles. I tried to place it back to where it had been while all these car alarms started going off. Pen rejoined the party a hundred yards down the road leaving me behind. It was like travelling abroad with Frank Spencer. He was a bloody joke!

By the time we got to New York, the other lads had got so fed up with him that they threw his bag out of a window 18 storeys high. Pen went down to get it and was gone about half-an-hour and when my dad came in, he looked around the room in search of you-know-who and asked me where Pen was. "Don't worry, he'll be back," I said, and, thank God, he sauntered in about five minutes later, out of breath saying, "Christ that was a long way down, I couldn't believe it! And my shoe's gone – who's got it, come on? Where's my shoe, then?"

Pen got so annoying that the other lads wanted to throw him in the hotel swimming pool and would have done if I hadn't stopped them. The trouble was, the pool had a plastic cover over it, with leaves on top of that and it would have likely wrapped around him like a piece of shrink-wrap plastic and drowned the poor bugger. We managed to make it home in one piece, eventually. Hardly surprisingly, the only time I really got in trouble at Rovers was through Pen. I rode over to his house on my bike to go to training with him later that evening. It turned out he was injured and wouldn't be going, so he asked me to go into town with him and his mum, which I thought I had time to do, and we ended up watching a film at the cinema. Immersed in the film, I forgot about the training and halfway through I thought, "Oh, shit..." I said I needed to get to training quickly and Pen's mum said she'd take me. I needed to get my bike first so I could get home afterwards and by the time I'd done all that it wasn't worth going, so I rode home from Pen's instead. My stomach churned as I turned into my road because I could see Gordon Bennett, sat on the wall, waiting outside our house. I pedalled a bit slower but eventually drew level with him. He was furious and he tore a strip off me like you'd never believe.

"I thought you were gonna make it! I thought your attitude was right! I wasn't sure you were good enough but I'd have put my house on you, but now, there's a black mark against you in my book. What excuse have you got?"

"I forgot and..."

"YOU FORGOT?" he bellowed. "Training's that important to you then, is it?" He continued the hairdryer treatment and told me Pen's involvement in the matter was unimportant because he was injured. "You should have remembered," he said ruefully as he turned and left. I was only 12, but he was right and if he'd wanted to force home a point, he'd done it with relish. I went into the house, devastated, and dad glanced over his paper and said, "Yeah, well he's bloody right, isn't he?" Mum called me over and told me everything would be fine – as mums have done since time immemorial – and the 'red eye syndrome' kicked in. I was embarrassed and felt a bloody idiot. All the hard work and focus counted for nothing at that moment and I'd have to work even harder from there on in. I cursed Pen, though it wasn't his fault and I don't think I was ever late for anything again.

Chapter 3

She's The One

Something had stayed with me from the time mum went into hospital when I was a kid. As far as I was concerned, she'd just disappeared off the face of the Earth for a week and it's fair to say I had a slight separation problem and was pretty insecure in many ways. It would manifest itself from time to time, particularly when I moved schools. I grew up with a lad called Mark Shail who lived a few doors down from me and we were close friends during childhood, so when he and his family moved about a mile away, it killed me for a while. We'd been through a lot together including a time when his dad Terry had caught him smoking in the back garden and, following in the great fatherly tradition, he made his son sit in the lounge and smoke a big fat cigar. As Mark turned green, his dad turned to me and said, "And you can stay there and watch this you bloody idiot." I think he got a taste for them after that because Mark still smokes today!

We kept in touch, though didn't see each other half as much as we used to, but the good thing was that Mark was going to go to the same secondary school as me and as luck would have it, the house he'd moved to was only a short walk from the new school. I was never that comfortable being in school all day and, being an unbelievably fussy eater, I started going back with Mark and his mum Judy to eat lunch at their house every day. They were like a second family to me and the daily break from school life made things much easier for the five or six years I was at Sir Bernard Lovell.

I was pushing on with my football and was totally dedicated to making it as a player with Gordon Bennett's bollocking still fresh in my memory. My mates would ask me to go down to the cinema or down to the youth club, but though it was hard at times, I'd tell them I was training later and I couldn't come out the following day, either, and so on.

I was at an age where even the other lads at Bristol Rovers were starting to have their heads turned by one thing or another, but I remained focused. It wasn't that I wasn't interested in being with my mates, it was just that I didn't feel I had any second chances at Rovers and if this was my one chance to make it, I was determined to give it everything I had. Things were ticking along nicely in Ian Holloway world until, bang! I was hit by a freight train – or at least that's how it felt at the time.

I used to walk to school with a lad called Gary Thomas, another kid I'd known all my life, and one particular morning I called at his house and his mum, Vera, told me he'd be ready in a minute and made me a cup of tea while I waited. He finally came down, looking a bit dishevelled, by which time I was totally pissed off with him. I hated being late and as we left the house I said, "Come on you idiot, we've got to run for the bus, now." He was bigger than me, but I used to bully him a bit, I suppose. We just managed to catch the bus before it pulled away and went and sat on the top deck where the only seats left were right at the back. I was like a dog with a bone. "That's half my dinner money gone now, you great pillock." I kept moaning at him until we got to school and everyone lethargically started to get up. At the front of the bus, four girls stood up and among them was one that made me stop in mid-sentence, my jaw dropping wide open as she went down the stairs followed by a smaller girl who looked just like her. She hadn't seen me but I'd seen her and I said to Gary, "Who the hell is that?"

"Eh?" he said, still rubbing sleep out of his eyes, but she'd gone by then. "Who do you mean? Which kid?" He probably thought it was a lad from the school team or something because I never showed any interest in anything unconnected with football.

"It was a girl, you plank," I said, but he hadn't seen her and she'd disappeared from view merging into a crowd heading towards the gates. He smiled and said, "I told you we should go on the bus more often."

We made our way off the bus but there was a sea of bodies in various versions of the school uniform so we carried on arguing about him oversleeping instead until we reached class. At break time, Gary found me and said, "I think that girl you've been going on about is called Kim Mitchell." He'd asked around, describing her to a few girls at assembly and the fact that she had what was obviously a smaller sister who looked like a twin had made the search easier. She was in a different House to me and because it was such a huge school, that meant she went to different assemblies from me, which is probably why I couldn't recall ever seeing her before. I didn't have a clue what was going on but I knew I had to find her and discover more about her. I searched the school with no luck for several days until Gary told me that a kid that lived down the road from us, Mark Nicholls – better known as 'Nipples' – not only knew who Kim was, but where she lived, too. Nipples was a full-time whinger and I didn't have that much time for him, to be truthful, but I needed information, and quick, so I had to go round his house and pretend to be half-friendly with him. I think he knew as much and enjoyed his position of power, but I was like a lovesick puppy and was prepared to humiliate myself if necessary. I made idle chat for a minute before cutting to the chase. "Gary tells me you know a girl called Kim Mitchell, is that right?"

"Yeah, yeah, she's in my maths group," he said flippantly.

"She's not bad is she? Where…" I didn't get chance to finish. Nipples, who was oblivious to the nickname we'd given him, wasn't about to waste this opportunity to make me squirm even more than I already was.

"You don't like girls!" he laughed.

"Shut up. Listen, I really like her a lot," and as those words left my mouth, guess who was coming up my road? I couldn't believe it. "There she is!"

"That's not her," Nipples said, then, "Oh hang on, it is." With that he got on his bike and rode towards her as I began to shrink on the spot. He stopped in front of her with a lame back wheel skid and, obviously being as tactful as possible pointed back towards me and blurted out, "He fancies you!" My stomach began doing somersaults. I couldn't take any more so I just turned and walked to my house a few doors down without saying a word. I went and hid in my room, snatching a sly glance through the net curtains. Kim was talking with Nipples for about five minutes. She had her smaller sister – a proper Mini Me – and her friend Rose with her, and when they finally left my mind was made up. This was the girl for me. I was totally smitten and managed to pluck up enough courage to ask Gary to ask her out on my behalf, but after he'd told her, she showed no interest whatsoever.

I found out as much as I could about her and about a month later, it was the school sports day and despite it being a huge field packed with kids taking part or just watching, I found out where she was and went and stood right behind her. Had I been slapped with a restraining order, I couldn't have complained because I couldn't have made it more bloody obvious. She was lying on the grass, resting on her elbows, watching the events and then she turned round and saw me stood behind – from the legs up. I was in shorts because I was due to take part in a race and my thighs were probably my best feature because I'd been working on them for years! She turned back around again, but it was the closest I'd been to her and I felt encouraged for some reason. I was 15, she was 14 and I was totally in love. I found out where she lived and plucked up enough courage to finally ask her out myself. I went along with Gary for moral support and got about two yards from her garden gate when her dad came out the front door so I backed off and waited till he left.

I then made Gary go and knock on her door and Kim answered. He got her to come outside for a moment and after a brief chat, she told him she would go out with me, but only if I'd ask her myself. He asked her to walk to where I was waiting and as they approached Gary subtly said, "You've got to ask her to her face." He walked off and left us alone and I finally asked her out – and she said yes. "Okay," I said, "I'll see you tomorrow in school, then." She went back in and that was that. I was chuffed as a badger and ran off punching the air, before realising I hadn't arranged where we should meet and what time! So, via a network of friends, I got a message to her to meet me by the coffee machine in the main corridor, which she did, but as soon as she saw me she went back into her classroom and I mistook that for not liking me after all. I found her and asked what was wrong. "I really like you," she said, "but I'm just really shy."

I could relate to that, so we arranged to meet with a few others around, including her sister who never stopped chatting. I should have fixed her up with Pen! A week later I went round to Kim's house, but the whole experience was horrific – absolutely horrific! I came from a council estate and she lived in a very smart private house and everything was totally alien to the world I knew. Her mum had given birth to Kim when she was just 19 whereas my mum was 31 when I was born and initially I thought her mum was her sister! Walking into that house was like going into a different world. They had bespoke furniture, really modern stuff, and nothing like the old fashioned gear we had at our house. The wallpaper, carpets – everything was completely different. I sat down in the lounge and it seemed most of the Mitchell family was there and I was feeling understandably quite nervous – but there was much worse to follow and I still can't believe what happened next. All Creatures Great and Small was on TV, with James Herriot, the vet. Everyone was quiet and engrossed in the story while I was thinking that if I'd been at my house, it was more likely that Benny Hill would have been on with my dad going, "Phwoar! Look at her knockers! Cor blimey! I'd give her a portion given half the chance!" Mum would just tell him to shut up and if any intimate scenes ever came on during any programme, she'd go and make a cup of tea. I didn't have much education on the birds and the bees front so when old James Herriot soaped up his arm I wondered what was coming next and then, on my life, wham! Right up the cow's arse! I started to get a bit hot under the collar, squirming with embarrassment. My mum would have been brewing up by that point and Christ knows what dad would have said – though I could imagine – when all of a sudden Kim's sister pipes up, "Mum, do cows have a clitoris?"

I thought, 'What's she on about? What's that?'

Her mum didn't bat an eyelid. Had I misheard her? Had she asked if cows liked liquorice?

"Well, that's a very interesting question," her mum said. "Terry, what do you think?"

"I'm not sure," he said. "Why not ask your teacher tomorrow?"

Eventually, it was time for me to leave, thank God, and I made my way home to what I considered to be a more normal home environment. You can probably see this coming, but as soon as I got home, I had to ask so I said, "Mum, what's a clitoris?" Yes, I really was that naïve.

"Ask your dad," she said putting the kettle on, which should have given me a clue! I did ask dad and he said, "I dunno, ask your mum, I'm still trying to find one!" and burst out laughing. I decided to leave it until I saw my mates at school and, of course, they took great delight in informing me what it was and where you could find it. I never did find out if a cow's got one or not!

So Kim and I were up and running, even though it had taken 11 weeks to finally go out on a date with her. It was typical of the way I am that I wouldn't have given up, even though there'd been lots of times when I'd thought she didn't like me, and persistence finally paid off. My life changed completely from the moment I saw her on that bus trip, one that I should have never really been on in the first place and had Gary not been late that day, who knows what might have happened? It felt weird, but it really was love at first sight – at least on my part.

Things changed in my daily routine too, and while I'd been discouraged to go out with my mates in the evening, dad did let me out with my girlfriend, though I had to be back in by 8.30pm at the latest so it didn't interfere with my football. He told me not to lose my focus and Gordon Bennett even met Kim, telling her that he hoped she understood I had a chance of being a footballer. I had career choices to make and that meant missing school discos and parties and suchlike, but I had to beg my dad to let me go to one particular youth club because Kim went there and he relented – so long as I was in by the normal time. In fact, he gave me a half hour extension because it closed at nine, though it was only once a week.

My mates were chuffed that I was finally going out with them in the evening, but I had to convince them to leave 10 minutes before the club closed for one reason or another. I'd casually walk round the corner and sprint as fast as I could the half-mile to our house, otherwise I would never have made it back in time and that would have been the end of the matter. Dad never took his eye off the ball and wanted me to remain disciplined at all times and at Christmas time, his mates would stop by and dad used to go straight to the shelf he kept his spirits on. "Go on, have a drink," he'd say when anyone called in over the festive period, and on Christmas Day he'd pour us all a little glass of whisky and then look at me and say, "You don't want one, do you." I left a question mark off that last quote because he wasn't actually asking me, he was telling me. If I did get one it would be watered down so much with lemonade it would be a joke, but I understood that he didn't want me to get a taste for alcohol because he didn't want that to stop me moving forward.

He eased off a little as I got towards my later teens, but he was still strict on sleep and what I did in my social life. He needn't have worried because I was totally focused on making the grade and my discipline was about to be rewarded.

"Come on goody two shoes," my mates would bait me when I turned down their offers of going to this place and that, and my work ethics during my apprenticeship had some of the other lads calling me a creep. It didn't bother me because I knew why I was doing what I was doing. I put my heart and soul into everything I did, whether that was cleaning boots or sweeping the dressing rooms. I had no desire to act cool just to impress my mates and if I didn't fit in with some of them it was by choice. It was hard at times, but I did it.

Kim was a steadying influence for me through my teenage years and without her I suppose I could have drifted off the path. I had her, my close mates and my family and it didn't bother me that I was ostracised by the other apprentices – that was up to them.

I got injured an awful lot between the ages of 16 and 17 and I missed a load of games because of my attitude to training and the way I threw myself into it. I was doing things my body simply wasn't ready for yet and during the first year of my apprenticeship I played just 11 games. I was up against it and I knew I had to pull out all the stops in my second year if I was to earn a professional contract on my eighteenth birthday.

At the start of the second year, Gordon Bennett said to me, "Whatever you do, don't worry, they like you. You're only small but you've not physically developed yet so keep on the way you are."

I played in an FA Youth Cup match at Swansea and I asked Gordon whether I should ask the club about the likelihood of being kept on prior to the game, but he advised me not to ask just yet. So I played, we won 3-1 and I scored probably my greatest goal ever, cutting in from the right and curling the ball over the keeper and into the top corner. The next day, Gordon came around to our house and said, "I suggest you ask the question on Monday morning young man after a goal like that."

I was just about to turn 18 and I'd been waiting for him to say those words, so I did ask the club what the future held and fortunately I was offered a contract. My dad played it down, of course, saying, "You haven't made it yet, you know? Wait till you've played 100 games, son. This is just the first rung of the ladder." But though he always kept my feet on the ground, I found out in later years that he was quite the opposite when it came to talking about my progress with other people. I got a letter in 2007 from a bloke who used to be dad's boss at a dye-cast factory. He told me dad had helped him through a very difficult period when he had a lot of problems with the unions over job cuts.

Dad told the union rep, "Look, it's not the gaffer's fault and I don't agree with all this. We're shirking our jobs and we've got to help him out," and he returned to work, not because he was some kind of scab or had his own agendas, but because he made his own mind up and stood up for what he thought was right. This bloke told me dad used to speak about me with great pride and added that, knowing Bill Holloway as well as he did, that he probably never told me. "Let me assure you, Ian" he wrote, "your dad was immensely proud of you."

Dad didn't praise me because he thought it would affect the way I was, to the point he was almost paranoid about saying anything at all, but I knew he had nothing but my welfare in his heart.

With my first Rovers contract signed, it seemed I was finally on my way, and Kim was making her way, too, training to be a hairdresser. Things took another turn for the better when Terry Cooper took over as manager of Rovers and he included me as a sub against a team from abroad. He threw me on in the second half, too, and I fed a ball through that led to a penalty being awarded. Cooper shouted that he wanted me to take it, so I did, putting us 6-1 ahead. I knew that Cooper liked my style of play and I was now on the fringes of the first team. It would be a traumatic season for Rovers, with the South Grandstand burning down, forcing us to play six home games at Ashton Gate. Imagine the irony if I'd made my home League debut at City's ground, considering the offer they'd made me almost a decade before. Things were also moving in my life and, aged 18, I was named as sub for Rovers' penultimate game of that 1980/81 campaign, away to Wrexham. I replaced Mark Hughes towards the end of a 3-1 defeat and though we were relegated to the Third Division that year, I went into the summer on a massive personal high.

Chapter 4

Holloway (o.g.)

I had a bit more money and had been courting Kim for three years and it was around about that time she asked me for an engagement ring. That hit me like a bolt from the blue, but at that point, I wasn't sure what I was feeling regarding our relationship. The situation at Rovers had me feeling a bit like jack-the-lad, so I told her a ring wasn't on the cards because I wasn't sure whether I loved her or not. Bang! A hell of a statement to say and part of me couldn't believe it was my voice even saying the words. I felt pressured, but of course, I didn't realise that I felt that way because I actually loved her so much, and whoever came up with the phrase, 'love is blind', knew what they were on about. I was walking around with my eyes wide shut and wasn't mature enough to realise what I had in Kim. Over-confident and being a bit egotistical, I asked for a bit of time and space to think things over and Kim took it really badly.

I ended the relationship and we went our separate ways, but within a month I was missing her terribly. I'd been a bloody idiot but my pride was holding me back. The new season began and I bumped into her mum, who was a member at Cadbury Heath Social Club where I was playing snooker and I asked how Kim was doing. She told me I should go and talk to her and, needing a haircut, I went to her where she was working. I had every intention of asking her back out and I think she was expecting me to say as much, but for some reason I bottled it and said I still wanted space and all that crap! What was I thinking? I've got a beautiful girl whom I'm as besotted with as the first day I saw her and I'm behaving like a bloody idiot. Not only that, but I tell her while she's cutting my hair. Her revenge was swift and she murdered my hair exactly the opposite to the way I usually had it. She shaved it up the back and left a big lump on the top and I looked like a member of Kajagoogoo – she did a right number on me, but good on her because I deserved nothing less.

I'd entered a different world to the one I'd loved and felt secure in, and things were about to get even worse as my dad had a heart attack, shaking the foundations of our family to the core. I think what happened to dad came as a result of his pride as much as the condition of his heart, because he was an immensely proud man. He'd help anyone out and give his last penny if he thought it would help, but on this occasion his body couldn't keep up with his good intentions. He'd always been incredibly fit and looked younger than his 52 years and I think that might have actually worked against him on this occasion. As per usual, he went out to see a Sunday League game the day after watching me play for the reserves and I'd normally go along with him, but for some reason didn't that day. He'd watch the game, then go and have a pint with his mates at the club and be home in time for Sunday dinner. On this occasion, he came home about an hour earlier than normal and sat down in his chair. His face looked grey and I could sense something was badly wrong.

"Is your mum in, son?" he almost whispered to me. I said she was. "Call her down for me would you?"

Mum came in and he looked at her and said, "I don't feel very well, love. I'd like you to call an ambulance." Mum asked what was wrong and he said he had a really tight chest. She held his hand and made to go over to the phone but as she did he grabbed her and said, "But I've got to tell you, I played football this morning. They were a man short and I couldn't let them down." Mum said for him not to worry, but it summed him up that he'd had to tell her the truth, because that was what he was all about. It was an awful time and the hospital later confirmed he'd had a heart attack and kept him in for a few days. They did some tests and discovered he had angina and would have to take tablets to help him keep it under control. It had been a real scare for all of us.

I had dad on my mind constantly and I was missing Kim more than ever by now and being apart was tearing me up, but it had been my own doing and I still couldn't summon up enough courage to tell her how I felt. I'd borrow my mate's dog just so I could walk past her house and if she saw me she'd come out and walk with me for a while, telling me about her new boyfriend, which didn't come as a surprise because there was always going to be a long queue.

I kept tabs on her all the time and my mate Phil Kite, who was the goalkeeper at Rovers, gave me regular updates because his mum used to get her hair cut at Kim's hairdressers in Kingswood. Time moved on and I tried to get on with my life and took another girl out at one point, but I treated her badly and was off-hand and rude to her and nobody deserves to be treated that way. My progress at senior level also seemed to be at a standstill with Terry Cooper gone and Bobby Gould replacing him as the new manager. The one game I did get during his first season in charge was during a 1-0 defeat at Wimbledon. Wearing the No 2 shirt I made my full debut playing right-back. I thought I was doing well enough in the reserves but Gouldy obviously didn't agree at the time.

I was all over the place mentally, and though it seemed like a lifetime since I'd split with Kim, I still harboured hopes we might get back together some day and would regularly call to see her to chat and go on the odd walk. I needed to concentrate on my football and dad encouraged me to channel my frustration into positivity on the football pitch, which I managed to do, finally breaking into the side during the 1982/83 season.

If I wasn't playing first-team football, I always thought there was something wrong with the manager rather than look at what I was doing negatively, because I always believed in my own ability. My chances under Gouldy had been limited, mainly because he brought in some top names – well past their prime – over whom there was no chance on Earth I would ever get preferential treatment. Mick Channon came to Rovers from Newcastle, which was fantastic for a club like us, but he took my place in the team. When Gouldy did play me, I'd get stuck out on the right wing, but that was all I needed because I was damned if I was about to let him drop me again.

I wasn't happy with the way Gouldy was treating me, though I could see he was under pressure because Channon's wages would have been substantial by Rovers' standards, and if he didn't produce the goods, it'd be his neck on the line.

Mick was larger than life, immersed in his horses and an amazing bloke, really, but he was the reason I wasn't in the side and I'd felt I was establishing myself up to his arrival. Mick arrived in October 1982 and Gouldy stuck him on the bench for the first two games, which inspired me to score my first senior goals, one during a 4-0 home win over Millwall and then two more away to Orient. Unbelievably, Gouldy dropped me for the next match, bringing Mick in claiming I was "mentally tired." I was fuming, but I had to get on with it. Later on, we drew Plymouth away in the FA Cup second round and, having won my place back, I'd put my bag under the No 7 shirt. Gouldy read the team out and I wasn't even on the bench – Mick was back in the side but I hadn't been warned and was seething at Gouldy for that. Mick could see this and went into his bag and brought out a sealed bag containing £1000 and said to me, "Here, go out and buy yourself a coffee." I went to take it from him and as I did he pulled it away and started laughing. I was steaming. I sat in the stand and Gouldy came and sat next to me. Mick had missed two sitters and he put his arm around my shoulder and said, "Do you think you'd have put those chances away?" and I said, "Yes, I do, but YOU don't."

He didn't like that and told me to see him on the following Monday morning. I had ideas above my station but I needed a streak of arrogance to push on. I never had a problem with Mick, who was a fantastic bloke, it was the manager I didn't agree with for not selecting me on merit. Whereas I was focused and committed, Mick was more interested in how his horses were doing and it'd be like, "Oh my horse just bloody lost. I'd better get my kit on." He made more of an impact on the coach and in the dressing room than he did on the pitch because I don't believe we were really good enough to play with him. He left for Norwich just before Christmas and was outstanding for them. Maybe he needed to play at a higher level to perform to his maximum potential and I think he needed quality players around him to be at his best, but what a treat to be able to train and play with a bloke of that calibre. Alan Ball arrived after Mick had gone and what an absolute pleasure it was to have him at the club. It was another coup for Gouldy who proved he could pull in the big names, and I wanted to learn as much off Bally as I could.

He was a terrific character and the lads were in awe of him because this guy had seen it, done it and was still wearing the T-shirt. He loved his horses, too, but that was for his spare time because when he trained and played, he was outstanding. I was picked occasionally, but mainly out of the team at the time, but after a couple of games alongside Bally, I was dropped again for an away game at Wigan. Gouldy told me he was going to play Bally out on the right and said he just wanted me to watch what he did and absorb it all in. In all fairness,

I believe I witnessed one of the best performances I've ever seen that afternoon. Gouldy said, "You won't ever get a chance to see another player who knows his next pass like Alan and on his day, he can run a game, and I think today just might be his day." Bally was outstanding and we won 5-0 and I think he created them all. I was sat on the bench with Gouldy next to me and he kept nudging me saying, "Look at that," or "Did you see that?" Eventually, I snapped and said "I can bloody see it!" He was 36 but had lost none of his brilliance and was four or five passes ahead of everyone else that afternoon, and to this day, I've not seen anyone who has played better. Bally was always first class with me and the lads and there was one occasion we turned up for training one time and Gouldy said, "We're not training this morning, we're training this afternoon so go away and do what you like." He was like that, always changing things or doing unusual stuff but it was good because it kept you on your toes.

Bally looked up and said, "Is there a café around here, lads?" There was one called the Monte Carlo so Bally said that we had to go there. I'd not long passed my driving test but he threw me his keys and said that I could drive us there if I wanted. We went outside and there in front of us was a brand new Mercedes 500 coupe parked. Bally, sat next to me at the front with his training kit and cap on, marking his horses off for the afternoon, and he didn't look up from his paper even once on that journey. He paid for us at the café without us knowing and we nipped in and out of the bookies next door for him over the next few hours. I chatted to him and asked him about his family, and he told me he had three kids and that he and his wife had adopted another. I asked why and he said, "Well, we've been lucky and had a good life. We just wanted to help someone else who'd been less fortunate. He was a proper fella – outstanding in fact – and he was a World Cup winner, but would you know it? What a top man and I really can't speak highly enough of him.

As for me, I was still a young kid and a bit erratic at times, too intent on proving Gouldy wrong rather than getting my head down and concentrating on my own game. I was making mistakes and was guilty of perhaps trying too hard, but I was still producing enough to warrant selection, creating a few goals and scoring here and there.

I had the pleasure of scoring the winner against Bristol City, in the Gloucester Cup Final when I smashed a left-foot shot into the top left-hand corner – on my life it was a stunner! Terry Cooper, by then City's manager, said afterwards,

"I worked with him for years and know he hasn't got a left foot. It was a total fluke." Cheers, Coops!

I wasn't physically the strongest or the quickest and there were always a lot of quality midfielders at Rovers during that period. Dave Williams, who went on to play for Norwich, Frankie Prince, Geraint Williams and Tony Pulis were all good players and older than me, so it was a constant battle to be in the starting line-up. I was forever arguing with Gouldy because I never felt he gave me a chance, but looking back, he did, because he did play me, even if it was sporadically. It was when he brought in a couple of lads who played non-League football and played them ahead of me that upset me the most, and even though both lads did well, I just didn't feel it was right at the time.

Dad had always taught me to confront someone if I felt the need for an explanation so I said to Gouldy "What's wrong with me? What do you want me to do?" and I kept asking the same kind of question, which annoyed him, I think. But I trained hard and kept my head up and the insubordination was just part of my prickly character at that age. I wanted to show him he was wrong and that I wasn't going to put up with it. I mithered him on the bench so much one time that he just gave up. "Go on, put me on, I'll get us the win, come on, stick me on…" and on that occasion, I did score and we did win, but I was cocky with it. "See, told you I'd do it." I had to be fairly happy with my return of seven goals from 26 starts – I was still only 20 and it was a solid base for me to build upon.

Gouldy left for Coventry City and I now realise the things he did or said were 99.9% right and I've a lot of respect for Bob. They should have awarded him a medal for putting up with a bolshy, headstrong little slugger like me, if truth be told. Dave Williams took over for the start of the 1983/84 season and I played 36 times and felt, with some justification, that I'd established myself in the team. I'd always had a great relationship with the Rovers fans who just took to me straight away, presumably because I gave everything every time I played and I was a local lad. They'd voted me Young Player of the Year in successive seasons when I was 18 and 19 and I hadn't even been in the first team at that point. Neil Slatter was 18 and a full Welsh international as well as a regular in the senior side and yet I beat him. How could that be? It was quite embarrassing, really, though flattering all the same.

I was full of anger in my late teens and early twenties and that was almost completely down to not being with Kim. I was doing all kinds of weird things like going on sun beds, wearing lots of gold, dyeing my hair bleach blond and going to the gym all the time to make me feel better about myself – egotistical stuff I would never have dreamed of doing normally. Looking back, I looked a complete pleb, but I suppose at least I can admit that.

I was nerveless on the pitch, though, where I would try anything to catch the eye of the manager. I remember one time I was up against an old centre-half, Les Chapman, playing against Preston, and Dave Williams played a ball out to me and as it came, I sort of nodded over Chapman, ran past him and whipped the ball in. The next time he came near me he punched me in the stomach and said, "You try that again and I'll snap you in fucking half and you'll get much worse than that." I just went for things and didn't care about the consequences because I always believed that was my time and if I didn't make an impression of some sort, I might not get another go.

Looking back, it was a miserable period and I was lonely and selfish in my ways. I bought an expensive stereo for myself and idled away my spare time listening to music in my room. I'd buy records like Tavares 'More Than a Woman' and dozens of others I could relate back to Kim – I'd even write my own lyrics to some songs – sad, I know, but I couldn't help it.

There were more reasons to leave Bristol than to stay and I felt my situation with Kim had to come to a conclusion before too long. I'd been thinking of moving on anyway.

Not being with her while still living in the same neighbourhood was killing me, in truth, and seeing her fairly regularly to chat to only made things worse, so I made the decision to keep away for a couple of weeks – at least. I had to move on and on one particular afternoon, I was handed the incentive I needed to leave Rovers, quit Bristol and start afresh somewhere else.

I was over at Phil Kite's house and his mum Miriam came in carrying a bag of shopping. "Hello Ian," she said. "I saw your ex-girlfriend today – isn't she stunning?" I just nodded and smiled. Funnily enough, I'd been talking to Phil and his girlfriend about the way I still felt for Kim just moments before and I noticed him in the corner of my eye attempting to shush his mum up, but she didn't understand and continued with her news. "I saw the ring – beautiful ring it was, too, she looks so happy." It was a tumbleweed moment and you could have heard the proverbial pin drop.

"What ring?" I asked.

Phil got up and said, "Come on Ollie we better be getting off…"

"She got engaged to that lovely boy she's with," his mum went on. "You don't like her anymore though, do you?"

"She's got engaged?" The colour drained from my face and I had to leave. Why hadn't Kim told me herself? Why did I have to hear it from somebody else? I spent the rest of that day thinking seriously about driving the fast car I'd bought straight into a wall and having done with it. I was an idiot and I thought I'd probably never be happy again, so why bother going through the motions? Eventually, I managed to calm myself down, went home and thought long and hard about what I wanted to do next. I still had a year of my contract left at Rovers and Pen had by this time come back to the club after playing for Mangotsfield United. I had good mates and my family around me so I decided to soldier on for another season at Eastville.

I arrived for training in July, still wanting to be somewhere else, but glad to be able to get my head down and start grafting again. There was a local pre-season tournament at Longwell Green that we were taking part in, mainly designed to build our stamina and sharpness up, and the heat was intense. Mickey Barrett was a brilliant winger for Rovers – a popular lad among the squad and with the supporters, but you could see something wasn't right. He kept having to come off during the games, which were only six minutes each way and was drenched in sweat and the lad just looked ill. Initially, we thought it was heat stroke, but afterwards his condition deteriorated rapidly and he was rushed to hospital. It turned out Mickey had hepatitis but, tragically, further tests revealed he was also riddled with cancer. Mickey, who was just 24, died a couple of weeks later. It was a total shock because he'd seemed a fit, young lad who was preparing to become a father for the first time. How do you get your head around something like that? More tragedy surrounded another of my team-mates, Tim Parkin, who'd lost his little boy to leukaemia not long before Mickey's death. The day after Mickey's funeral, one of my best mates, Phil Kite, left for Southampton, which, while nowhere near as devastating as the other events, still was a blow to me. I couldn't quite comprehend what was happening around me and the events of that summer made me look at life through different eyes.

With Kim engaged, the tragic loss of Mickey, and Tim losing his boy, it put my life into perspective and I had to get things absolutely clear in my mind as to what I really wanted to do, where I wanted to go and who with. I got on with the 1984/85 season and channelled all my aggression and frustration into football and probably had one of my best seasons for Rovers, capped off by scoring the winning goal in the Bristol derby at Eastville. I thought of Mickey and Tim's lad as the Rovers players and fans went mad and it clarified everything in my mind, and I decided I was going to dictate my own future as best I could from there on in. Dave Williams left the club and Bobby Gould returned as manager and after that I started having major rows at work. I told Gouldy about what was happening and how I felt about Kim and that it was destroying me, but he either didn't understand or more likely didn't care. "Go on holiday, get your head together and if you happen to catch anything from being with another girl, just get a jab in the ass. Stop being such a bloody soft arse." Terrific. Cheers gaffer – next time I need good, solid advice I'll know to keep walking when I come to your door. He offered me a new deal with my contract now expired, but any slim chance that I might have stayed disappeared when I was on the end of what I felt was a total stitch-up.

The lads who had come through the ranks a year ahead of me had been given a loyalty bonus of £5,000 for staying with the club and agreeing new deals after their initial contract expired. When it came around to my turn to sign again, the loyalty bonus had been taken out of the agreement. I couldn't believe it. I'd been with Rovers since I was nine and was prepared to give them the best years of my career, but all of a sudden the loyalty payment is off the menu? I told Gouldy, "Look, Bob, I'll sign the new contract provided I get the same as Geraint Williams and Mark Hughes did when they re-signed."

He said, "We've changed that now. It's not my fault, but we're not doing it anymore." I told him I wouldn't be signing anything then, and he told me I couldn't do that. "I can and I am because it's not fair and it's not right."

My situation with Kim had come to a head anyway and I'd been thinking of moving because I hadn't been getting on with Bobby Gould at all but that was just a minor irritation compared to the bigger picture. I can understand some of the things he did and said now, because I'm a manager, too, and it wasn't anything personal on his part or mine – I'd just had enough.

Kim, as the song goes, was always on my mind, but instead of pining away for her from a distance and watching her slip ever more out of my life, I decided it was time to grab the bull by the horns and tell her exactly how I felt – how I'd always felt and that I was leaving. I plucked up the courage I needed and went round to Kim's house, a little angry and very emotional and said, "I know you're engaged and you won't understand why I'm doing this, but Mickey Barrett died suddenly and I don't want me to die or you to die without you ever knowing the truth. The truth is, I've always loved you – I always have and always will – and I know I can't change things because you've chosen him, so I've got to leave. I can't stay in Bristol with you still here and I want you to be happy, so I'm going. I just needed to tell you that."

I left her standing at the door, turned and headed home. The time was right to move on. I asked Gouldy to be placed on the transfer list and hoped the move would come quickly. I didn't like the person I was becoming and wasn't going to stick around and make things any worse. A fresh start was what I needed and I couldn't do that by staying with Rovers and living in Cadbury Heath. I didn't know it at the time, but it was to be the beginning of an even more dramatic chapter in my life, when being away from home would actually be the last thing I needed.

Chapter 5

Holloway Prison (London)

I was placed on the transfer list and it wasn't that long before Dave Bassett from Wimbledon came in for me with an offer of £40,000. Bobby Gould tried one last time to get me to stay and even said he could sort out the £5,000 loyalty payment, but I told him he could stuff it up his arse. He then accepted Wimbledon's offer, thus creating a new Rovers transfer record in the process. I agreed a three-year deal, though I'd have probably signed for Hartlepool at the time, if it meant being out of Bristol. As it was, the Dons were in the old Second Division and had been moving up the leagues impressively during the previous few years so it looked like a reasonable career move. Lennie Lawrence's Charlton had shown strong interest, too, but I spoke with Gordon Bennett, who was by that time Rovers' chief executive, and he thought Dave 'Harry' Bassett would be a good man for me to work under, so that's where I went.

Harry's first words to me had hardly inspired me and in truth, left me wondering why he'd bothered to sign me in the first place. With his assistant manager at his side, he pointed to him and said, "He tells me you're the next Brian Marwood, but I think I've already got him in Dennis Wise, but he's away in Sweden right now with England. His arsehole is on fire because of you. I've seen you once and I didn't think you did very well, but he tells me that after watching you 14 times, you're the one we should get." I just said, "Oh, cheers."

But it didn't stop me signing because of the old I'll-show-you streak.

Chairman Sam Hammam grabbed me on my first day at the club, got me in a headlock and punched me a couple of times in the ribs saying, "You gonna be all right with us, eh?"

I moved to London and felt positive about the future and myself for the first time in what seemed like years. Training began in early July and was going well and the world felt all right again. I scored a cracking goal on my debut during a pre-season friendly, but Alan Cork was ruled offside. He was in an offside position but was nowhere near to interfering with play, but the ref wasn't having any of it. I was gutted, but the other lads just thought it was funny, but I suppose I should have known what the infamous Crazy Gang would be like. Then, in the same game, I burst through and was pulled down in the box, but the referee, fellow Bristolian Roger Milford, waved play on. Those two decisions – a goal and a penalty – could have changed my time with my Wimbledon, I'm a big believer in the path of fate and destiny, but as it was, the road ahead would be as bumpy as the Plough Lane pitch. I actually scored seven goals in pre-season – and all of them from right wing – so from a playing point of view, things had still started positively. I went home to see my family whenever I got the chance because it had been the first time I'd ever lived anywhere other than the family home. I'd been a Wimbledon player for no more than a month and I drove back to Bristol to see mum and dad and was hit with a sledgehammer as I settled down for a cup of tea.

"I've got to tell you Kim's not very well, Ian," Mum said.

"What do you mean she's not very well?"

"Well I bumped into her mum and dad and they told me she's got a problem with one of her lungs."

It turned out that she'd been on holiday with her folks and her lung collapsed, but they couldn't work out why. She'd been out of breath and tired all the time and even needed a piggy back up a gentle slope because things had got so bad, so she was admitted to hospital to undergo tests and it was decided that she had to have her lung drained off.

The news that she was ill made my mind up – I had to see her and sod the consequences. I made my way to the hospital with mum and found out which ward she was on. I just wanted a few moments alone with her, but as I walked in the room, her fiancé's brother was sat there. Kim looked really pleased to see me (she later told me the one person she wanted to walk through that door was me, silly old sod), but I think she was a little embarrassed that I was there, too. It's fair to say that this lad's brother and I didn't see eye to eye because he'd been round to warn me from seeing Kim in the past, but I told him I would only stop if she asked me to stop seeing her. "Would you give up on her if you were in my position?" I asked. Of course, when they became engaged, I stopped the visits myself and took it that Kim just hadn't had the guts to ask me not to see her again. I told his brother that I was only visiting Kim because she was poorly and he said that his brother wouldn't have a problem with that – not as though it would've stopped me because in all honesty, I didn't give a toss what he thought. Still though, this guy was there in the room with us and the private moment I wanted and needed so badly just wasn't going to happen. He started chatting and laughing with Kim and I looked at her and realised I didn't know what had been happening in her life for the past few months and I felt I didn't know her anymore, a feeling that absolutely killed me at the time.

I had to leave Bristol and head back to Wimbledon knowing that there was nothing I could do about the situation, which, of course, had all been originally instigated by my immaturity a few years before. It's fair to say I was in bits and up to that point had never felt so bad in my life. My whole world had stopped, but my mum was brilliant, as ever, and she said, "This isn't about you, now. Hopefully she'll get better and you can go in and see her again." I said I couldn't, not while her boyfriend was there – how could I? I wasn't even part of her life anymore. About a week later my mum called saying I had to go back home because Kim had asked to see me and her mum wanted to see me, too. Then, the words that I'll never forget, as she added, "She's finished with that lad and wants to start seeing you again."

"What do you mean finished with him?" I asked.

"She's given him the ring back and doesn't want to see him anymore." Apparently Kim had tried to end it before she'd fallen ill, but he'd blackmailed her by saying he'd kill himself or suchlike, but now her life was on the line, his threats didn't seem to matter and he was gone, exit stage left as they say. So I drove home to see her and she asked if we could start seeing one another again and that was it – it was the easiest question that I'd ever been asked.

I'd go back to Bristol whenever I could while the doctors tried to get to the bottom of what was wrong with her. She was allowed to go home and to go on days with me and one occasion, Kim turned her head to look at something and I noticed two lumps on her neck. "What are they, then?" I asked, and she touched them gently.

"I don't know," she said, but whatever they were, they didn't look right. The following day, the doctors did a biopsy on the lumps and the results revealed she had non-Hodgkin's lymphoma. I'd just got Kim back after nearly losing her to another bloke and now I had the very real possibility that I could lose her to cancer. It was unbelievable.

The focus and clarity Kim had from that moment on was utterly inspiring because she told me she was going to deal with this illness and meet it full on. She started her treatment once a week and I'd travel home and be there as often as I could while she underwent the course of chemotherapy. On each occasion we tried to make the most of our time together because we never knew whether or not each meeting would be the last one. We had some fantastic times, sharing moments neither of us will ever forget, not knowing if the future we yearned for together would ever become reality or not. Kim later told me that those days we planned had given her a target to aim for and no matter how poorly the treatment made her feel, she knew that the next course would also be just a part of another day for us to be together. She looked forward to it as much as I did, though I felt incredibly guilty that I wasn't on hand all the time, and tried to get home as much as possible. It was hard to travel back and forwards all the time because all the while, I was trying to carve out a career with Wimbledon and during the season, your time's not really your own. My energy levels were in the red and I was running on fumes. I was tired all the time and had little or no strength, something I'd never suffered from before, but it would be a while before anyone would actually diagnose my condition not as exhaustion, but as glandular fever.

I either slept after training or was spending every spare minute travelling back to Bristol and that didn't go down too well with the Crazy Gang, who regularly had little get-togethers, partly why their team spirit was strong back then. I was ostracising myself away from the other lads, unintentionally – though I couldn't honestly give a shit about that, even to this day. I had something much more real and important to deal with and if they saw me as an outsider who wasn't going to come in, so what?

My brother John lived close to Wimbledon and as I was in digs at first, whenever Kim was well enough to come up, we stayed at his flat. We were just about getting by, but I felt physically weak and mentally all over the place but I had to keep going. What other choice was there?

Wimbledon Football Club was quite a strange place to be and the Crazy Gang were suitably led by Harry Bassett, who was crazier than anybody. Harry was an open and honest bloke whom I really liked. They had a good squad, too, with the likes of Dennis Wise, Lawrie Sanchez, Wally Downes, Stuart Evans, Nigel Winterburn, Alan Cork and Kevin Gage. I was finding training difficult because of the fatigue I was suffering from and I'd wake at night sweating, with my sheets soaked through. Harry told me to ease off a little in training, thinking that the effort I put in was exhausting me.

"No, I'm fine and that's how I've always trained," I told him. "There's something wrong with me." Behind my back, however, the physio was telling Harry that there was nothing wrong me and that it was more likely to be down to the fact that I couldn't handle playing at a higher level, cheeky fecker. They told me I was dehydrated, had a chest infection and also diagnosed me with several other ailments, but basically the truth was my immune system was knackered by the glandular fever, which nobody had yet picked up on or even considered. Geoff Taylor was on the coaching staff and he was a big help during my time there. The lads used to call him 'Ballbag' because after every training session he'd shout, "Put them bloody balls back in the bag will you?" He'd been with Harry for years and also worked with the kids a lot and he was probably the only person who showed me a little bit of sympathy regarding what was happening in my life at that time. Mick Smith and Lawrie Sanchez were different class, too, because they would do anything to help me and stayed out of the piss-taking and wind-ups. I made other good friends in Kevin Gage, Glyn Hodges, Nigel Winterburn and Stevie Galliers, but the fact I couldn't really socialise with the squad and get to know them better meant I was viewed as some kind of outsider. I wasn't a country bumpkin, but I just thought some of their antics and humour went over the top. I became the butt of a couple of the lads' jokes and though I've always believed I've got quite a good sense of humour, some of them went too far. I felt it was a London thing, if that makes any sense.

"What's it like dating a baldy bird," was one of the comments in reference to Kim's chemotherapy. Wally Downes and a couple of others found that really funny and in later years I would confront him about it. He has since apologised, but it was clear we were never destined to be great mates. There were a lot of piss-takers and banter always flying around and they even had their own pub, The Plough, at the end of the ground. They'd arrange little get-togethers there but I never went along to any of them because I didn't have the time and I'd put any one of them in my shoes and I bet they'd have done exactly the same thing.

The one occasion I did go out with the lads, I realised not being out with them regularly was a bonus after one of them spiked my drinks. The next day I had to be brought off at half-time, but none of them told Harry why I was struggling and that it hadn't been my doing. There was definitely a bullying culture at the club and if you were on the receiving end, as I was quite often, you'd better have thick skin otherwise they'd destroy you. Wally liked to dish it out and he could be quite ruthless with some of the things he said, and you either came through it and became one of them – or you didn't. I wasn't used to it because it hadn't been like that at Rovers, but I accepted that was their way. Harry had a couple of chats with me about it, saying I was too honest and had to lighten up, and then came out with the classic line, "You've got to be more like Wally." I didn't want to be anything like Wally because I cared about people, and for my manager to tell me that, it was a bit much. I understood what he meant, thinking I had to be crafty and have a bit more about me – or at least more than I was showing at the time, but he was the last person I wanted to be like. Some of the things the lads did to each other, like cutting the bottom of your jeans pockets so your money falls through or cutting out the crotch of your pants so when you pull them up they go right up to your chest, just didn't make me laugh, even though it was happening to other lads. Even if I had been in the right frame of mind, I still would think it was childish at best, because it's not my type of humour. Lawrie Sanchez was on the end of a lot of Wally's wind-ups but he wasn't having any of it and just let it wash over him. He'd read a book, listen to music or concentrate on the successful wine bar he owned – he didn't give a toss what they thought and I admired him a hell of a lot for it. Lawrie was in the team, though, and doing well, so he also had that to fall back on – I had nothing. But, what doesn't kill you makes you stronger and I learned from those experiences, and even though I initially wanted to fit in and be one of the lads, I don't think I was ever accepted in that respect and it was a hard time for me.

Chapter 6

Bee Stung

All the travelling and worry was exhausting every bone in my body, but the love of the game drew me in, even though I felt like death warmed up, and on one occasion I could've got into serious trouble with Wimbledon – had they ever found out.

I was out of the team so I went back to Bristol for the weekend and while I was at Kim's mum and dad's, her old man cajoled me into playing for local amateur side, Cadbury Heath. They were short of a player and he convinced me to come along as sub, telling me that nobody would know who I was because it was an away game deep in Somerset. I thought, 'What the hell?' – it couldn't do any harm and the way things had been going, what if my club did find out? Kim came to watch and stood on the sidelines with me, and Cadbury Heath went 1-0 down. We needed a win to stay up so they stuck me on in the second half and everything I did went right for the first time in what seemed like an age. My first touch almost set up a goal and my second resulted in a run and cross that set up the manager Steve Risdale to equalise. Steve ran past me with about 10 minutes to go – and by this time we were 2-1 up – and he said out the corner of his mouth, "For fuck's sake, do something wrong!"

"What?"

"Give the ball away. Trip over the fucking thing. Anything!" Their sub must have been growing suspicious because he shouted, "How come he didn't fucking start, then?"

Before the 'ringer' suspicions grew any stronger, I tripped over one ball and let another one go out of play and that seemed to make a few of their fans settle down again. It was fantastic to be just playing football again, real football at that, and I played just for the sake of it, and all the worries and concern about Kim and my own health problems were forgotten for 45 minutes, and all in the silver wrapping of Cadbury Heath. I got a lot of self-belief back in that game, though probably broke every rule in the book in doing so. Cadbury Heath would have probably been relegated and I was in breach of contract with my club, but that afternoon nothing mattered except playing just for the love of it. I felt a little guilty about it and the next day I was at dad's and he said, "I heard you had a game yesterday. How did you go on?"

"All right," I replied sheepishly.

"I heard you did better than that," he said. I should've known better than to think my playing would have escaped his network of sources!

I was still constantly tired and my next visit home was a few weeks later, by which time I'd moved on loan to Brentford, and this time I got mum to book me in to see the local GP. Just talking to him was enough for him to surmise that he reckoned I had glandular fever. He added it was no wonder I wasn't playing football, because, in his eyes, it would be almost impossible. He took some blood and water and a week later I received an urgent phone call telling me that if I was playing, I had to stop because it had been confirmed I did have glandular fever. Frank McClintock at Brentford had asked to take me on loan to Griffin Park and I took the opportunity to go there and play some football again. I wasn't bothered about moving back down to the Third Division and Bassett thought I could build my fitness and confidence back up so everyone seemed happy. In fact, Wimbledon were looking a good bet to go up to the top flight for the first time in their history, so they weren't overly concerned about whether I was around or not.

I played a few times for the Bees before I was told about the glandular fever, and I told Frank that I'd been advised to stop playing and rest, but he said I'd been doing really well and asked me to carry on, which like an idiot, I did. It got to the stage during the week where Wimbledon thought I must be training with Brentford and Brentford thought I must be training with Wimbledon where in fact I was in bed, ill at home. I managed to see out the season with the Bees, and Wimbledon won promotion in my absence. I had two years of my contract left at Plough Lane but Brentford were keen to buy me and had offered £25,000, so I spoke to Harry to find out where I stood in his plans and he said, "Look, son. I like you, but it hasn't gone that well. I'd like you to marry my daughter, but I don't want you playing in my team sometimes because you're too honest. Try and get a bit more like the others we've got here, or you can go to Brentford. It's entirely up to you." In all honesty, I didn't spend that much time thinking about it and decided to jump out of my contract with what was now the equivalent of a Premiership club, and join a Third Division club instead, which in hindsight was absolute madness. The Ian Holloway prior to the illness would never have done that because I would have had a point to prove at Wimbledon. I was only 23 and would have had a chance to play at Old Trafford, Anfield, Maine Road, White Hart Lane and Highbury, but I made the wrong decision – big time.

After I signed I take no pride in admitting that I was rubbish at Brentford and had a torrid time there because the illness appeared to come and go, and some days I'd feel okay and others like a zombie. I think they all thought I was making excuses for some reason or another. I got them to sign my mate Phil Bater from Rovers and they also brought in Paul Maddy and Gary Stevens. Frank felt we had a decent squad and was convinced we were going to get promoted, but I couldn't do a damn thing right. I was the original weakest link. Brentford employed Terry Mancini to help Frank when Johnny Doherty, his assistant, left for Millwall, because things were going so bad for the team. I was being left out of the side on merit, or lack of, as their patience ran out and I didn't get on with Terry at all, probably because he spoke the truth when he told me I was crap and wasn't doing it for the team.

Frank was telling me one thing and the next day Terry would say, "Look, Frank gets a little bit excited so I want you to do this instead." It ended up with me going to Frank because I didn't know whether I was coming or going. "What is it with you two?" I said. "He's telling me one thing and you're telling me another. I've had enough of this bullshit – any chance of speaking in the same feckin' language?"

"Do you think he's after my job?" Frank asked me, and I said I didn't know what he was after. I added, "I wish Terry would just shut his mouth and I'll play for you."

I didn't believe I could play as a winger as I was being asked to do, especially the way I was feeling. I'd sometimes look at the full-back I'd be up against and defeat myself before I even started – that wasn't me because my nature was to enjoy that type of physically mis-matched challenge. I'd talk myself out of a game and I thought, "Jesus, I'm in trouble, here." Finding out why I was thinking that way and the real reason I was so weak was a massive relief, because I knew it would pass out of my system as time went on.

It's such a shame that I couldn't have enjoyed my time at Brentford because I doubt I'd ever find better people to work with in Frank and Johnny Doc – two terrific characters that refused to let us get downbeat. Even if we lost it would be Frank and Johnny that got up and started the singing and there was a fantastic spirit in the camp. The trouble was, we just couldn't turn camaraderie into results and everything poor Frank tried to do that year just went wrong. In his thick Scottish accent he came in one day and said, "Jesus Christ what's going wrong with me? I went for a run this morning and got bit by a fucking dog and for Christ's sake, I started apologising to the owner! I came away thinking, 'Jesus, Frank, why didn't I kick the flea-bitten bastard in the bollocks?' I'm becoming someone I didn't want to fucking be – lads, please, help me out – I'm gonna get the fucking sack." It was funny because of the way he said it and even then, he could laugh at himself and I loved him for that.

There were other characters knocking around like former Chelsea veteran, Mickey Droy, who were coming towards the end of their careers. Mickey loved a smoke in the dressing room and probably would've taken a light out with him on to the pitch if he could have got away with it. Former Ipswich and Villa striker Dave Geddes was there on loan, too and these lads must have been on a fair whack at the time, and the fact we weren't winning games was piling the pressure on Frank. He had the quality, but nothing went right for him and when Johnny Doc left to take a job at Millwall, it was the beginning of the end of his reign at Griffin Park because Doc left just when Frank needed him most. Having said that, I was probably the main bugbear of that bloody awful season we had. It just goes to prove that Ian Holloway in red and white just ain't right.

Frank was finally put out of his misery by the board and one of the lads he'd brought in towards the end, Steve Perryman, took over as boss. I was still suffering from bouts of chronic fatigue, but Perryman was a man I idolised as a kid and I even used to have his poster on my bedroom wall. Despite all that, it wouldn't take long to figure out that he hadn't a clue where my strengths lay. During his first few games he'd be on the touchline shouting, "Run at him, go on, run at him!" I wasn't a winger and was fed up with the way he was trying to play me so I wrote a long list of things out – rightly or wrongly – and gave it to him. I thought I had nothing to lose, but I don't think he took too kindly to that.

Dad came up to watch me one week and I had a stinker. Later, as I drove him back to Bristol, he said, "Why don't you just come home, son. Come back and play for Bath City. I can't watch you playing like that anymore."

I was so crestfallen I couldn't even reply, because he was the one who had always made me believe in my own ability, and for him to come out and say what he had must have meant it had been torture for him to see me so unhappy and out of sorts. I felt like I'd failed him. I had to prove that I still had it in me to be a success. First, I had to get back to full fitness, and in truth, I could began to feel some of my strength was returning. It was too late to save my Brentford career, though and I was dropped from the side. Perryman came up to me and said, "Look, I've had a couple of phone calls about you, how do you feel about going out on loan?" I said I was fine because I needed to keep playing and maybe put myself in the shop window again. One of the sides interested was Torquay, which I thought wasn't that far from Bristol so I decided to go there for a month. I spoke to their manager Stuart Morgan and what a breath of fresh air he turned out to be. He kept telling me how good he thought I was, which is what I needed to hear at that time, and that he'd seen me when I played for Rovers and he reckoned a few weeks in Devon would do me the world of good. Frank McClintock had taken me on the strength of my days at Eastville, too, which suggested I hadn't done much since. Those days seemed an age ago and I wished I could play half as well as I did during my time there. Morgan said that he didn't care what I did or where I went training, so long as I met up with the lads on a Friday, which would earn me the nickname Robinson Crusoe (Man Friday) with the lads.

Torquay thought I was training with Brentford and Brentford thought I was training with Torquay, but as before when I'd gone out on loan, the truth was I was back in Bristol in bed, trying to regenerate my body. I did well for Torquay, probably because I'd preserved what little energy I had during the week for the match at the weekend and each time, I found I had just enough to see me through 90 minutes. We won three games in a row, which Torquay hadn't done all season. It was just the fillip I needed and it restored some confidence when

I'd been running on memories for the best part of two years. Kim and I would stay at a bed and breakfast in Torquay and we just relaxed, and I felt totally detached from it all. I broke my toe against Notts County while I was at Plainmoor after I kicked the underside of Big Sam Allardyce's boot and it was bloody painful. I told Stuart Morgan that I thought I done some damage and he told me to get treatment back at Brentford so I'd be right for the following week.

I went in to see Ron Woolnough the Brentford physio and a man with more scams on the go than Arthur Daley. I never really got on with him because I was always complaining about feeling ill and I think he thought I was a malingerer. I never thought he was thorough enough with me, and thought he could have picked up what was wrong with me through blood tests or whatever, so with trepidation I went to see him about my toe.

"If you've broken your toe I'll eat my bloody hat," he said.

"I think I need an X-ray Ron." "No you bloody don't. An X-ray won't change anything because the treatment will be the same." He then asked me to run up some steps – unbelievable! I sorted an X-ray out myself and the guy said, "Oh yeah, you've broken your toe, mate." I asked him to mark on the image where the bone was broken and then took the film into Ron, with a hat. I said, "Do you want some salt with that?" I asked. "Go on then, you'd better eat that hat." He didn't see the funny side and maintained the treatment was the same regardless if it was broken or badly bruised and I said, "Yeah? Well the doctor said I wasn't supposed to run up feckin' steps on a broken toe."

"Get on the bike, then," he said and got on with treating somebody else. It felt good to prove Ron wrong and he couldn't say a word this time.

I returned to Torquay to play one more match after having a pain-killing injection in my toe, but my loan was up after that. They needed results to go their way to avoid relegation out of the Football League – and their fate rested on the teeth of an Alsatian dog called Bryn. On the last day of the season Torquay lay second bottom, with Burnley one point behind them and Lincoln City one above. A win would keep them up, but they were soon 2-0 down at home to Crewe, and the news that Burnley were winning filtered through. Torquay did pull one back, but despite throwing everything at Crewe, they looked doomed to defeat. In the pandemonium of the last few minutes of normal time, as the crowd threatened to run on the pitch, a police dog bit the Torquay skipper Jim McNichol as he made to take a throw-in. The game was stopped for four minutes and, despite the news that Burnley had won, Lincoln City had lost at Swansea. If Torquay could get a point they could escape on goal difference. Three minutes into time added on for the police dog incident, Paul Dobson scored and Torquay retained their League status with just seconds remaining on the clock. It was an unbelievable escape and I only wished I could have been part of what must have been an incredible day, and I was delighted for the lads, fans and for Stuart Morgan who'd restored my belief again.

Wimbledon were in the top division and doing well and Torquay had just avoided becoming a non-League side. I'd literally gone from one extreme to the other and I seemed powerless to stop the slide downwards. It was a joke!

At least one happy thing happened during that period as Kim and I got engaged and had moved into a flat together in Croydon in 1986. We had no furniture at the start and I remember us watching the Mexico World Cup on a few cushions scattered on the floor. It was just us and we had our whole lives in front of us. It was magical. We'd had long conversations about the future and what it meant for us both. With her treatment over and Kim given the all-clear by her doctors, I asked her to marry me. We'd agreed there was no point doing anything until she was well again but now she was, I wasn't going to lose her again and I'm happy to say she accepted. There was no bending down on one knee, but things were crystal clear in our minds. We had a life to get on with and there was no time to waste. We arranged to get married the following summer and though the doctors had told her that the chemotherapy would likely render her infertile, it didn't matter. There'd always be other options open to us in future years if we wanted to take them. The flat wasn't up to much, but we were together and that's all that mattered. We got married in May 1987, though it was a quiet wedding with just a few close friends and family, and a month later, Kim missed a period and we wondered… was it possible, despite being told otherwise? We got a pregnancy testing kit and both watched as a little dot appeared in the middle window. We were ecstatic and it was the icing on the cake for us – it's potent water up in Croydon! It proves the old saying, never say never, because nobody can really predict what path your life will follow, and for us it was a genuine miracle.

I returned for pre-season training with Brentford as we prepared for the 1987/88 season, though I was still suffering from bouts of fatigue from time to time. New faces began arriving and it seemed there was no future at Griffin Park for me under Steve Perryman. The only way forward was to leave. A Swedish club came in for me, wanting to buy me for £12,000 and Perryman told me about it, adding that he didn't think I had what it took to play for his team. I asked him if they were going to watch me in a practice game we had between the first team and the reserves and he told me they were. "Well stick me in centre midfield for God's sake," I said.

"You're not a centre midfield player," he said. I said I was and he relented and said he'd go along with it, probably thinking he'd do anything if it meant me finding another club. Desperate to show Perryman what I could do, I scored one and made another as the reserves won 2-1 as the guys from Sweden watched on the sidelines. Afterwards, I was told that if I wanted to, I could sign for the Swedes within 24 hours, but I wasn't sure what to do. I had a baby on the way and wasn't sure what would be the best thing to do. I was up for the move, but called Gordon Bennett at Rovers to see what he thought about it. He told me straight, "Whatever you do, don't sign. You'll go over there and you'll get forgotten about. See it out at Brentford, tell Perryman to stick it up his arse and that you're not leaving."

What Gordon said made sense, so I told Perryman I was staying and he reacted by sticking me on the transfer list. He didn't want me and my career just seemed to be drifting aimlessly, at least that's how it felt. Shortly before the new season began, I played against Aldershot in a friendly – on the left wing for Christ's sake – and Gerry Francis, now manager at Bristol Rovers was watching in the stands. He called me later that day and said, "We've been given permission to talk to you Ollie, and we've agreed a price of £12,000. I saw you today and I thought you were crap."

"Why do you want to buy me then?"

"Because I can make you play better than that. Left-wing? You're having a laugh, aren't you? You've got to be either on the right or in the middle and I'm sure I can get you playing better than that, plus I know your dad's not been too good, so why don't you just come home, spend some time with him and get playing again? I'll give you a day to think about it."

I thought about what Gerry had said, but was puzzled as to why he'd mentioned my dad. Dad knew a lot of people and some of them were close to Gerry and Rovers, so I supposed that his heart condition wasn't a secret as such. He had angina and I supposed that it must have been fairly common knowledge he was on the waiting list for a triple heart by-pass operation, but as far as I knew, he was doing reasonably well. He had always been a fit bloke and was always running around doing this and that and keeping himself active. Plenty of people had heart attacks and made full recoveries, so why not him? As far as I was concerned he was going to be around for another 30 years or so, but all the same, it placed a seed of doubt in my mind that perhaps he wasn't doing as well as I was being led to believe. I looked at Kim and we spoke about it and then she said, "Well why don't we go home?" Why not indeed? It wasn't happening for me in London and had never felt right since day one, admittedly, mostly because of what had been going on in Bristol. I liked Harry Bassett a lot and he was always fair and straight with me but I'd never settled at Plough Lane and hadn't exactly been welcomed with open arms by Steve Perryman, who clearly didn't rate me, so it was the easiest footballing decision I'd ever had to make. I called Gerry back and said 'yes' and informed Brentford I was leaving. It felt right, and for the first time since I'd left Bristol, going back to my home town, back to my boyhood club, back to my family and friends with the girl I loved on my arm and a baby on the way, was what I believe they call today a 'no-brainer'. I still called Gordon Bennett to see what he thought and he said, "Oh, I wouldn't go back. It's not good to go back." He'd told me not leave Wimbledon, but I had, and now he was saying don't leave Brentford, and though I could see his logic, it felt right for Kim and me, and so we did. It was probably the first time in my life I hadn't put my career first. This was a personal decision and for once, it was the right one.

Chapter 7

Back Home

We gathered our belongings and hired a truck for the move back home. A great mate of mine, Keith Millen, a centre-half at Brentford helped me pack up the truck and that one-bedroom flat suddenly became like the inside of the bloody Tardis. I couldn't believe how much stuff we'd accumulated and it took an age to load it all up. We must have looked like the Beverly Hillbillies as we pulled away with only a rocking chair missing from the roof of the truck. We left at 5am the following morning and by the time we approached Membury Services on the M4 – about halfway back to Bristol – we couldn't see more than a couple of feet ahead due to thick fog that had descended. I was panicking a bit because we were running on fumes but we couldn't see anything and had to trundle along at a snail's pace. Finally, we saw the signs for the services and managed to make it to the petrol pumps, only for a bloke to come out and tell us that we'd have to take a service road over the motorway to the other side because they'd run out of diesel. Fantastic. I wasn't sure we'd make it, but we drove onto the service road up a hill and over a bridge and as we came down on the other side, the road seemed to veer sharply to the right. I came to halt in the grass verge and I heard a noise and looked out to see what it was, only to be greeted by a cow looking over a fence, inches away, just staring at us. "What are you bloody looking at?" I asked just as a car flew past us at speed and was gone in a flash. I asked Kim, "Did we really just see that?" Had it not been for old Ermintrude, I reckon he'd have rear-ended us – maybe worse. I found the petrol station, filled up and we crossed back over the motorway and slowly continued on our way. We moved in with Kim's folks and stored the furniture in her dad's garage while we looked to find a new home, and within a few weeks we'd found a lovely old house in need of renovation and I came up with a hair-brained scheme to do the work myself. I took my dad round and he absolutely slaughtered it. "What are you doing you idiot? What are you thinking about? This is a hell of a job and you've got no chance of getting this into shape…" He went on for a bit, but we bought it anyway. I think he could see it was going to be a bit of a money pit, but we could see what it could be like, and with a baby on the way, we were determined to get a big family home ready for the winter. With the help of my mate Paul Lewton, who was a workaholic builder, we reckoned we could just about do it. I'd been away once and come back to Bristol and I couldn't ever see myself leaving again, so we put our heart and soul into the renovation work and on my afternoon off, Kim and I would nip off to Bath and browse antique markets and bric-a-brac shops looking for knick-knacks, fittings and furniture.

Dad would come around and give me a hand from time to time, but he wasn't well and was getting chest pains – probably much more severe than he let on. Kim used to despair when Pen would turn up unannounced and take one look at me covered from head to toe in dust and say, "Coming out for a game of golf, Ollie?" He hadn't changed a bit, though in truth, after my experiences at Wimbledon, it was good to see him again. Kim would invariably tell Pen I was busy – in so many words – and on one particular day I told him I had to get on with painting the skirting boards. The next day at training, I walked in and all the lads were on their hands and knees painting imaginary skirting boards around the dressing room. Pen was a bloody nightmare but because he was a fully qualified plumber and could have helped me out, I called him up and told him I needed a plumber urgently and he said, "No problem, mate, just look in the Yellow Pages under 'P'," he laughed at his own joke and then hung up. Like I said – a bloody nightmare. Who needs mates like that?

I was always in a rush to get things finished and on one occasion I almost paid the price for my haste. I was doing some tiling and had to take the light switch off, but didn't turn the mains off first. As I was doing the last few tiles I touched a live wire and electrocuted myself. I couldn't get away from the bugger and as the doorbell rang, I somehow managed to fall backwards on to the floor with my hair stuck out like an Afro. With a distinct smell of singed flesh in the air, dad walked in the room and shook his head. "I shall have to live till I'm one hundred and fifty to look after you, you silly sod."

We had some laughs doing that house and we weren't far off finishing when dad fell ill. We'd prepared the kitchen for plastering and later on he'd gone to watch a match with his mate, but on the way back he asked to be driven straight to hospital because the pains in his chest had worsened. He'd had another heart attack and this time it was major one.

The warning signs had been there, but he carried on anyway, never really telling anyone if he was in pain, and now he'd landed back in hospital, seven years after his first attack.

I went to see him every day, and four days after he'd been admitted – it was a Wednesday – I left hospital in high spirits because he'd perked up and was laughing and joking again. I'd taken Devon White with me and Devon was a tall, strapping striker from Rovers who was also doing the wiring on our house. Dad looked up at him and said, "Hello mate. Good God! I wouldn't like to argue with you! You're a big 'un aren't you my old mate?" He seemed almost back to his old self after a few days of not really seeming to have been there at all, no doubt partly due to the morphine he was receiving. I went back to the house feeling happier about everything, and started mixing the plaster for Paul. Not long after there was a frantic knock at the door – it was my sister Sue and my heart sank. "You've got to come quickly. Dad's taken a turn for the worse." I was devastated. I hadn't seen him that long ago and he'd improved loads from the day before. We rushed to hospital and from start to finish, it was just a horrific experience. To us, he was getting better and there were no indications that anything untoward would happen, yet there we were, at his bedside, watching him slowly slipping away. All the immediate family were there but after a short time we were asked to go into another room – he had another attack and they managed to resuscitate him, but his breathing was awful, heavy and laboured, and it was torture to listen to. We were told he probably wouldn't last the night and mum stayed by his side, but had to come out a couple of times while they revived him again. He'd lost his blood pressure and time passed into the early hours and we all knew we were just waiting for him to die which is the most terrible thing I'd ever experienced.

I had a game to play later that day and I couldn't stand it any longer. I didn't want to see dad suffering like that so I said I was going home because I had a match to play for Rovers, and we left about 7am, though it killed me to do it. I knew dad would be angry if I didn't play because he'd spent his whole life making sure I turned up on time and was properly prepared to play. Within an hour, we had a call to say that he'd died – he was just 59, which is no age at all, is it?

A woman who had been in the next bed to dad called mum a few weeks later to say that after each time he'd been revived he asked the doctors what they were doing. "It's my time to go…why are you doing that?" he'd almost whispered. That wasn't my dad because he loved life and lived it to the full. He'd always told me to live each day as if it were my last, because one day it would be, and for him to want to leave and be at rest meant he couldn't take the pain any longer. He also said he'd been to a lovely place and that he hadn't wanted to come back, and I think we all took a little something from that. For me, hearing what dad had said meant I had to wipe my blackboard clean, because he'd always been the one who told me that when you died that was it, and this contradicted everything I'd been taught and believed in.

We'd at least had the opportunity to be with him and say things we needed to say but knowing the way he was, if he had pulled through that night, chances are he wouldn't have been the same man, and that would have made him unhappy. If he could have, I reckon he'd have said, "I've had a hell of a go at it and enjoyed every single day, but when your time comes, that's the way it's meant to be."

I was in pieces when I heard he'd died. I wanted him to be okay and get better and just be my dad again, but you don't always get the things you want in life, do you? He couldn't have done any more for me than he did and I think he did the job of two dads – the one he didn't have himself and the one he wanted to be for us. Everything I ever really wanted, I got, and for that I'll always be eternally grateful to both my parents. Everyone knew Bill Holloway, and my brother-in-law, Phil, always said he thought dad was the richest man in the world because wherever he went he gave warmth to others and they gave it right back to him. He's still with me, though it's getting harder to hear his voice in my mind. From that moment on, I vowed to get my career back on track and use the loss, pain and grief I felt by channelling it into my football. It was the only way I could deal with things and it was the start of a new chapter in my career. Whether he was around to see it or not, I was going to make him proud of me.

My decision to play just hours after he'd died, I believe, was one of the best I made during my playing career. It was obviously one of the hardest, too, but I called Gerry Francis to tell him what had happened and that I wanted to play that night. We had an FA Cup replay against VS Rugby at Twerton Park and Gerry asked if I was sure I'd be alright and I told him I'd be okay.

"That's fine by me, then," he said. I'd intended on keeping the news of dad's passing to just very close family and Gerry so that I could get on with the game without anyone mentioning it to me. The last thing I wanted to do was to break down in front of 8,000 fans, and I thought that was the case, but when I ran out to warm up before the match, there were a few people who did seem to know. I had to run straight back in. It turned out somebody from the hospital informed the Evening Post and they'd run a brief story about it – I was fuming, but I still had a game to focus on.

None of the lads seemed to know and if they did, they kept it to themselves, but anybody watching me that night probably guessed something wasn't quite right. All the anger and grief I was immersed in came out in one of my best performances ever for the club. The ball was all I cared about and I could hear dad saying, "Always believe it's yours. Make it yours." Every time the ball dropped near me I was in for it first and won it, and it was as if all the self-doubt, fear of failure and hesitancy I'd been carrying with me throughout my career just lifted from my shoulders. If he was ever with me during a game, it was that night, because I could feel him there in my boots. I played like a man possessed and was all over the place during a match we won 4-0, and after the game I finally broke down, overcome with the events of the past 24 hours.

In truth, things hadn't gone at all well at Rovers since I'd returned and for the first time I'd started to hear a few moans and groans around the ground. I remember a ball came to me and it went straight under my foot and out of play. There were one or two boos, which I'd never had before, but Pen ran 30 yards to me and said, "Come on Ol, get on with it, get on with it!" A few minutes later we had a corner and little Phil Purnell, another lad I'd known all my life, ran up and said, "Come on Ol! Come on son!" and I realised I needed people to get through this. I knew that if I could get through that and play after what had happened, I could do anything and my fear of failure had gone in an instant.

I later went to the chapel of rest but I didn't kiss dad goodbye or touch his hand because as a kid I'd been to see my grandfather at rest and given him a kiss on the cheek, but he was stone cold and I hadn't expected it. I didn't want that to be my last memory of dad so I just popped my head in and as I looked at his body I felt – not heard – him say, "That's not me anymore." I felt that wherever dad was now, it wasn't there in the chapel of rest. He looked like he was made of plastic and it was bloody awful. In my mind I could see him fresh and young, running around, joking and full of life. I almost wish I hadn't gone and seen him lying there because he didn't need me to do that, and I would rather not have that memory of him. Everything felt different in my life. I felt very lonely. If I had a problem with my house I couldn't just pick up the phone and talk to dad about it anymore and the feeling of loss was all encompassing. Probably the hardest thing for me was knowing he'd never hold my child, who was due just three months later. He'd had such a special relationship with his first grandson, Sue's little boy, Luke, and he would have been the same with my little one. He'd go round to Sue's house every Friday, pick Luke up from school then stay for his dinner and play rough and tumble with him. It was wonderful to watch. Luke still misses his Granddad today, some 20 years on.

Mum took on a full-time job the week after dad's death and showed her inner strength by getting on with her life when she could have just as easily hid herself from the outside world while she grieved.

The funeral was one of the weirdest experiences I think I've ever had because I felt as though I was watching everything from afar, as though I wasn't actually taking part. There were hundreds of people at the service which was at a crematorium in Bath for some reason, and the wake was held at a club dad used to go to with all his mates. People were saying things to me about him, but I can't remember anything because the whole day seemed to be played out in slow motion. I saw some people look at me and then look away and I just thought they were cowards because I had a lot more respect for the people who tried to say a few words, even if they couldn't quite get them out. We all managed to keep it together on the day, even though we were all in something of a stupor, but I felt angry and cheated because he was just 59 for God's sake. My only advice to anyone reading this is to tell the people you love exactly what you think of them while they're here. Tell them you love them and how much they mean to you and, like dad always told me, never go to bed on an argument, because if you lose somebody without doing any of that, you'll regret it for the rest of your life.

Another one of his sayings was "One out, one in," meaning that for every death in a family there would be one birth, and the old rascal was right, because our first child was born just a couple of months later on March 6, 1988. Kim went into labour and the moment I knew the baby was coming I rushed her to hospital because I had an irrational fear of the baby coming quickly and me ending up like Frank Spencer trying to deliver it myself. We got there, but the baby wasn't born until 9pm at night, by which time I was in the bad books after moaning about how long it was taking. My off-the-cuff comment, "I wouldn't be here for just anybody, you know!" during a heated discussion, ended with Kim verbally launching into me. I think I probably just about deserved it. I nipped out to get something to eat in my sister's car, 'Bluebell' – a beautiful blue VW Beetle – and I found a chippy nearby, but there was a fair old queue and the woman behind the counter said there was a five minute wait for chips. I had an odd feeling I needed to get back sharpish so I just asked for a pasty and set off back to see Kim. All the while, Kim was ready to give birth and was holding on as best she could. The midwife asked if I'd be upset at missing the birth because the baby was ready to come out at any second and Kim said, "Bloody right he would!" Just then, she heard me whistling in the corridor, not a moment too soon. Kim was sure we'd have a girl and was shocked when our first born turned out to be a boy. I was in floods of tears and the midwife wrapped him in a blanket and handed my little son to me and at that moment, everything felt right in the world and I understood what life was all about. I knew why dad had been like he had with me and if I could have hugged him at that moment as I was hugging my baby, it would have made my world complete. We'd been planning to call him Jacob, but Kim was more than happy when I asked if we could call him William after his Granddad. It was an amazing, life-changing event, but that, of course, is when the really hard part began.

Paul Lewton, who'd worked ever so hard on helping us get our house finished, had just finished his nursery by the time we returned home, and I'll be forever grateful for the way he got on with things on his own. I quickly learned, however, that babies don't sleep to order. William sounded like a little warthog, snorting and grunting, and I asked Kim if he was going to be like that all the time. I was paranoid about getting my sleep, especially around matchdays and after three weeks he had to go in his own room. He was given his first red card – he invariably had an early bath each day anyway – and after another month or so, he slept all the way through the night – thank God!

Things were going well for us but something happened that made me wonder about things like guardian angels and whether maybe dad was keeping a watch over his grandson after all. It happened when Kim, alone at home with the baby, was out in the garden and she heard somebody call out her name. She thought it was me – or my dad's voice – I've been told I sound a lot like him. "Kim…Kim…Kim…?" It was so clear that she wondered if somebody had come around the side of the house because they'd been knocking at the front door. She went in the house and opened the front door but there was nobody there. Then she heard William's muffled screams from upstairs. She ran up to find him underneath his blankets, red faced and in distress. How can you explain anything like that away? Derek Acorah eat your bloody heart out! We took a lot of comfort from that moment and I think mum did, too. Mum forged a tight bond with baby William and I think he helped her through that difficult first year without dad. She'd come up once a week and take him away for the day to give us a breather. She loved taking him out shopping or round to see her friends, and they are like two peas in a pod to this day. So I'd lost one William and gained another. One out, one in, just like the silly old sod had said.

Chapter 8

Ollie and the Chocolate Factory

My first year back at Rovers had been an emotional rollercoaster for me, and sometimes I wonder how I managed to get through it, but football is a wonderful panacea and for me, playing regularly in familiar surroundings was exactly what I needed. I say familiar, but we were now playing at Twerton Park, home of Bath City FC, and it wasn't quite the same old Rovers anymore.

Gerry Francis had gathered together a great group of lads, many of whom had gone out of league football into non-league, and then come back into the league with Rovers, but I knew virtually all of them and they were good, down-to-earth people. Twerton was a ramshackled old ground and I think visiting teams found the sloping ground and facilities tough to deal with. The visitors' dressing rooms were horrendous and I don't think anybody really fancied playing us there. We liked it though, because the pitch was quite narrow and tight, which suited our style of closing teams down, and I quickly learned just how organised Gerry was as a manager. He was very positive and methodical and you knew what day it was just by the training session we were doing. He'd been a winner all his life and he was a winner in everything he did. He had a great eye for a player, too, as proved by the goalie he'd brought in from a Cornish non-league side called St Blazey. A lot of people have claimed to have discovered Nigel Martyn, but if I reveal the true identity of the undercover scout to be Vi Harris, our tea lady from Eastville, it might just about sum up Bristol Rovers FC! Vi had been on holiday in Cornwall and she invited Nigel up after seeing him play in a game while she was down there. Can you imagine Dot the Tea Lady at Arsenal inviting some kid down to a session for Arsène Wenger to run the rule at? No, me neither. Vi told Gerry that she'd asked him to come up for a trial and when he arrived he was absolutely spot-on. Des Bulpin put Nigel through his paces with the reserves and then ran over to Gerry and said, "My God, I think we've got one here. Come over and have a look at him." Twenty minutes later, Nigel was training with the first team and no matter what we tried, we just couldn't beat him. We already had a fantastic keeper in Nicky Carter, but Gerry signed Nigel on anyway. You wouldn't think it could happen that a bloke just walks in off the street and is taken on, would you? But that's exactly how Nigel began his career.

Big Devon White was another lad who'd come back into league football from non-league. Gerry remembered playing against him a few years before when he was looking to bring in a powerful striker and he thought of Big Dev who was then at Shepshed Charterhouse, playing part-time and working as an electrician. In a way, Gerry was building a team of renegades – lost souls, if you like.

Everyone got along well and I'd missed that kind of camaraderie during my time with Wimbledon and it was the kind of atmosphere I needed to be among. Another member of the squad, Andy Reece, was discovered in much the same way as Nigel Martyn, only his was more like a dream come true.

Kenny Hibbitt was still living in Birmingham and he was walking his dog one morning when he stopped to watch Goodyear Tyres playing a game on a nearby field. One player in particular, Andy Reece, caught his eye and at the end, Ken went over and asked him if he'd like to come to Rovers for a trial. Andy thought he was being wound up by one of his mates, because he was a huge Wolves fan and Ken was one of his heroes. Andy came up, impressed Gerry as well and was signed on, so we had Nigel who had been stacking shelves in a supermarket and Andy who had been working in a tyre factory. Andy was on such a high because for him, it was unbelievable to be there, and that lifted everybody.

I still wasn't playing anywhere near my best and was out on the right wing. I was lucky the Rovers fans remembered me from my first spell because they were patient with me when in truth I was toiling a bit. Then, at home to Sunderland, Kenny Hibbitt was on the end of a nasty tackle that broke his leg.

That inspired us to go on and beat them 4-0, but it also meant I moved into the middle, with Andy Reece alongside me and David Mehew switching from up front to out on the right. We formed quite a solid unit with Phil Purnell on the left and Pen up front. Gerry kept working with us to make us better, too.

I think the main ingredient to the team was that almost every one of us had something to prove. There were no stars, everyone was equal and the spirit we had was fantastic. We trained at Fry's Chocolate factory out at Keynsham, where the facilities were outstanding – but not owned by us – and typical Bristol Rovers, our dressing room was a portacabin out in the car park. We'd have our lunch with the factory workers – some were City fans, some were Rovers, and we'd occasionally go on factory tours and have skittle nights with them – it was a nice atmosphere.

Our kit man Ray Kendall was superb – he did everything and was Mr Bristol Rovers in my book. He used to say, "I can do a thousand jobs, but not a thousand and one, Ollie."

He'd pack the kit, take it over to Twerton in a van, make the place ours, then go and serve drinks in the boardroom. He'd take down all the Bath City pictures and put ours up and it must have been like moving house every week for him! He was an absolute ringer too for Darren's boss out of the old TV series Bewitched – a fantastic character that everyone loved. He did more for that club than anybody I knew and, as an example of how bad things had become financially at Rovers, there was an occasion when we had a game cancelled a few hours before kick-off and Ray was up in the boardroom and the chairman, Mr Dunford Senior, saw him preparing to throw a tray of sandwiches away. He told him, "You can't throw those away, Ray. You'll have to take them home and freeze them." Ray said he wouldn't, so the chairman took them instead and brought them back a week or so later for the re-arranged date. The sandwiches had just about thawed when the referee decided the game couldn't go ahead on that day either, and called it off again. Mr Dunford was about to take the sandwiches home to re-freeze again, but before everyone was struck down with salmonella, Ray said, "Sorry Mr Chairman, they've got to go in the bin this time." Mr Dunford once told him that he was being extravagant with his sandwich making, telling him, "Ray, cheese is fine, we don't need to use tomatoes as well."

If any of the lads would moan about the kit or suchlike, Ray would come out with these gems and say, "You lot think you've got it hard? You should try doing my fecking job for a day." He probably kept that club together single-handedly, and he was woven into the fabric of Bristol Rovers. People like Ray made me glad to be home again.

Gerry Francis is a fierce competitor, but I didn't realise quite how bad he was until we travelled to play a friendly in the pre-season of the 1987/88 campaign. Gerry hates losing at anything and I'd put money on him blowing a fuse if he lost paper, scissors, rock. Kenny Hibbitt was still playing, and I didn't know either of them that well when I re-signed for Rovers. We arrived early for the friendly and Gerry asked me and Pen to play him in a game of darts. He teamed up with Ken, who said he didn't really play, but Gerry coerced him into it and I felt a bit sorry for him because he clearly didn't want to.

Pen and me were OK, but no great shakes, but were winning all the same. Pen started winding Gerry up and I thought, 'Christ, you don't want to upset this bloke, Pen.' Gerry had quite a temper but Pen knew him better than I did and he could get away with things the rest of us couldn't. The next thing, Gerry starts having a row with Ken. "Come on!" he said. "What's the matter with you? Why aren't you taking this seriously?"

Ken said, "Shut up! I didn't want to play in the first place!" They continued arguing and Pen was loving it, chuckling away to himself. I thought, 'My God, what is this bloke all about?' I was on the end of a bollocking from Gerry once as well – you tended to only upset him once if you could manage it – you wouldn't want to do it twice. I'd been having a beast of a game away to Torquay and during the team-talk I started to say, "Come on, let's…" Gerry turned to me.

"Shut your fucking mouth. I'm speaking. Shut the fuck up." He carried on talking to the team and I muttered something under my breath and he turned back to me. "Right, get fucking off and shut your mouth or I'll put you through that fucking wall you little (C U Next Tuesday!)" It shocked me I think, because I felt he'd meant what he said. As the lads went out Gerry waited until there was just me and him in the dressing room and said, "Look, I didn't mean anything nasty by that, but there's got be just one voice. I'll see you tomorrow." I tucked it away in my top pocket because I agreed with what he said. It was all part of learning and Gerry epitomised winning, for me. I'd run through a brick wall for someone who wanted to win, because that's the way I felt and I'd finally met somebody who I felt was just like me, only he'd played for England, too.

He'd lost a few years from his career because of a back injury so he still had the drive to succeed and it was bloody infectious, trust me. I'd always wanted this for Rovers – somebody who believed and cared as much as he did and he made us all feel valued as well. Looking back, he was a bit like my old man. He'd have a bark up every now and then, but I had a total respect for him. Then I lost my dad and I suppose it was Gerry that I was now trying to please instead and I think that really helped my career. What I didn't know at the time was that this was just the start of a long association with him, nor did I realise what an influence he would have over my playing and managerial career. He did things in training that couldn't help but inspire you to learn and do better. He'd been retired for a couple of years but we couldn't get the ball off him or Ken in training, and it was like that for about two-and-a-half years – they were, in fact, better than the players we were up against every Saturday. Their legs might have been slower but their brains were still razor sharp and with them both having played in my position, it helped me again.

Gerry had a knack of changing players' positions to great effect, more so than any other manager I'd ever worked with. Ian Alexander was a winger and he put him at full-back and with Pen playing in midfield, he said to him, "Your talents are better suited up front, son." It was funny in a way because Pen had played up front as a kid and I'd been a centre midfielder back then, but we'd ended up playing out of position for the majority of our careers up to that point. Gerry looked at our strengths and weaknesses and decided to move us around to what in fact were our natural positions, and it takes a top drawer manager to do that in my opinion.

We only had a small squad with no resources as such, so he had to work hard with the players he had and to a man, he made us all better players. We knew that if we made a mistake during one game, we'd half a chance of putting that right the following week. The Rovers I'd left three years earlier had actually been a bigger club because we had an A team, a reserve side that you had to play well to get into, but all that was gone and the focus seemed to be on penny-pinching and cut-backs rather than investing in the team. I noticed a huge difference, but it actually had resulted in making it a closer-knit club – more human – because we were up against it and all in it together. The club was actually being run as though it was in administration, so it was good practice for me considering what was ahead for me in future years. We had an attitude of 'we might not have much, but what we have got we're going to make the best of.' It was a very special feeling, hard to describe in fact, but we all had points to prove and a drive to do better – and none more than Gerry who'd come to Rovers from Exeter City, where things hadn't gone too well for him. It was Gerry's last chance saloon and we all bought into his enthusiasm and belief. I worked on my fitness and got my head together again after dad's death, and I used the grief and anger I had still in me to positive effect. I still felt cheated that dad wasn't around but I did feel he was with me every time I played. We finished the season with a winning mentality, having won nine of the 13 games prior to our final match at Brighton. We lost that 2-1, but Gerry was really good at putting things into perspective and he always had a pile of stats to back up what he was saying. He said, "All we need to do is turn six or eight of the defeats we've had this year into draws and we have a great chance of going up, but you've all got to listen to me, because where the hell were you lot heading when you did what you thought was right? Make sure you listen and we'll do OK." He held a group of people in the palm of his hand. We were hungry, determined and all had points to prove. He made us believe we could do it. I was back to my best and relishing my football again. We finished eighth in the 1987/88 season, which wasn't bad considering we were all still knitting together, but I think we all knew we were on the verge of something good. Pen had finished top scorer with 24 goals in all competitions, endorsing Gerry's decision to play him up front and we thought we had a really good chance of going up the next season.

I felt good in myself and was still only 25. Kim and I were very settled in Bristol, I had my little boy and I was ready to push on and show the world what Ian Holloway was all about. It was upwards and onwards from here on in. Or was it...?

Chapter 9

Rise of the Gas Heads

We made a solid start to the 1988/89 season and were there or thereabouts for most of the season. William was coming up to his first birthday in March '89 and then we had the news that would change our lives forever. We'd always wanted any kids we had to grow up close together and not too far apart age-wise, so when Kim discovered she was pregnant again, we were obviously ecstatic, but the first scan showed we wouldn't be expanding our little family from three to four – it was going from three to five. I'd been watching the scan on the monitor and thought there was a little blob of gel on the screen and the nurse said, "Oh, you know what that means don't you?"

Kim said, "Yeah…"

I said I didn't and the nurse said, "That's two heads you can see, there. Identical twins." She got a doctor in to try and find a separate sack, but there clearly wasn't one, meaning they would be identical. It was pretty amazing and I was absolutely made up. All of a sudden the family I'd wanted was going to be here inside two years. "Great!" I said, "There'll be no arguing." But Kim grasped the gravity of the situation a lot quicker than I'd done and she realised how hard it was going to be. I was floating on air and it wasn't long before we were out looking at double buggies and kitting out their room. If I ever saw anyone with twins I'd go up and ask them what it was like. I couldn't wait for their birth and it was like all my dreams were finally coming true.

The football was great too, and Rovers were powering towards the play-offs and we'd beaten City away thanks to a fantastic goal from Pen in front of more than 23,000 at Ashton Gate. Winning at City is always a fantastic day for a Gas Head – the name Rovers fans are known by because of the two big gas tanks that used to sit behind Eastville. Our fans called their lot 'the Shitheads', because the river that ran close to Ashton Gate didn't always smell the best, or more likely our fans are that unimaginative that they just tagged the most insulting nickname together. Pen was on fire and banging in the goals for fun, and with five games left we had a real chance of going up – but we chose a shocking time to hit a patch of bad form and we failed to win any of them, including two games against teams just above us in Fulham and Port Vale. We finished sixth, meaning we would play Fulham in the play-offs. We'd already beaten them 2-0 away and drawn 0-0 at Twerton so we weren't afraid of them at all.

The first leg was at home, but the date of the game caused a big problem for Geoff Twentyman who was scheduled to be best man at his brother's wedding the day before the first leg. Geoff had asked Gerry at the start of the season if he was OK with the date and he said it was no problem. He didn't say that it wouldn't be OK if we got into the play-offs so when he told Gerry he'd have to miss training the day before our match with Fulham, he was understandably upset when Gerry told him, "You miss training because of that and you won't be playing in my team."

Geoff said. "I am going because you gave me permission," and a right ruck followed, which was badly-timed to say the least. Geoff did miss training and I feel he was right because it was only a training session. Gerry was a stickler for preparation, though, and training was his time and his chance to get things right, so where perhaps other managers might have seen it as not the end of the world, Gerry saw it as being as important as the game itself in many ways. I think we could have gone through the set-plays he particularly wanted the day before, but that didn't happen. We were all pretty brassed off about the situation but I was good mates with the lad who would be taking Geoff's place – a man we called 'The Judge' because he'd sat on the bench so many times that season – Billy Clark. He called himself 'Splinters' but he was obviously happy to be playing. Pen told everyone, "Don't worry, I'll get the goals that will take us up," and he did score a great goal to win the first leg 1-0 in front of a sell-out Twerton Park.

The second leg was something close to football heaven for our lads. It was like the Alamo in the first half and Nigel Martyn was absolutely incredible that night, saving shots that looked impossible and keeping us in the game up until half-time. Had it not been for him, I reckon we'd have been dead and buried after just 45 minutes. As it was, we were still 1-0 up and after the break, we ran away with it. Our first goal came from a set play and The Judge scored with a header at the near-post, and not long after that, they had a lad sent off and then collapsed. We went 3-0 up in a short space of time before I made it 4-0 with a deft little chip over Jim Stannard – biggest keeper in the world – pick that out you big lummock! All that stood in our way now was Port Vale for a place in Division Three.

Pen scored a screamer to put us ahead in the first game and then they had a shot that was going miles wide – until Robbie Earle threw himself at it and equalised with a diving header to make it 1-1, and he scored what would be the only goal of the return game with just a few seconds remaining at Vale Park. There was one thing from that game that, despite the pain and disappointment we felt, still makes me chuckle today. Just after they scored, I was walking back towards the centre spot and I looked over to Pen as their crowd went bananas, spilling over onto the pitch, and he was laughing and pointing at something. I thought, 'What's he found so funny?' and looked to where he was pointing to see one of those little turquoise disabled cars absolutely bombing down the touchline knocking fans over as he went. Whether the driver was celebrating or trying to keep people off the pitch, I'll never know, but it was surreal and even though I was pissy as hell, I had to laugh because I'd never seen anything like it. We just about kicked off again and the referee blew for full-time. We were absolutely shattered, but as we slumped down in the dressing room, Gerry gave one of the most poignant speeches I think I've ever heard from any manager. He said, "Don't you be ashamed to cry." My dad had always told me not to cry and would give me a whack when I did, but now my 'new dad' was telling us all it was OK and I looked around and there wasn't a dry eye in the place because the thought of all that hard work and the 50 games we'd played had all been in vain, was just too much. Gerry went on, "For all those days when you think it's hard, think about every game, think about how fit you need to be and think about how hard we're going to work next year and how we're going to keep this pain in our heart like a burning ember, and make sure we don't ever experience it again. You can do it, you're good enough and we lost out on promotion by one goal. Remember that." You could have heard a pin drop by the time he'd finished, and then he told us how proud he was of us all and that we should be proud of ourselves. It felt like a ray of sunshine slicing through your body.

By the end of our coach journey home, I think it was cemented in our minds. It sounds daft, but we knew we wouldn't fail next time. Gerry's words made us focus on what we needed to do. It was inspired stuff and the mark of not only a very clever manager, but a great man, too.

The club took us away shortly after the defeat to Vale and we flew out to Majorca. It was the first time I think they'd ever done anything like that and whenever I bumped into families with twins, I'd stop and talk with them for a while. Kim only had a few months to go by that point and was huge. There were also a lot of rumours that Gerry would be leaving, and as he wasn't on the trip, we wondered whether he'd still be there come August.

Kenny Hibbitt was sort of in charge, which was rare, because Gerry never let him do too much. I don't think it went down too well with Kenny's missus and he'd been reluctant to go because of that, but we were all glad he had because he was a top man with a very dry sense of humour. I'm not sure how I got away on that trip while my wife was heavily pregnant with twins with a one-year-old baby, though I can assure you Kim had an opinion on it! It was a comical few days because everywhere we went people were mistaking Ken for his brother Terry Hibbitt of Newcastle United. Pen and Andy Reece were always winding him up about it and on one particular day we met a bloke who used to play for Crystal Palace and he was chatting to Ken all day around the hotel pool. When this bloke went for a drink, Pen said, "Oh he knows you then?" and Ken said, "Yeah, he does. He won't get me mixed up with our kid, no chance." An hour or so later, as we all got up to leave, the Palace player shouted, "Terry! Terry! You've forgotten your towel, Ter!" Ken didn't want to turn round because he knew he'd never hear the last of it – and he didn't. Ken's mistaken identity wasn't the only entertainment on that trip. Pen, Reecey and I spent the entire week engrossed by this bloke's attempt to windsurf. Each day, he'd get up, fall off and try again. This went on for hours each time and Reecey ended up doing a commentary on it, with me and Pen in stitches. Finally, on the last day, it clicked. He got up, stayed up and then the wind caught his sail and he shot off like a bullet into the side of a glass bottomed boat.

Relaxed and still full of belief from Gerry's speech, we started the 89/90 season on fire. We played Brentford on the opening day and beating them 1-0 felt good because I knew after that game that coming home had been the right thing to do. I also knew it was going to be our year. We won our first three games and we'd only lost once in the opening 10, and after a 0-0 draw at Bury, my two girls were born and we named them Chloe and Eve. They arrived two weeks early and I hadn't learned a thing about the birth of our first child because the moment Kim told me her waters had broken, I went into a blind panic. We made it to hospital at speed and Kim was given an epidural. Chloe arrived first after about seven hours, but as she came out, Eve dropped down inside Kim's tummy and she was born breach, backside first and was in a bit of trouble for a few minutes. I was rammed against a wall as the doctors tried to help her come out, because she was having difficulty breathing and it was a frightening experience to say the least. We had to wait for the top man to come in and sort it all out and I could hear him sauntering down the corridor, whistling. He walked in eating a sandwich, cool as a cucumber and took about a minute to assess the situation before freeing Eve and bringing her out into the world with a couple of swift moves. It was incredible and thank God there are people like that on hand when you need them. She was blue, and it seemed like an age before she started crying and I felt the relief wash over me. I was given Chloe wrapped up in a nice clean blanket and not long after I was handed Eve. I was sat in the chair, looking at two little miracles and was chuffed as a badger, I suddenly thought, 'How can I put one of them down?' It was a simple thought, but it was the first clue that these two little angels/rascals were going to have an incredible impact on our lives, though we could never have guessed quite how huge that impact would be. I went home and was still floating on air, and my mum and brother were waiting and I called up my sister, and it's fair to say the Holloways were a bit emotional that day.

I took William in to see his new sisters the following day and I was told by one of the nurses that there was a call for me in their office. I went along expecting it to be one of the lads' wives – Sue Jones, wife of Rovers centre-back Vaughan Jones, was who the caller claimed to be. I thought she was calling to congratulate us both and as I said hello, a woman on the other end said, "I hope your kids die you bastard!" It took me by surprise and it was upsetting, if I'm truthful and I walked back to Kim feeling a bit shocked. Why bother doing something like that? It was beyond me, but in hindsight maybe it was a

Rovers-City thing – I'll never know for sure.

A few days later and Kim and the twins came home and after about an hour I said to her, "Is this how they are all the time? Dear me!" They were crying and screaming for food constantly – it was unbelievable! I'd put one down, pick the other one up, then there was William to tend to – the maths just weren't working out. We upgraded our car to a black Sierra Sapphire and had three baby seats in the back. This was going to be the biggest challenge of our lives, but of course, it was one we'd desperately wanted.

Back at Rovers, Pen proved too valuable for the club to hold on to and he went off to Watford for £500,000. He'd been linked with a number of big clubs and Gerry had told him that if a top six side came in for him, he'd let him go, but when Glasgow Rangers made an offer, he didn't let him go! He said, "Well they're not a top six club in England, are they?"

Pen wanted to go because he wanted to better his career and everyone understood that. He didn't want to stay because he didn't feel the club were looking after him financially – at one point he'd threatened to turn up at training with his plumber's bag and demand the club ripped up his contract and he'd return to plumbing. He'd have done it as well because he was a bloody hot-head when he had a mind to be. Eventually the best thing seemed to be for him to move on. Gerry brought Tony Sealy in on a free as Pen's replacement, and then four games later, Nigel Martyn went to Crystal Palace for £1m – and in return, we got their keeper Brian Parkin as part of the deal. I called Parky 'Mr Glum' because he couldn't understand how he'd gone from being Palace's No 1 and playing all the previous season, to picking up an injury in pre-season, missing the first 10 games and then finding himself at Bristol Rovers – I suppose he had a point! I told him to shut up and get on with it because he was now our first choice goalie, and to be fair to him he bought straight into our collective thinking and was absolutely superb.

So we had a million and a half in the bank and we were still winning games and playing well. Then, going into the New Year, Gerry finds a fella called Carl Saunders. He'd looked through the previous couple of years' goal charts and he saw Carl had scored 18 goals one season when he played as a striker, but was now playing at Stoke City as a full-back. He sent Kenny out to see him, liked what the report said and signed him as a striker. Carl scored two goals on his debut and a hat-trick in his third game! Not a bad start. We played fairly direct and he fed off Devon White, though he didn't score another league goal that season. Gerry had us well drilled and we were playing some great stuff. We had David Mehew and Phil Purnell on the wings, Devon and Carl up front. Steve Yates gave us plenty of pace at the back, Geoff Twentyman was dominant in the air and we also had two fantastic full-backs in Ian Alexander, who didn't understand the meaning of the phrase 'lost cause' and would never give anything up, and Vaughan Jones who was a terrific left-back. We had it all, and it was between us and Bristol City, would you believe, for the title.

Chapter 10

None Shall Sleep

Back home, Kim and I were having to get up to feed the girls every hour throughout the night. It was exhausting and the only thing that kept us sane was our family support network which was second to none. My sister would take all three kids on a Friday night and it could never come around quickly enough. Without Sue and her husband Phil, my mum and Kim's parents, I'm not sure whether we'd have managed to get through that intense period without losing the plot completely. Friday gave us something to look forward to because we knew we had two nights of sleep to recharge our batteries. The girls' arrival meant that, being a natural worrier, I didn't have time to worry anymore.

Back at Rovers, we proved what a gutsy bunch of sods we were by going on an incredible run in the spring. There were six games where we trailed 1-0 down in each match, and came back to win 2-1. We won one and drew three of our next four games leaving us with five games to go, and we still had to play three of the teams around us. Bristol City looked home and dry and were well clear of everyone else, and the remaining place was realistically between Rovers and Notts County, managed then by Neil Warnock. City needed one more win to go up and would be our penultimate game of the season. We had been scheduled to play them a few months before, but it had been postponed. They wanted the re-arranged game to be as late in the season as possible because obviously, we weren't going to make it easy and it wasn't unthinkable that they could win promotion on our own ground. Gerry told us to ignore that because there were enough matches left for things to change. We had an immense belief and team spirit and were still tapping into the pain of the previous season.

We went to Notts County and lost 3-1, which was a nightmare because they were the only team who could catch us, so it was very much game on again after that, but all the while, City couldn't buy a win and we'd made up a few points on them. A win over Shrewsbury, thanks to a penalty from muggins, and another poor result for City put us just a point behind going into the derby at Twerton with the knowledge that if we won, we'd be promoted. If we drew, they'd be promoted and if they won, they'd go up as champions. We had to win, and didn't even consider any other possibilities.

The night before the game, I got a call at home at around half eleven. Our phone number was in the directory and it was another crank call, this time from someone threatening to burn my house down. Apparently they knew where I lived and if I tried too hard against City the next day, they'd carry out their threat. I thought, 'you're not having me, my friend,' and wouldn't put the phone down. They tried to hang up a couple of times and Kim wanted me to hang up, but I told her I wasn't going to let them beat me. I kept the line open until one in the morning and it didn't bother me about the sleep loss because I was used to it. I knew it was all bullshit, but I still wasn't happy about it. The next day I went into work and Gerry was just about to start a speech and I said, "Gerry is it OK if I just tell the lads what happened last night?" They were all fuming about the call and there was no need to do a team-talk because we used it as our motivation, so more fool the idiot that made the call in the first place.

Twerton was rocking and as we waited in the tunnel to go out, I could see that the City skipper Rob Newman was petrified. Twerton could be an intimidating atmosphere and was live on local TV and we set about City like men possessed because this was our last chance. They couldn't handle Devon White and the first chance he got, he scored. The ball went out to Dave Mehew, whom we called either 'Cringer' or 'Battle Cat', both characters from the Masters of the Universe cartoon. Vaughan Jones, Andy Reece and I would leather him and start giving him digs before the game saying, "Are you with us tonight, son? We need Battle Cat tonight." So Mehew goes to cross the ball, but scuffs it to their full-back. He showed Battle Cat determination by winning it back and crossed it in again. The ball went under City defender, Andy Llewellyn's foot and rolled on to Devon who scrambled it into the net. At half-time, Gerry, very calmly said, "Lads, we're the better team. All you've got to do is keep your head. Make sure you keep doing the same thing." We went out for the second half and I lost the ball and City almost equalised and would have, but for a fantastic save from Parky. He got up straight away, hoofed it down the field and within a few seconds Devon and Carl Saunders linked up well and Devon made it 2-0. Job half done. Then came the maddest bit of football I'd ever experienced, and it seemed time stood still for a few minutes, for me in particular. City were still in it, but we broke again and Phil Purnell fired in a shot that was palmed off the line by a defender. Dave Mehew knocked the rebound in, but the ref had already blown for a penalty. Their keeper Keith Welsh needed treatment before I could take it but for some reason, having scored two penalties in my previous two games, I felt as cocky as hell. I knew this would be the final nail in their coffin and I'd practiced taking penalties against Parky the day before, and he'd advised me to change the side I normally put it if we got a penalty. While all this was going on, the City fans were losing it big time, and Joe Jordan walked from the dug-out down to the City fans' enclosure before things got too far out of hand and I reckon he probably stopped a riot that day. They were ripping parts of the enclosure up and throwing it onto the pitch and trying to get at the Rovers fans. I walked over to place the ball on the spot, flicking the ball up with my feet as I approached to show the City fans they weren't going to get to me, stepped back and tucked it into the bottom corner for 3-0. I hardly celebrated at all and just jogged back to the middle, very businesslike and the whistle went a few moments later. We'd done it and the place went wild. I ended up on the balcony and I wore a hat I'd been given by the parents of a young boy who'd been killed outside his school by a car a few months before. He'd gone to run around some people who were between him and his mate on the pavement and as he stepped on to the road he was struck and killed. It was awful, but his mum and dad sent me his Rovers hat. I'd taken it with me in my kit bag ever since. I'd been away and failed, but after 18 months back at Rovers I'd become someone's favourite player again, so that hat meant a hell of a lot to me, and I thought of that kid as I celebrated and when I came to speak on the mic, I told the Rovers fans about him and felt that he was with us everywhere we went. I was a bit emotional but it was a special moment and what better occasion than when we'd just been promoted against our biggest rivals? Notts County lost their game in hand the next night so City were promoted too, without kicking a ball.

We still had to win our last game at Blackpool, who'd already been relegated, and beat them 3-0 to be crowned champions on what would have been my dad's birthday – May 5. City won their last game 4-1 but we'd done it and went back to Bristol to celebrate in a local pub, Rovers-style. The next day I bought the paper which contained the best advert I'd ever seen. It showed the league table with a big red ring marked around us and City and underneath it said 'Looks like a Dry Blackthorn day.' Fantastic. We had all that and a Leyland DAF Cup final at Wembley to come against Tranmere.

We had an open-top bus tour but when it arrived to pick us up, there was a bloody brass band (including Helen Chamberlain off Soccer AM's dad) sitting upstairs! We couldn't believe it – had they expected the players and our families to sit downstairs while the band played on? Only Rovers could plan an open-top bus tour from the lower deck. I started moaning and got up a bit of a mutiny and eventually they got another bus for us to go on with the band following behind. That was followed by the worst planned do ever, with both Rovers and City invited to a civic reception with the mayor where we were presented with our championship medals. The City lads didn't get anything and it was embarrassing and humiliating because the only people there to applaud us were the City players. It went down like a lead balloon and Joe Jordan was the only person who stood there and clapped. In fact, a policeman I knew told me Joe had been something else during the derby at Twerton. He'd had his own fans spitting on him and hurling abuse at him and he just shouted, "They deserve this, don't you spoil it for them." He refused to be shouted down and while we were all jumping around in the dressing room after the game, he came in and shook everyone's hand – the dignity that man showed in defeat was unbelievable and I shall never forget that.

After the bus tour, we came back in and Gerry gave us a right bollocking! "You think that's it? I want winners and I don't want you to think you're champions, we've got to play Tranmere yet. I can smell an atmosphere and I don't like it, so you're gonna run."

And boy, did he run us. We had two weeks before the final and the first four days of the first week he ran us into the ground. He said, "I've played at Wembley and it's the biggest pitch you'll ever play on in your lives and you've got to be fitter than you've ever been to close them down the way I want you to." Coming off the euphoria of winning the title, I think we would have been fine if we'd done our normal routine, and I think Gerry got things a bit wrong on that occasion.

We'd had an exhausting league season and the extra running meant that we ran out of steam in the final, despite going 1-0 down and pulling it back to 1-1. Normally, I think we'd have gone on and won because it was almost engrained in our psyche at that point, but we had nothing left and eventually lost 2-1. I think Gerry got that one wrong. It was a disappointing way to end a memorable year and with 32,000 Rovers fans inside Wembley, we all felt a little flat when it was all over, but considering we only had a 16-man squad and sold our two best players, we'd not done badly, had we? Better still, the fans voted me their Player of the Year which I was absolutely made up about.

Family life was as hectic as ever but one particular day, when the girls were about six months old, Kim called me in to see her in the nursery. Chloe was in her cot and Kim said, "Watch this." She was saying 'Da-da' to Chloe and Chloe was mouthing the words, but not actually saying them, which seemed strange. The girls could laugh and cry like any normal babies, but their screams were very high-pitched, which again suggested something wasn't quite right. It began to make us wonder and we started to notice other things, too. They played differently, too, and would pass toys to each other and pass them back again and looking back, they were learning to communicate in their own way without making noises.

We were in the middle of house renovations and were having some major work done in the kitchen on one occasion. The bloke who was fitting some new units knew the girls were asleep in the room next door and he asked if we wanted him to wait before he began drilling. We told him to carry on and despite the noise, which was bloody loud, they slept through without even stirring. I put it down to over-tiredness, but Kim had a mother's instinct that the girls had a problem.

We took them for a hearing test where electrodes were attached so they could see what brain activity there was when certain noises were made, and eventually, having failed those tests, though not conclusively because it was hard to tell with them being so small, a lady who worked for the Hearing Impairment Team, called Sue Horne, came out to our house to assess the girls. She told us that, in her opinion, the girls at best had a severe hearing problem, but it was more likely they were profoundly deaf.

I asked her how she could be sure and she said, "Well watch this." She got a large bell out of her bag while the girls were playing on the floor with their back to us. Sue rang the bell and it was that loud it hurt our ears – but the girls didn't even flinch or look around. It was hard to take in and I wanted her to be wrong, even though deep down she was only confirming what we'd suspected. I questioned certain things and said that whenever I came into a room, they always looked around or seemed to know I was coming. Sue said they were just feeling the vibrations on the floor and they were learning to rely more on slight draughts or temperature changes, seeing shadows and reflections and so on, to know someone was coming. To confirm the girls were deaf, shortly after Sue's visit we went for a thorough hearing test that would conclusively prove the level of their hearing capabilities. The results proved the twins were, as she'd said, profoundly deaf. It was odd being told that, because we wondered what that actually meant for us. We were advised to find out all we could about deafness and decide how we wanted to teach language to our girls because there were several ways it could be done and probably no two families are exactly the same, though sign language is obviously the most common.

We felt we needed to communicate with them as quickly as possible and we decided to learn everything we could. Kim was incredible, as ever, and devoured book after book, because we felt we were playing catch up and needed to teach them a language quickly. They were now 14 months old and though they were communicating in their own way between themselves, we needed to unlock the door for everyone else, and sign language was the way forward.

Eve and Chloe would have severe tantrums and it was all down to them not being able to get across what it was they wanted to say. If we thought they wanted a drink and got out the milk when they wanted juice, they'd go down on the floor and start screaming and kicking because we hadn't understood them properly. It must have been unbelievably frustrating for them.

We were starting from scratch, too, and it was like learning English before you could talk to your children. We started with the basics like the sign alphabet and then moved on to animals, numbers, shapes and so on. There are guidelines, but there can be family variations unique to your household, too. It was fascinating, and deaf teachers would come to the house to help us learn sign language. We agreed to be part of a study from Bristol University for several weeks because we thought it could only help things move along, but though they videoed us and did various other things connected to their research, we didn't actually get that much feedback so it didn't really help us at all. We learned quite a few things off one of the team members called Jenny – on a personal level – and she's remained a good family friend to this day.

We had to learn to think in pictures, because that's what our girls did. They don't see or think of words as they communicate, they just think of images and how they will sign them. From our part, talking and signing don't really go together and you should really do just one or the other. There were three different languages – British Sign Language (BSL), Sign Supported English, where you talk and support it with sign, and English.

We needed to teach them that a bird was a particular sign, then show them how to read lips by saying 'bird' and then writing it down so they could read it. If we could manage that, they'd have half a chance of understanding, though whether they'll ever actually hear the word as we do is another thing all together. It was going to be tough for all of us, but at least we were on our way. The whole of Kim's family and mine began to learn the basics of sign, and as our friends got to grips, each person would have their own way of communicating.

Gerry Francis came to the house one day and said hello to the twins and then sort of froze, realising he'd said hello to deaf kids as if he'd committed some kind of capital offence. Phil Kite couldn't sign but he had his own way of greeting the twins and he'd pick them up, twirl them around or do something visual that worked in his eyes. I was getting a lot of things wrong and basics such as discipline were totally different with the girls compared to William.

You'd only have to raise the tone of your voice to Wills and he knew I was serious but that would never work on the girls because they couldn't hear you. They'd do things to wind me up because they thought it was hilarious, and when I'd start to tell them off they'd just cover their eyes. We had to do things in a different way and that meant learning new methods that would prove effective. I saw one lady at the hospital who was fantastic. I was having a beast of a time in all honesty and needed guidance, and while I was talking to this woman the twins were playing up, grabbing my legs, and I said "Help! I don't know what to do!" She said, "Watch," and got down to their level and used sign to say, "Stop – daddy's talking." They looked shocked and she asked if I'd let William get away with that, which of course I wouldn't. She had a room next door with a two-way mirror and we put the girls in there and walked out. She told me to watch what happened. "They're only acting up for your benefit," she said, and she predicted everything they would do next and got everything spot-on. She told me they were acting up just for me and said they'd come and find me and then start acting naughtily again. A few moments later they came in and started rolling around on the floor and whingeing again and the woman said, "It's your fault they are like this because you are rewarding bad behaviour."

We had to try and introduce hearing aids into their lives, too, which wasn't easy and really tough to begin with. We had to decide whether we wanted to keep the girls' deafness a private matter or share it with the world and ultimately we decided to share it in the hope it might make others more deaf-aware. There were so many things we discovered connected to deafness and one of the most perplexing things for me was that depending on where you lived throughout the country depended on how your deaf child would get taught – and the authorities ask you your opinion about that when we are not qualified to give an opinion. When you discover your child is deaf you are confused and not sure where to turn, so when a so-called expert asks what you think should happen next, it doesn't actually help that much.

One thing we did learn was that the visual side of the girls' perception was fantastic and what that actually means is that your kids spot every little idiosyncrasy that each human being on this planet has and they mimic them. If they aren't careful, it's so obvious who they are talking about it's unbelievable! We'd never be able to play charades with them, that's for sure, but gradually, we noticed the girls seemed to be getting happier because now they knew that their previous methods of communication hadn't worked either, so now if they wanted a drink of juice, they'd grab your hand, take us to the fridge and point. The frustration was still there but we were all learning now and life was going to be a lot better from the moment their deafness was confirmed. We were cooking on gas, it was just that the knob was turned on full power!

Chapter 11

Capital Gain

There was yet more speculation about Gerry leaving before the start of the 1990/91 season, but he wanted to see the job through and see how far he could take us, and we all enjoyed going to places like West Ham, Sheffield Wednesday, Wolves, Portsmouth, Watford, Newcastle United and Ipswich. The standard was obviously much higher but we held our own, finishing in mid-table, and I played in every league game that season, scoring seven times. In the spring of that season we had another piece of fantastic news – Kim was pregnant again – bloody hell! From being told we probably wouldn't have any kids, we'd gone to having three in three years with No 4 on the way – four little miracles, rascals, call them what you will, but this would complete our little family unit while probably condemning Kim and I to the asylum at the same time. We were very happy, though poor Kim must have felt she'd actually been pregnant for the best part of four years.

I'd reached the end of the season but things were starting to turn a little sour. There was a fight at the Player of the Year do when things got completely out of hand, and it was the beginning of the end of the team spirit we'd built. Devon White had been stabbed by a neighbour during the season and the club was rumoured to have bought his house to get him out of the area he was living in, which you'd hope they would, but some people didn't like that. There was a lot of jealousy and rumours of an in-crowd suggesting that Gerry had rewarded his favourites with new deals, but not others – it was all bullshit and it got a bit stupid. I think it stemmed from some of the wives making mischief and it culminated with Gerry having to physically throw Devon out of this awards do and telling him to get out of the way and cool down, because Devon had been furious at something that had been said, and you didn't want a giant like that losing his temper when our fans were present as well. One of the wives had told one of the others to fuck off and everything just snowballed from there. It was all about who was getting what and who wasn't – it was pathetic and the cracks were beginning to show. Gerry could see that and not long after, he left to take the manager's job at QPR, where he was still a revered figure. I was out of contract and getting pissed off because nothing seemed to be moving forward. Martin Dobson, the ex-Evatt on midfielder had taken over at Rovers but things weren't going to be the same anymore and I wasn't convinced I wanted to work for him after a couple of clashes with him. Gerry had also privately promised he was going to come back and get me depending on where he ended up, and said if he was in my shoes, he wouldn't sign a new deal with Rovers. He told me I was better than their offer and I knew a few players who'd been brought in were earning more than I was so I became a little anti-establishment about the whole situation. I needed to bring more in to look after my ever-increasing family and I wasn't happy with some of the discussions I had about money with the club. One director said, "Well you've had all the fun and now we've got to pay for it." I told him he should have had a lot of fun watching me sweat my guts out for the club each week over the years… I felt they were taking me for granted and I was reluctant to lose the momentum I'd steadily built up in my career, but when Gerry did finally come in for me, Rovers wanted too much money and he told them he couldn't afford it. I was in limbo and moved on to a week-to-week contract, so Kim and I decided to go on holiday to Majorca for a week. We booked a late deal and asked the girl in the travel agency if the hotel was in a flat area because of the kids and the prams, but mainly because Kim was expecting. She assured us it was, but we arrived to find it was actually on the side of a bloody hill! From that point on, everything went wrong. It was too hot, the girls were suffering from glue ear and they weren't sleeping. Glue ear is a really painful condition that made them scream in agony at night and I'd have to grab them and run out in the cool night air to help relieve their suffering a little. We were in the middle of toilet training and God-knows-what else, too. It was the archetypal holiday from hell. Kim was too tired to do anything and I was chasing them all around the edge of the pool because they were too small to swim – I was having a nightmare. The girls had learned to rip their nappies off and were peeing or dumping everywhere and I was chasing after them picking up Richard the Thirds in nappy sacks – I even had to make a dive Gordon Banks would have been proud of to keep one from landing in the pool – and we'd gone for a relaxing week away! The Holloways could never be accused of doing things by half, that's for sure. It kept me fit, though, and I needed something because trying to get the kids asleep all at the same time during the day so I could have a run, was almost impossible. We came home feeling much more tired than before we'd left.

At least our house had sold reasonably quickly. I was determined we were going to leave and I didn't want to have the problem of selling up as well as finding my feet at a new club. We rented a house in Bristol for a brief period until finally it was time to get back for pre-season training with Rovers. I spoke to Devon White before we went back and Dev was the most placid bloke under the sun, but he was still furious about what had happened a few weeks before at the club's awards do, and he was going to have it out with one or two of the lads. He wasn't going to take any shit anymore, and I thought there was going to be trouble, so I met Martin Dobson for the first time and he asked me whether or not I was going to agree a new deal. He told me his grand design for Rovers and said he was going to change the style of play and cut out the long-ball, and I said, "What do you mean? Have you seen us play? You can't have seen us play because we play some nice stuff." He ignored that and said he wanted me to stay, but I told him I didn't want to and was looking to move on. I said I wouldn't be signing anything and even if the club did offer me what I'd been asking for, I probably wouldn't sign up on principle. Plus my heart and mind were already in Gerry's camp at QPR, not that Dobson was aware of that. I was about to tell him about Devon White and of his intentions when he said, "I don't care, get out."

"What do you mean? You're inheriting a problem and if you don't understand it…"

"I'm not interested in tittle-tattle, not from someone who's not going to be here and isn't committed. Get out!"

So what happens? Devon goes in and all hell breaks loose. He had words with Vaughan Jones, Ian Alexander and a couple of others, but my God, he

Intended to settle the issue that day. He started on Ian, and Steve Yates tried to stop him, and Dev put one arm out, pushed him away and he fell out of the dressing room, down four steps and cracked his head on the floor. I was next door and I heard it start to kick off so I ran out shouting for them to stop and then Dobson sprints over and I said to him, "Well, so much for not wanting to hear what I wanted to say. You didn't want to listen and you could have stopped this."

So we've got Yates with a banged head, Dev's driven off saying he's never coming back and Dobson could have diffused the whole situation by dealing with it beforehand – it was a joke and he's stood there blowing his bloody whistle like Ivor the feckin' Engine! I couldn't believe what I was seeing, but of course my observations made me public enemy No 1, and later he called me in and said, "You're not allowed in training anymore. People who are not committed to this football club are not allowed to train with my lads."

I was a bad influence, according to Dobson so I had to train on my own with an old team-mate, Tony Sealey, who was now with a non-league side, and he put me through my paces, kept me sharp and finally, Rovers accepted a bid of £230,000 for my services. I was pretty chuffed with that price because I was no spring chicken anymore. Kim and I went up to have a look around Loftus Road and it was fantastic. I was 29 and was finally going to play in the best league in the world and play at some of the best stadiums in the world, too. I'd served a long apprenticeship, paid my dues and even allowed myself to entertain the notion I'd earned this chance.

We had to find somewhere to live and went to see my old mate Keith Curle, who was at Wimbledon, at his house in Camberley. He was going to show us around the town because it was easy to get from there into London and then he gets a call from Manchester City to sign for them, which he jumped at, of course. Camberley wasn't a million miles from Bristol, either. Curley said that now he was off to City, why didn't we buy his house? It would be fine for our needs though it was a mock Tudor stereotypical footballer's house and not one we'd have chosen ourselves. He was moving out the next week, so we could move straight in. It worked out a treat and all of a sudden we'd moved from having an old house in Bristol to a big new one near London, and it was a different world. We felt like the poor relations – a culture shock of sorts because we were just Kim and Ian in a world of millionaires. We were invited to Ray Wilkins' house for a barbecue, and walking through his front door was like walking into an expensive hotel. He'd invited all the players and staff from QPR and I mentioned to Ray that he had a nice garden. "Thanks, yes I pay someone to do it for me." It wasn't a big thing, but it was one of a collection of little things that just didn't happen in our lives. We'd never had a gardener and I couldn't ever imagine having one, either. I wouldn't say we had an inferiority complex, but it wasn't what we were used to. The kids were with us and one of the wives asked where our nanny was? Kim wasn't impressed and said, "Well we look after them ourselves, actually."

I was chasing them around and changing nappies as usual and I think we caused a bit of a stir because you could tell it wasn't the done thing, but it was all we knew. Worse still, I didn't have anything to wear because we hadn't had the chance to bring our stuff up yet and all I had was the club tracksuit. Everyone else was wearing expensive casual shirts and trousers and I think they thought I was some kind of freak. Who would have thought I'd end up as manager of Rangers one day? There were other things said that day that made me feel a bit uncomfortable. One of the lads said, "Oh I can remember the days when I used to buy my suits from Burton's," and I was thinking, 'Christ! I've got one at home I got from Asda!' I hadn't progressed as far as Burton's yet!

Kim thought some of them were so far up their own backsides because of the things they were coming out with, and to be fair, she had a point. It was like they'd left Planet Earth and the people that lived there and had joined a new race of beings where you were judged on the label on your shirt and how many minions you had helping you along the way. I really liked Ray and his wife Jacqui, though, and they were a very nice, genuine couple and I certainly never felt they looked down upon us. There was no edge to them yet they had more money than anyone else at the party. I think the lads had just got suckered into something I called 'a London thing'.

I'd missed out on the pre-season tour of Sweden but I was on cloud 9 about the move to QPR. I used to sit watching Match of the Day when I was at Rovers thinking 'I can do that' – I just didn't think I'd ever have the chance, and had it not been for Gerry, I doubt it would have ever happened. Now I'd have the chance to prove it and when I looked at the fixture list, I had to pinch myself that I was in a team who'd be playing at Liverpool, Arsenal, Spurs, Manchester United and Aston Villa. Obviously I had to work my way into the team but, as ever, I had belief in my own ability and knew that Gerry would give me an opportunity at some point. When I'd signed, he said to me, "I want you to rub off on the others because you're infectious – I don't know if you'll play but I want your enthusiasm to spread round the others, especially in training." It wasn't exactly what I wanted to hear, but I knew what he meant and I was determined I was going to play, anyway. He knew how to work me, so he was probably trying to squeeze a bit more out because he knew I'd never settle for that. I was a good trainer, even if I say so myself, and I made other people try hard, too.

Gerry's words were still fresh in my mind by the time our first game came around – defending champions Arsenal away – lovely jubbly! I thought I'd be watching from the stand and it would be a while before I got anywhere near the first team, but come the day and I'm actually sat on the bench. It was amazing, and I looked at the lads around the Highbury dressing room and just tried to soak it all in. There was Ray, Simon Barker, Andy Sinton, Alan McDonald, Dennis Bailey, Les Ferdinand, David Bardsley, Roy Wegerle, Clive Wilson – whom Gerry switched from midfield to left-back – and the squad was huge. There was competition for all positions, plus younger lads like Kevin Gallen, Danny Dichio and Bradley Allen coming through – completely the opposite to what I'd been used to at Rovers where we just about managed to field a team each week. I was just chuffed to be part of it all and to start my career at Arsenal was unbelievable. The kit man, Ron Berry, had come up to me during the week and said, "You won't be needing your two tickets this weekend, will you?"

I said, "You're joking! Two tickets won't be enough!"

"Nah, all the new lads give me their tickets, son!" He was a typical Cockney – a lovable rogue and a right character – a typical kit man, in fact. I had played at Arsenal once or twice during my career, but to stand on that marble floor at 29 and be part of a very good side, was something else all together – a dream come true in fact. During the game Ray had to limp off with an Achilles problem that would keep him out for the next couple of months, and I came on as his replacement. My first touch was part of a move that almost saw Andy Sinton score the winner on a break away, but it finished 1-1. It had been everything I'd expected and a bit more – the pace, the skill – everything.

I came down to earth with a bump in the next game, though, when Norwich beat us 2-0 at Loftus Road on my home debut. It was a bit worrying because we'd been outplayed by an unfancied team and I hadn't played very well, either.

I was gutted to be honest, but when I went up into the players' lounge, nobody was hurting – nobody – and I could understand why. They were all having a laugh and a joke and were totally relaxed. I got a bit annoyed and at training the next day as Gerry held a meeting to go over the previous night's performance, I decided I had to say something. I hadn't come to the club to take the money and forget about why I was being paid, so I said, "I can't understand this. What the hell's going on? Nobody seemed to be bothered last night after the game."

Les Ferdinand said, "Well that's how it is at this level, Ollie. You can win any week and you can get beaten any week, too, we'll be all right."

I said, "Well I'm not used to that. I want to win every week." I'd come from a team where we'd die not to lose and if we did, we were distraught. I thought it was a bit weird and I didn't want to be in an atmosphere like that. I reckoned if we could adopt some of the same values and passion that we'd had at Rovers, we do all right. I was back in London and while not exactly the Crazy Gang, there was definitely a clique element to the squad, but I wasn't about to stay on the outside this time, but then again, I wasn't going to be a shrinking violet, either. I don't think speaking up the way I had at my first meeting had gone down particularly well, but I wasn't going to let this pass me by, so if anyone had a problem with me, fine. I was here to win games and I think Gerry was quietly pleased I'd said what I'd said.

We drew our next game against Coventry City and then lost at Liverpool and Sheffield Wednesday, where I had a real stinker. It couldn't have begun much worse and we were bottom of the league. We went another three games without a win and the pressure was growing on Gerry – from the media, not the fans, because they loved him. We'd gone eight games without a win and Luton were next up. Gerry had brought in Paul Walsh on loan and Garry Thompson by that time, and both players had absolutely worked their socks off to help us win 1-0. Our team had a habit of not grafting like that, but they'd proved what rolling your sleeves up could achieve. We had brilliant individual talent within the side with players like Roy Wegerle, but their attitude was more like, 'Oh dear. Never mind,' when we got beaten. They just didn't care enough. There was no doubt we were missing Ray Wilkins because, let's face it, I'm not exactly Ray's replacement, am I? I started to play more like the way I could – and should have been doing – working hard and putting my foot in here and there, and Simon

Barker started scoring goals from midfield, though the partnership still wasn't anywhere near as fruitful as I'd hoped it might be. The potential was there, however. The win at Luton helped, but the QPR fans didn't think much of me – our relationship was rubbish and I think I was no more than an annoyance and a nuisance for them because they loved flair players, not industrious little Bristolians who cared so much about getting beaten and giving one hundred per cent each time I pulled on the shirt. It didn't really bother me, though, not after my experience at Brentford, and I was never going to lose my self-belief and confidence again.

One thing I did notice was the sprints and runs I used to win in a canter at Rovers, were a different league in every sense at Rangers. I'd be lucky to get in the early teens in terms of finishing. The longer distance stuff was still mine and Gerry used to do a training routine called 'box-to-box' where we'd do shuttle runs from one box to another, and I'd win them, too. The more we did, the further in front I'd go, and when we first started them, Les Ferdinand was useless and one of the slowest at the club. After a couple of months of hard work, however, he was miles ahead – he was so quick and strong, he was frightening. I'd been doing the same routine for more or less 11 years and believed in it and I'd been at Bristol Rovers, where they believed in it, too, but I wasn't so sure this lot would. There was a lot of moaning and whingeing, but Gerry wanted us to be fit to play the way he wanted. I felt like one of Gerry's soldiers and would have run through a brick wall for him.

During the poor run, he had to play 3-5-2 because of the players he had, and I was just praying he'd go back to 4-4-2 because he knew it like the back of his hand, and eventually, he did and we started winning again. So I'm holding down a place in the team, feeling reasonably settled in Camberley when our fourth child, Hattie, arrives. Within three months we had a hearing test done on her and it came up as exactly the same as Chloe and Eve – our third daughter was also profoundly deaf. We'd been told the chance of having another deaf child was akin to winning the lottery five times over, yet here she was. Hattie being deaf hit me even harder than the twins because I was not expecting the next baby to have any problems – we'd been told as much, hadn't we? I didn't take it very well, but Kim was totally the opposite, and she had an outstanding take on things, which was, "Well thank God for that. She's come to us and we're already a family who knows what they're doing with deaf children so it was meant to be."

I'd wanted another hearing child for Will because we'd been going to hospitals and clinics for one reason or another for the past few years and here's this poor little mite having to spend hours on end in waiting rooms and not able to speak with his sisters. It was silly, really, and thank God for Kim being Kim. She drives me bananas because she's so right, all the time. She sees things exactly the way they are and, well, I'd be lost without her – I just don't like to say all that while she's around in case her head gets too big to go through the door! In retrospect, that little baby coming to us was spot on, and where it had always been 'poor Chloe and Eve', with Harriet we had her ear moulds done from the off so she became used to people examining her ears, and in fact she still plays with ears today to help herself relax. The signing with Hattie was an absolute joy and she had none of the frustrations her sisters had had at all and she was a very happy baby, always laughing and smiling. She cried a lot – particularly with me – and she didn't like me at all, but I think she grew into it! She was perfect – unplanned – but God-given.

I had the snip after that because I couldn't be in the same room as Kim without her falling pregnant and from wanting two kids close together, we'd had four in four years, and Hattie was the perfect ginger bundle anyone could have wished for.

It all tied in with my life as a Rangers player and though we'd got off to a poor start that first season, I was still living every minute of it. It was so professionally run compared with Rovers – 'Ragbag Rovers' as we called them when I was there. The hotels were better, the food was better, the preparation was better, as I suppose you'd have expected. The volume of noise as we ran out in stadiums such as Anfield and Old Trafford was incredible and even arriving at the ground was different. Our coach would have to slowly make its way through a sea of people whereas at Rovers the driver would stick out his head as we neared the stadium and ask a bloke, "Can you move your dog mate? We're trying to drop the lads off here."

We even had a mid-season break at La Manga and in the past we'd have had to have won promotion to be rewarded like that. Everything you did was scrutinised and replayed so you daren't put a foot a wrong, and the reports in the paper were twice as big.

Gradually the belief grew as the season went on but there were massive highs still to come. We were building up a head of steam and I was now often playing alongside Ray Wilkins rather than filling in when he wasn't available, which was another huge confidence-booster. I was, as they say, in my element, and felt something like my old mate Andy Reece must have done when he joined Rovers from Goodyear Tyres. If that was the case, I was more than happy to tread the same path.

Chapter 12

Double Ham & Eggs

Pen signed for QPR and it was great to have him in our lives again. He arrived during my first season at Loftus Road after things hadn't gone that well for him at Aston Villa and he moved just down the road from us in Finchampstead. A few of the QPR lads didn't take to Pen at all. He won a sprint and did a forward roll in celebration and a few of them made comments that I didn't like. I said to Simon Barker, who was moaning about him, "Look, you don't know him yet. Give him a chance because he's not the person you think he is." Pen had always been straight with me and after a couple of weeks watching me train, he noticed I was doing things I'd never done before like step-overs and fancy flicks. The other lads could do it and I suppose I'd been trying to keep up with the Joneses. Pen pulled me to one side and said, "Ollie, what the hell are you doing?"

I asked him what he meant and he said, "That ain't you – that's never been you. He brought you here to do what you're good at – don't try and do what some of the others are doing, you idiot. You've got to stick to what you know – don't try and change it. For Christ's sake, sort your life out. It doesn't make you any less important. Just do what you do and keep it simple and quick, and you'll be alright."

That really helped me, and it hadn't been the first time he'd talked perfect sense to me, and it wouldn't be the last. He made his debut against Leeds and though we won, he went to Gerry and asked what he'd thought, and Gerry said "That was shit." Pen needed to hear that because he had to re-discover his old self again, and he came to QPR despite interest from Chelsea because he knew Gerry would get him playing again.

There were a couple of lads being bullied with banter and on one away trip, I think Pen and I turned everything around. We were having a right slanging match on the coach with him calling me big nose and I'd say he had wax ears and had worn a hot bowler hat once because his ears were turned over at the top. We knew each other so well that we could say anything to each other and not be insulted. Then Alan McDonald joined in, calling me something or other and Pen said, "Why don't you shut up pizza arse? I can say that to Oll, but you can't. Just because you sat on a pizza and it stuck to your arse, doesn't mean you can join in." He stood up for me after giving me all that stick and after that, a few of the lads who'd been on the end of some pretty cruel banter, started to fight back a bit, Rufus Brevett among them.

A couple of games later and things really came to a head for all of us, and I had to let rip at one or two of the lads. It was a horrendous day, but it was time to fire in one or two home truths because there still wasn't the camaraderie and togetherness we needed to push on, and Gerry didn't really have the dressing room at that point. We were away at Man City and Gerry had changed the system again, with Dennis Bailey and me among the subs. We went 2-0 down in the first half and in my opinion, Roy Wegerle, who could run like the wind when he wanted to, was hardly trying when he didn't have the ball. So we go back to the dressing room at half-time. I was in the toilet and I heard one or two players moaning between themselves about the formation and tactics. They clearly hadn't accepted Gerry yet and seemed to still be thinking of Don Howe, the previous manager at Loftus Road, which was understandable I suppose because Don was fantastic. I told them to shut up because I was trying to listen to the bloke. So Gerry changes to the tactics they like, we go out and score two goals to draw 2-2 and Wegerle is chasing everything and working his socks off.

So there's a meeting after the game and I'm fuming inside because I'd said some things that Gerry hadn't, and for me, it was all about winning, not the formation we played and whether it suited certain players better than others. It wasn't about Don Howe or Gerry Francis – it was about us beating Man City, and for me, the only consistent thing you should give your manager and – more importantly – your supporters, is your effort. It isn't about your ability, it's your goddamned effort – so Roy could do what he liked and because he could do things with a ball nobody else could, no-one said a word to him, but I wasn't going to accept him not working as hard as the rest of us.

When Gerry said well done, Roy pipes up, "Oh it was the tactics, Gerry. They suited us better in the second half." Alan McDonald, the skipper, sort of said the same thing and I said, "That's absolute bollocks!" Gerry looked a bit shocked at that, but I was going to say my piece. "The difference is, Roy, you worked your ass off in the second half and ran, chased and put your foot in. In the first half you didn't put a fucking ounce of effort in because you didn't agree with the tactics." Alan McDonald stood up and said, "How dare you say that to Roy Wegerle."

I said, "Fuck off! You're the captain so you should have been saying that to him instead of me because he hasn't worked as hard as you did in the first half, but you've got a problem because you are letting him get away with it!"

Roy said, "Sometimes it's just meant to be, Ollie."

I said, "Yeah, but isn't it meant to be that you run back and put a foot in as hard as everybody else? I'd rather go back to Bristol because we didn't like losing there, we worked our ass off, there wasn't anyone who was better than anyone else and you know what? I miss those lads. If this is what playing at the highest level is all about, I don't want it. This is bullshit. If you're in the same team as me we go out and try to win every game, not just one week and not the next. You're meant to chase back and put a foot in."

I sat down again and started to get changed. I'd got it off my chest and stood up to them, and in later years I asked Gerry why he hadn't said that to them, and he said, "Ollie, you don't understand. It's the politics of a football club." Now I'm a manager, I do understand but I still say exactly what I want to my players, over and over again, no matter what the goddamned politics are. If you're poncing about claiming that if you get the ball, you'll win your team the game, it's not good enough and I wouldn't pick somebody who said that.

Sometimes I stepped in where perhaps Gerry could have, but he hadn't heard what was being said behind his back in all fairness. It wasn't about being a creep to the boss – I believed in Gerry and felt everybody else should, too.

We'd needed a clear-the-air talk and sometimes it works, sometimes it doesn't, but there was a definite upturn in certain individuals' attitude and just a few games later – having not been beaten since – everything came together in one of the most incredible 90 minutes of football I'd ever taken part in.

There was no prouder moment for me as a player than when we went to Old Trafford on New Year's Day 1992. What a day that was! It was the first time I'd played against Manchester United and it was live on TV, too. I spent most of the pre-match on the toilet – it was all happening and my hors d'oeuvres had completely gone. I'd been told at the hotel I was in the team and I was so excited and nervous that when Gerry shouted for us all to gather round for his final team talk before the game he said, "Where's Ollie?"

I shouted from the toilet, "Carry on, I'm gonna have to stay in here while you do it."

A few of the lads were laughing, but when I get nervous, my system goes into overdrive. I wasn't the only one who was feeling it, and Darren Peacock and a few others were suffering, too, but when Gerry called out the United team, there were two or three big names missing, including Ryan Giggs and Andrei Kanchelskis. Fergie obviously thought that with United being top of the table, he could rest a few players because they were playing QPR, and we took something from that. I hadn't touched the ball with 15 minutes on the clock yet we were 2-0 up – unbelievable! Simon Barker and Dennis Bailey had scored the goals. It was absolutely amazing, but Bailey was playing without fear and giving Bruce and Pallister all kinds of problems. We went in at the break still two goals to the good and then made it 3-0 in the second half through Bailey again. United pulled a goal back but Bailey completed his hat-trick to make the final score Man United 1, QPR 4. It was a fantastic day for me and a proud day for our club. We ended the 91/92 campaign full of confidence and with a great team spirit.

The first game of the 92/93 season was also the first ever Sky Monday Night Football match. The First Division had become the Premiership and we were away to Man City. There were cheerleaders, fireworks and a PA system that was shaking the whole ground. The times they were a changin', as some American singer once said. One end of Maine Road was just a building site as they rebuilt the Platt Lane, but there was a great atmosphere and you could see that as a player, the Premiership was going to be the only place to be. We went 1-0 down to a David White goal – he always seemed to score against us – but Andy Sinton fired home an equaliser and we left with a 1-1 draw.

Another game that sticks in the memory from that season was against Chelsea, who'd brought in Ruud Gullit as the first really big-name foreign import. Gullit was a man-mountain and an incredible talent, and Gerry told me

I had to mark him! Let's just say things didn't go so well that afternoon and there was a moment during the game when Gullit was in front of me. I knew I had Rufus Brevitt about 10 yards behind me but Gullit just pushes the ball about 15 yards in front of himself and runs past me with a couple of strides. He glided past despite my best efforts but I thought Rufus would catch him because he was quick and would tackle his grandmother, given the chance, but he left him for dead, too, and got in a cross which Chelsea almost scored from, and I say, "Jesus, were you trying then, Ruf?"

He shook his head and said, "Bloody hell! How quick was he?" Ruud reminded me of the alien in the movie Predator – same haircut, same build, plus he seemed to be equipped with advanced weaponry. He was brilliant, and the closest I got to him was in the bar after the game. It was an absolute pleasure to be playing with or against the calibre of player he was. I never lost my will to play or sense of justice, though, and appreciative though I was, if something didn't feel fair, I wasn't going to just sit there with a sycophantic grin on my face because I'd come to a top-flight club from Ragbag Rovers. On one occasion I learned I'd been dropped and replaced by Ray Wilkins and I didn't think I deserved to be dropped, so when training came around I decided I was going to have Wilkins – it wasn't his fault but he was my target to redress my sense of justice. He knew it too, and I have to say that I was given the biggest runaround I'd ever been given by anyone. Ray was laughing during the session and I was four passes behind him every time – he was thinking that far ahead of me. At the end, he was the perfect gentleman – as ever – and he shook my hand and said, "I apologise for being selected ahead of you – thank you for helping me train as well as we did this morning." Then he added, "By the way, if your mate Penrice can play like he did this morning on a regular basis, he should play for England."

As we walked back to the changing rooms I said, "I don't ever want to give the ball away," and Ray said, "Well I don't look at it that way. I don't ever want to be caught with the ball – if you're caught with the ball it means you don't know your next pass and you're not thinking the right way." I took that into my game immediately and it made a hell of a difference. He added, "You have to keep hold of your self-esteem too, because your confidence belongs to you, son."

Ray was different class and to illustrate the point, when Gerry brought big Devon White to Loftus Road, the Rangers fans were laughing at him because he was gangly and looked awkward, but Ray would say to him, "Come on, son! You're better than you think! Come on, you can do this!" and the difference it made to Devon was immense, and it proved to me what a class man Ray was, as well as a top player.

Midway through the 1992/93 season the club began to discuss a new deal with me and I extended my contract by a further two years. Our standard of living improved after I'd agreed a pay rise and the club got me a better car. Things were going well and one game that sticks in my mind was all down to the wit and wisdom of Pen. We were playing Swindon Town in an FA Cup third round tie at Loftus Road, and we beat them 3-0. I had a bit of a good game that night and Pen scored, too, so we were both quite happy on the journey home. I was driving and Pen says, "Oll, I'm starving, pull over." We stopped outside a Kentucky Fried Chicken and he asked me if I wanted anything – I wasn't hungry so said 'no'.

"Go on have some."

"No, I don't want anything. Not that, anyway."

Pen has an annoying habit of not listening to you, so I shouldn't have been surprised when he came out with two boxes, one for him, one for me. "There you go, mate."

"I told you I didn't want anything." "Go on, have it." So I did. I know I didn't have to, but he'd talked me into it. A day later and I was crapping through the eye of a needle. I had the military two-step – I couldn't be more than two steps away from the toilet. I was being sick, too, and I couldn't go into work. It was that bad that I went to see my local GP and he told me I'd got food poisoning. Cheers, Pen. I called him up and told him and a bit later, he came round to see me. He couldn't stop laughing at me and I was laid up for two days and had lost a stone. He came into see me before the trip to Middlesbrough and Pen says, "Jesus, Oll – you've lost some weight haven't you? You look like a nose with eyes." To be fair, he was right! He carried on taking the piss and I said, "I didn't even want it, you idiot."

He carries on laughing and says, "How's your luck, then. You get the dodgy one, I get the good one."

As it turned out, he played at Middlesbrough and his luck was out this time because he broke his leg, and a few days later, his wife drove him round to see me. He had a full leg cast on and was on crutches, and as soon as he saw me he said, "Oh you don't have to say it! I took the piss out of you, you don't have to say it."

I said, "Well that's great isn't it? I'd rather have what I've got than what you've got. In a week I'll be fine, you idiot." Pen sees the funny side of everything and he's a nightmare, but a great mate, and totally irrepressible. One in a million, in fact.

Ironically, I picked up a bad injury away to Aston Villa that kept me out of the last nine weeks of the season. It was bloody painful too – a knee up the arse from Shaun Teale, their central defender. I had to go in five days a week for treatment on what turned out to be a fractured pelvis. At first the physios thought it was no more than bruising and five weeks in I started running again. I set off and after about three minutes, my leg went completely numb so I had to stop and x-rays showed there was a small crack in my pelvic bone. Gerry didn't like injured players and was always trying to get me to play. "Come on, it's only a bloody bruise, what's the matter with you?"

I said, "Actually Gerry, I think it's a haematoma..." The minute the words had come out, I regretted it.

"A haema-fucking-toma? What the fuck is that?"

It wasn't until Gerry's – and my – third season at Loftus Road that things really began to click. We started with a couple of heavy defeats, 4-1 at Villa and 3-1 at home to Liverpool, but we lost just three of the next 16 league and cup games and by the time we were due to play away at bottom-of-the-table Swindon Town, we had a chance to go second in the Premiership. It was a midweek game and we were doing so well, but we lost 1-0 and it was infuriating. I still felt we didn't have enough fight in the side and every time we had a chance to put pressure on the leaders, we blew it. We didn't have the ruthless streak needed to become champions and I wondered if we ever would.

Then came a point in the season when we all started arguing and there was a lot of moaning and whingeing. There were rumours that Darren Peacock was going to be sold for £2m and on one particular day I was on my way to the treatment room when I heard Dave Bardsley say, "Oh, yeah, he's a real ham and egger." My old mate, Steve Yates, a fantastic young centre-half, was rumoured to be on his way from Bristol Rovers and as soon as I walked in, it went silent. Dave, Les Ferdinand and Alan McDonald were all sat waiting for treatment and were three of the biggest wind-up merchants at the club. They'd all been at the club a while and maybe one or two of them felt a bit threatened by Yates arriving. We were also possibly bringing Trevor Sinclair in as well, with Andy Sinton set to leave, so it was a bit of an unsettling time for one or two of the lads. I put two and two together and said, "I hope you're not on about my mate being a ham and egger." A ham and egger was another way of saying 'useless' or 'rubbish' – you were either ham and eggs or caviar. Dave said, "What do you mean?"

I said, "Steve Yates – I hope you're not calling him a ham and egger."

"Yeah, but Darren's done really well and Sinners..."

"You are, aren't you, Dave?" Les Ferdinand had begun chuckling by this point because he always found me and Pen quite amusing, but I hadn't finished yet. "How can you be so judgmental? Were you born and bred a Premiership player or did you signed on from Blackpool? By the way, if Yates is a ham and egger at £750,000, what does that make me? Double ham and eggs?"

Macca piped up and started to say something along the lines of I was taking things too seriously, and I said to him, "the trouble with you lot is you're too judgmental. Yatesy hasn't even signed yet but he's a damned good defender and if I was you Macca, I'd be worried because what if Gerry doesn't sell Peacock? Yatesy is a brilliant centre-half so you might be out of a job. Bit worried are you?"

Macca said, "Why don't you get your international caps on the table, then Oll?"

Macca had played for Northern Ireland fairly regularly and Les Ferdinand was just breaking into the England team. I said, "Hang on, how many international games have you actually won? It's alright getting a load of caps but if you lose every time you play, what's the point?"

I had the raving hump by that time and we were due out for training. They were trying to hush me up as we lined up in a circle outside, but I wasn't having any of it. "Les has got a real cap Macca, but you ain't." Les was chuckling away to himself by this point so I turned it around on myself and said, "Anyway, I could have qualified for the Faroe Islands, but they told me they weren't interested, but even they've won more internationals than your lot, Macca."

I carried on for a bit, telling them to let the "ham and egger," have a go when it was my turn. I christened myself 'double ham and eggs' after that. I spoke up when I thought I needed to and I stood up for others when I felt it necessary –

I was just doing what dad had told me to do all those years ago and I hoped he'd be proud of the man I'd become. I don't want this to come across as though I don't like Alan McDonald, because I did. Macca was a great bloke and you couldn't help but like the fella, it's just sometimes I didn't agree with some of the things he said or did. He was actually one of the best centre-halves I had the pleasure of playing with and he could pass it like a midfielder, it's just that we didn't always see eye-to-eye, but the secret of that is to not take things personally. He'd been at QPR a long time and sometimes, as I'd find out when I later became a manager, that can become a problem. I think my biggest mistake was trying to make QPR into Bristol Rovers, which I could never have done. It was a totally different set-up, different players and different fans, but I didn't perhaps realise that until later on.

I was 31 by this point and I was thinking about what I would do after I finished playing. Working under Gerry had made me think about coaching because I believed in his methods that much. He actually taught players how to improve their game, no matter how many international caps they had, and he'd made teams from virtually nothing. I'd been keeping notes for years about training and different sessions I'd been involved with, so the seed was firmly planted in my mind. But I felt as fit as a butcher's dog and knew I had maybe three or four good years left in me. We finished fifth in the Premiership in 93/94 and were the top London club, which Gerry had a bit of a crow about. But I still wasn't happy because I felt we could have finished higher – at least third, but we just hadn't collectively turned up in one or two games, and Swindon, who barely managed to get double figures in points that season, beat us home and away, which sort of illustrates the point, doesn't it?

Chapter 13

Ray of Light

The girls' schooling was getting desperate by the time the season had ended and we couldn't continue the way we were. The twins were coming up to four and had to go in a taxi to their school in Reading every day and it was getting harder and harder for them, so we decided to move back to Bristol so they could attend an excellent deaf school in the city. There, they would have times in the day when they did BSL, then they'd do sign-supported English, then English, and we wanted them to have a grasp of all three languages to assist their development. Hattie would be able to go there too, in another year or so, hence it was a move that made complete sense. I was prepared to drive from Bristol to London five days a week because driving had never bothered me and the reason I'd be making the journey was well worth it. Plus we'd be back near our families and it'd be good for the kids to see their grandparents and aunts, uncles and cousins on a regular basis.

I went to see Gerry and said, "I've got a massive problem, here. My daughters aren't getting educated here and we've got to move back to Bristol." He was just brilliant and said, "That's not a problem. Fine." I hadn't expected that because he liked all his players to live within a certain radius and I was going to move 130 miles away.

So we upped sticks and moved home again – our families must have thought, "My God – we'll never bloody get rid of them!" But the journey to work wasn't as bad as I'd thought it might be. It gave me a lot of thinking time, which I never got at home, and if I left at 8.30am, I could miss the traffic and be at training on time, and because we almost always finished at about half-twelve, I'd be home before 3pm. Being injured was a problem because you had to be in by nine, Sundays included, which was a nightmare, but I've always believed that if your reason is strong enough, you can put your mind to anything. I was a very disciplined person and I knew what I wanted, and I was going to bloody do it and nobody was going to stop me.

We'd started the 1994/95 season terribly, winning just one of our first 12 games. We were in the bottom three and there were constant rumours that Les Ferdinand was going to be sold, which was annoying the hell out of Gerry. In fact, I think he'd had enough at that point because we just couldn't buy a win. There were one or two frayed tempers and one incident could have been a lot worse had it not been for Pen's irrepressible humour.

During training, Macca caught Trevor Sinclair a bit late, and the niggling carried on. Trev called Macca something not very complimentary, because he was pretty fiery when he got going, but things went a bit further. Gerry told them to calm down and go and get changed. Pen and I were already sat down eating dinner when Trev walks into the canteen. Pen wasn't going to let things die down too quietly and said, "That was a bit silly Trev wasn't it?"

Trev said, "It was his fucking fault."

Then Macca walks in behind him. Trev says something to him and Macca didn't like it again, so he says something back, and it's getting more and more heated. There were always jugs of orange on the table and I said to Pen, "Shut up, will you? Just leave it."

Macca was carrying an autographed ball and as he goes to the counter to get his food Trev throws a bit of food at him, hitting him on his shirt. Macca wasn't happy with that and told him to fuck off. Trev sits down and says something again so Macca drinks his orange leaving a little bit at the bottom which he launches in Trev's direction. Macca still has the ball in his hand when Trev gets up with a whole jug of orange and pours it all over his head. Macca was absolutely fuming and the first thing he could think of was to throw the ball at Trev and it pings off his ear-hole at some speed and goes flying out the double doors. At this point both of them are ready to go to war, and all of a sudden Pen pipes up, "Trev, Trev, Trev – for a future England international, you've got to sort your touch out, that ball you tried to control's gone 50 yards."

Trev starts laughing and so did Macca, and goes over to see Trev who apologises, and the whole episode is over, thanks to Pen being Pen. That's why you've got to love the fella, I suppose.

We turned things round with a couple of wins in three days against Aston Villa and Liverpool but Gerry wasn't happy with life at QPR. A lot of problems were to do with money and his decision to keep Les would prove a costly one. The board were keen to sell him and rake in the cash while Gerry was thinking how could he possibly replace a player like Les. So he decided to increase his money substantially and I think the board let that information be known to cause mischief among the other players. Gerry had promised Pen, who'd taken a wage cut to come to QPR, that if he did well he'd put him back to what he'd been on at Villa, so when he heard the rumours of how much Les was on, he was fuming. He wanted to see Gerry and before he did, he said, "And by the way, Oll. Your money's shite too. You ought to see him as well – it's fucking rubbish!" Pen wouldn't shut up about it and Frank Sibley the coach got wind of it and told Gerry who said, "I want to see you two in my office."

We went in and I was sort of caught up in it all and during the meeting Pen and Gerry started having a massive argument. I was playing regularly and wasn't happy about my money, but I'd signed a contract and was going to abide by what I'd agreed.

Pen laid into Gerry. "You bloody liar. You lied to me."

Gerry tried to explain it as best he could and in the end I said, "OK Gerry, I'm having it," and started to walk out. As we did, Pen said, "Well I'm not, you fucking liar. You shouldn't either, Oll." We went out to go for the training session, but the arguing had gone on so long that everyone had gone home!

Gerry wasn't himself and a couple of days later during a five-a-side game, I think he showed how much stress he was under. Gerry was on my team and Frank Sibley was referee. Gerry scores a great goal and ran off celebrating as normal, but I'd stepped in the box and held my hands up. Frank blew up and said, "No goal. Play on!"

Gerry said, "What? Fuck off Frank, that's a fucking goal!"

Frank said, "No it's not."

"Actually Gerry," I began to say but he told me to shut up. "Don't take the piss, Frank!"

Frank said, "No goal, play on."

"Gerry, I was wrong, I was in the box," I said.

"Shut your mouth, you – I haven't got a problem with you, I've got a fucking problem with him. Frank, you (C U Next Tuesday)!"

Frank threw his whistle down and said, "I'm not fucking being talked to like that!" and walked off. Gerry was shouting, "Come back here! I'll fucking kill you!" He'd fight anybody when it came to winning, but I couldn't believe it. As we walked back in I said I thought he'd gone over the top and he said, "You know I don't mean it. He'll be alright." It upset Frank, though, and I'm not sure things were the same between them again.

The next time we played, Rodney Marsh – who Gerry had never liked – was spotted in the stand and the rumours were that he was going to be brought in as general manager. So Gerry went to see the chairman to say he wasn't happy, and the next thing is he's taking over at Tottenham. I think it suited Gerry, if truth be told, and as he went out, Ray Wilkins came in. How did I feel about that? Fantastic! He gave me a new contract and doubled my money! He said he'd looked at what I'd been on and said that wasn't right, and I couldn't have been happier. I signed a one-year extension, but Pen was put on the transfer list because of his constant moaning.

Ray hadn't been able to convince Les Ferdinand to sign a new deal and he went to Newcastle for £6m at the end of the season, and Les just went into a different orbit after that. I was really pleased for him, too, because he was a wonderful bloke who'd do anything for anybody and what he got, he thoroughly deserved as far as I was concerned. I sent him a note saying that it was nice to see a good bloke get on, which it was.

Clive Wilson wouldn't re-sign, either, and he went to join Gerry at Tottenham, so we'd lost two of our best players by the time the 1995/96 season started. We didn't really replace them, either, choosing to bring in a couple of youngsters instead. At least Pen stayed, because Ray changed his mind about him. Pen still wasn't going to get the money he felt he deserved, but his staying wasn't because nobody came in for him, because West Ham were ready to do a deal. He still had the hump with Ray and one morning during training, Ray had us all in a circle with two in the middle trying to get the ball each time it was passed across. Every time Pen got it he picked out Ray and whacked it at him – not that easy with sometimes two players stood in front of him! Ray didn't deal with the ball too well on that particular day and it was so obvious Pen had issues with him that at the end of it, Ray, ever the gentleman, said, "Stop, stop, stop, stop. Obviously Gary, you'll have to see me at the end of training, but what I will say is, if you can sort your focus out, you are one hell of a footballer, because your accuracy at hitting me across the circle is quite outstanding."

Pen ended up training on his own, because he was like a spoiled brat, and he'd have to be driven in a mini bus to train away from the rest of us, but to be fair to him, he worked hard and eventually Ray picked him again. He was a talented kid when he put his mind to it, but if he had a beef about something it was like he had a wasp in his head. By November 1995, however, Pen re-joined Watford for £500,000 so things were changing and I wasn't enjoying my football.

We were struggling in the league and around Christmas, I started to hear that Bristol Rovers were interested in signing me again. The drive to London and back I thought I could cope with was now killing me. I'd developed sciatica and it was starting to affect my game, and I needed to think about finding a club closer to home.

It'd obviously mean no more long drives and rushing to get home, so I went to see Ray and he said, "Yeah, Ollie, you can talk to them. I knew you would anyway, but you've got my permission."

I went to see Rovers and they told me they wanted to offer me a four-year deal as player-coach, which sounded ideal with my days at QPR gradually winding down, and a return to something close to normality regarding getting to and from work. Everything seemed fine and then Ray comes back to me and says, "Well hang on a minute, Oll, I've changed my mind. They've not offered enough money."

I said, "Hold on Ray, I'm thirty bloody three, they're offering me a four-year contract and you're standing in my way? Jesus Christ, Ray."

Rovers had bid around £200,000 which wasn't bad for a player my age. So I said, "Well give me a new deal, then."

"No, I'm not going to do that, either. I don't have to."

I lost my head a bit, to be honest and I said, "Well why the hell did you let me talk to them, then? I want to go now."

"No."

"Well thanks a lot!"

The next day I got sent off in the reserves for only the second time in my life for swearing at a referee. Dougie Freedman scored a goal, but it was kicked away from a good yard or so behind the line and the ref waved play on. I told him that it was a goal and he said it wasn't, so I said, "You're a fucking idiot. Couldn't you see that you fucking idiot?"

He showed me a straight red, which I deserved, and it sort of straightened me out a bit. I decided that if Rovers were that keen, they might come back in for me in the summer, so I got my head down and started working hard. I wasn't disrespectful to Ray, but I had a bit of an edge to me and I'd got back some of the anger I used to have as a kid.

During the last month of Ray's first season in charge things were deteriorating at home, which was hardly surprising considering how much I left Kim to deal with by herself. She was under tremendous strain bringing up four kids virtually single-handedly as well as every other day-to-day activity that goes along with running a family and a house. Even minor things that shouldn't have been a problem were going wrong, like the big unruly dog we had at that time which was causing extra headaches. She would end up in the back of a police van for one reason or another almost every other day, usually because she was terrorising our neighbours after escaping from our garden. I needed to be around a lot more than I was. It got to the stage where I had to tell Ray I needed time off. I said, "I've got to do everything at home Ray for a while. I can't make training because Kim isn't even able to get out of bed at the moment."

He was terrific. "No problem. You do what's right for your family, they always come first, son." That was outstanding in my book, especially as I'd had a bit of the hump about not going to Rovers. And then he goes and offers me a two-year extension, which would have taken me to 35, but I was determined to go by that point and turned it down.

I spoke with Gerry Francis about it and he said, "Look Ollie, they might be thinking of taking you back as manager. Just be ready if they offer you the job, which they might well do."

I had to consider that was a possibility because there were obviously people on the board who really wanted me to go back and there were strong indications current manager, John Ward, was going to leave Rovers. I started getting a dossier together. Because I couldn't play for QPR, who were on their way out of the Premiership by that time, I went to watch Bath City and Stevenage play because Marcus Stewart was out of contract at Rovers and it was likely he wasn't going to sign, so I was planning on how to replace him, and while the kids were at school, I was writing down things – training sessions, the structure I'd want and so on – I'd always wanted to be a manager one day, anyway, so I was making my plans for Bristol Rovers. Thankfully, Rovers did offer me the position of player/manager on a four-year deal and the contract was on blue paper, which meant I was signing a PFA-backed players contract and therefore I couldn't be sacked. It was a dream ticket because that would take me to 37. It gave me the security I'd needed and it coincided with Rovers returning to Bristol by playing at the rugby union club's Memorial Ground. We would have a new training ground, too, so it was all pretty positive and the supporters seemed quite pleased about it, too, which was a relief. All I had to do was learn how to play and manage at the same time, but I'd become so engrossed in everything that I still wasn't doing enough to help Kim out of her depression. It was a time when I was seeing everything wrong and the things that were precious to me were being shoved aside in my quest to be successful in my job. My job was a gold whistle in a box that I kept in a drawer. I tended to that whistle and took it out, polished it and cared for it lovingly. It just shows you how wrong you can be. In trying to secure a future for my family it almost cost me my family and our future together. Kim was so exhausted and mentally drained at that time, and looking back and thinking about how old the kids were and also dealing with the girls' special needs, I wonder how she ever got through that period at all. I just wasn't there for her in the way I should have been, which is something I will always regret. I just wish I could have seen things with more clarity back then and got the balance right.

Chapter 14

Marvin Hagler's Eyes

Because I'd had time to prepare properly, I hit the ground running as Rovers' manager. First of all I had to convince Marcus Stewart to sign a new contract. We were already short of strikers so I'd have to get some new players in as quickly as possible. The first meeting I had to have was with Marcus because he was out of contract and the ruling at the time was that he could go abroad if he wanted to – and he was considering it – and we wouldn't get a penny for him. Huddersfield Town had offered £500,000 which was nowhere near enough, so I had to do something quickly or my entire transfer budget for the new season could go up in smoke. I knew his agent, my old mate Phil Purnell, but when I called him he said, "Ollie, there's no way you'll make up the difference. He's not going to re-sign and he's got the raving hump with the club, and the offer they've just made is what he should have been given two years ago."

I told him things were different because I was in charge now. "What's his favourite car?" He told me it was a Toyota MR2 – and asked what that had to do with it. I said, "Listen, that car will be included in the contract, just get him to meet me tomorrow."

I called a bloke who ran a Toyota garage and found out he was a Rovers fan and explained the situation. I told him that I would have to sell Marcus the moment he re-signed. "Hopefully, though, I will be able to get a top club to pay big money for him to stop him leaving for nothing – would you give us a MR2, which we can give to Marcus to convince him to sign? You fund it and when he goes, we'll buy the car off you."

He said, "Yeah, of course I will."

I got him to bring it to where I'd arranged to meet Marcus the next day and asked if he could put a big ribbon around it, which he did. Marcus arrived the day after and the first thing he saw was the car. I went out to meet him and I said, "There you go, that's for you. That's what they owe you. There's £23,000 worth of car there, but I need you to know that if you re-sign, I'm going to have to sell you, but when you go, this car's yours."

Marcus turned down the new deal in writing, but what he'd done by doing that, with the car thrown in of course, was turn down a much better offer, which guaranteed us getting a big fee for him at a tribunal. The better our offer the more we'd get, and ultimately Huddersfield agreed to pay £1.2m for him. They came back in and we told them he'd rejected a much better contract so rather than lose him, they paid the kind of money we'd been looking for. I'd never seen our chairman looking so happy!

Two players I'd targeted to lead a new-look strike force were Adi Akinbiyi and Jamie Cureton at Norwich. I thought they'd link up really well so I called their manager Mike Walker and asked him about them. Cureton was a Bristolian, but he had somewhat of a reputation for being a bit of a wrong 'un, but I knew him from a few years before. Gordon Bennett was at Norwich and he'd asked me to help coach a couple of his youth team to train during the summer when I was still at QPR. He'd wanted an experienced pro to help them along because, save for Jeremy Goss, he didn't feel anyone of the first-teamers at Carrow Road would help them. One of the kids was Andy Johnson, another was Jamie Cureton, so we had established a kind of relationship in that we both knew a bit about each other, and I knew he'd be keen to get away from Norwich because things weren't really happening for him there. Mike Walker said, "You can't have Akinbiyi yet because he's injured, but you can later on, and you can have Cureton now."

I said I'd take him on loan with a view to a permanent deal so we agreed a fee of £250,000 and in his first three games for us he scored four goals – an absolute revelation, and we signed him on. The board were made up with me because it looked as though we'd got a steal, but then he goes and plays like an idiot, maybe because he'd got his deal under his belt, scores one in six and I have to drop him. Welcome to the world of football management, Ollie! I thought that I wasn't going to have the little sod treat me like that. Then, Adi Akinbiyi comes up for sale and Gillingham went in for him. I told the chairman we had to sign him because he'd be perfect with Cureton, but he wouldn't do it. Despite having secured £1.2m from the sale of Stewart, he wasn't prepared to back my judgement thanks to Cureton's second month at the club. It wasn't an ideal way to start a relationship with my chairman and the truth of the matter was, I'd have rather signed Akinbiyi first, and if I'd have insisted and not spoken of Cureton, Mike Walker would have sold him to me. I got that one wrong. I was in the thick of it now, though, and I must say, I loved it.

I'd brought a few lads with me who had been released from QPR on frees in Matt Lockwood, Graham Power and Steve Parmenter. I added Tom Ramasut and tried to get Gordon Bennett to come back to Rovers but he turned down the offer – he did recommend a bloke called Richard Everson who I employed as my chief scout – and he turned out to be fantastic.

We'd actually begun my reign as manager by playing at Twerton Park against Peterborough. It was a weird day because after that match, we were moving to the Memorial Ground in Bristol, but we won 1-0, I had a bloody beast and Barry Fry was sat there with his shirt off – the worst sight I'd ever seen. It was daylight robbery because they deserved nothing less than three points, but I wasn't complaining – we were up and running. It was an embarrassing match in all honesty, and I wondered what the hell I'd done leaving Rangers in the first place. I'd managed to coax Geoff Twentyman, a former team-mate and then a sports guru at BBC Radio Bristol to be my assistant.

I was bursting with pride to be back at my boyhood club and be its manager. The fans seemed pleased and one bloke made a T-shirt for me to warm up with and on the back it said 'Ollie's back!' and on the front it said, 'Ollie's front', which made me smile. The first few weeks were a hell of an eye-opener but our next home game against Stockport was even more special because we were finally back in Bristol again. We drew 1-1 but one of the goal posts was about a foot too high at one end – the end we both scored at! The groundstaff at the Memorial Stadium only ever put up rugby posts and weren't used to putting up goal posts. As it turned out, I think theirs would have still gone in whereas ours would have gone over! We'd not lost any of our first three games, but lost my fourth in charge away at Millwall, and from the middle of October till the middle of February we won just three out of 19 league and cup matches – Christ it was hard!

Geoff Twentyman had left his job at BBC Radio Bristol open and decided he wanted to return to his old job, and I'm proud to say he's gone on leaps and bounds ever since.

Another old mate from my Rovers days, Phil Bater, was running his own gardening company so I called him up and asked if he'd like to be my No 2, and he said he'd be happy to come on board. Phil was hard as nails and scared everybody to death, and his influence was instantaneous and we won three games in a row after he'd joined us. I signed big Julian Alsop for £25,000 from Halesowen and the fans nicknamed him Bert the Brickie because he had a typical non-leaguer's attitude and was mad as a March hare, but a fantastic lad. I'd been under massive pressure at the time. He scored a vital equaliser at Peterborough (Peter Beadle scored the winner in a 2-1 victory) and we eventually finished 17th in Division Two. Both Phil and Julian had given us a massive lift at just the right time. We had five wins in the last eight games, which kept it from being a disastrous first year. The lack of investment meant that I reckoned we'd be a good bet for the drop if we didn't spend, so I said to chairman Geoff Dunford and his board, "If you want to see that again, don't add any players." One of the directors had suggested he was fed up with seeing the same "shit" as he called it, so I put the ball in their court and gave them a chance to change the "shit". They either backed me or we went down – it was as simple as that. I'd been a plate spinner and a juggler throughout that first year because you never really do just one job at that level. I'd had no idea about the politics Gerry Francis had often spoke about and I was seeing them at close quarters now. Talk about being thrown in at the deep end. To be fair to the chairman, he didn't take my comments personally and I signed five players during the summer and every one of them was a humdinger, even if I do say so myself! I still had a load to learn and was on a sharp learning curve that I just about managed to hang on to at times, but there were other aspects to being a manager that I hadn't grasped yet, such as how to deal with the media because I was a joke and took everything personally. I was too emotionally involved, probably because I was still playing, and I had trouble splitting the role of player and manager. I thought I could do everything, but the truth was I didn't do any of the jobs particularly well during that first season. Being back in Bristol and in the middle of the City-Rovers thing, I was like a walking ego, I have to say. It was frightening. I hope I never go back to being that bloke because if you get that engrossed in what you're doing, you'll almost certainly get it wrong, as I was proving. You need to be objective and you need to be able to see things for what they are. You need to be stood on a bank at the side of a stream and throw a big pebble in and see where the ripples go and how the water passes by to figure out what you need to do next. My problem was I was the pebble and I was fighting against the rapids, splashing around so that I couldn't see a thing – it was a joke. I still believed I could do the job and be a success but I swear had I not had the security of a three-year deal left, I'd have been out on my ear. They couldn't have afforded to pay me off and the fact the chairman and vice-chairman were the people who had wanted me as manager in the first place meant they had to stand by me or it made their judgement look rubbish. By the end of the season, it was just a total relief not to have been relegated and to be back in my home town.

I needed quality in my squad so I brought back my old mate Pen from Watford, which meant a great deal because obviously I thought a lot of him as a player, but he was also a terrific judge of players. I'd asked his advice the year before about Barry Hayles and he came to watch him play for Stevenage against Woking in a non-league cup final at Vicarage Road. He reckoned Hayles was a fantastic find, but added, "What about the centre-half for Woking? He's outstanding." I began to watch the lad, Steve Foster, more closely because I'd only been concentrating on Hayles, and he was right – he was playing out of his skin and marked Hayles out of the game. We ended up signing them both. I'd tried to get Hayles the year before, but Stevenage were adamant they wouldn't let him leave and told me even if I offered £400,000 they wouldn't sell. Then he broke his leg and we managed to get him for half that fee, with another £50,000 if he scored 25 goals in one season. Guess how many he scored in his first season? I wasn't complaining, though.

So Brian Gayle, Jason Perry, Steve Foster and Barry Hayles all arrived for a total of £350,000 which was a fair amount of money for a club our size at the time. The funny thing was, the fans were behind me in a 'back Ollie!' kind of way. It was weird in a way because I hadn't earned their support as such with performances from either the team or me, and even though I was still running round and putting my foot in, I wasn't the player they must have remembered. Perhaps I was living off past glories as a player but I still seemed to be in the honeymoon period and they'd never once got on my back.

I was pleased with my new signings because I thought they were all really good, solid lads and we began the 1997/98 season with a pre-season that dreams are made of. We won the first game 7-0 and Hayles scored a hat-trick, and two days later, I played two different sides in each half and Pen made his Rovers comeback debut in a 10-1 win at Bideford. I began to think our goals problem might have been solved and we followed that up with a 5-1 at Oxford City, and the board were getting excited by the way things were going. We'd nailed all our problematic areas down. It showed too, only losing one of the opening 10 games of the season, giving us a solid base to build on. My new signings were bedding in well and we were consistent throughout the year, so much so that we had an outside chance of going up. But with six games left, I lost Phil Bater as my assistant. Our youth set-up wasn't all that it should have been and he wanted to take control of it, which I didn't have a problem with because I knew he'd do a great job. I still needed a No 2 for what was a vital run-in and I couldn't think of anyone better than Pen, who accepted my offer of becoming my assistant manager.

With two games to go we were away to Blackpool and still needed points to be sure of a play-off spot, but my season was ended when Gary Brabin almost split me in two. I went to play a ball through and Brabin lunged at me and almost took my nuts off. I had to be carried off on a stretcher and was shaking I was in so much pain. Brabin actually scored a great goal that day and we lost 1-0, meaning we still needed a good result against Brentford on the last day. They were already relegated so we fancied our chances, but after 10 minutes Pen was sent off! Before the game he'd been fidgety and unsettled and eventually he came up to me and said, "I want to say something." What came out next was quintessential Pen, and I wondered what he was on about. He said, "Come on lads, we've got to have eyes like Marvin Hagler. We've got to be determined and believe we can do this." I let him carry on because he needed to get it out of his system but something still wasn't right. He was fired up and I said, "Are you OK?" He said, "Yeah, yeah, great!"

Brentford had Warren Aspinall in their side and I told the lads not to get involved with him, because he would stir it up given the chance. He was a tough cookie and wouldn't say no to a physical encounter but what I didn't know at the time was that Pen had had dealings with him in the past. With 10 minutes gone, we won a corner and as Matt Lockwood was on his way to take it, I notice

Pen by Aspinall on the edge of the box and next thing, Pen elbows him in the face, right in front of the ref! He gives him a red card and Pen's off, and I was wondering what he was doing. He'd lost it completely and started walking over towards me, muttering under his breath, "What have I done, what have I done?" The ref was looking at him wondering where he was headed because our changing rooms were in the opposite corner to where I was and I had to say, "You've got to go over there," and felt terrible having to point him in the right direction. It was the world's longest walk because he made an 8-yard walk about 160 yards. I was having a bit of banter with their manager Mickey Adams but I thought we could blow it so decided to throw caution to the wind. What I didn't know was Pen had gone to the dressing rooms, got his car keys and driven away still in his kit! He just couldn't deal with it and had to be somewhere else – he didn't know what to do and didn't know what to say so he went and parked up about a mile from the ground and listened to the match on his radio. We were actually playing really well and I said to the lads, "Just because he's had an absolute brainstorm – Marvin Hagler – what a bloody idiot – doesn't mean to say we can't win this game. I'm expecting you to win this game." I switched tactics around and Curo puts us 1-0 up. With Gillingham drawing, we were above them in the table, but with 10 minutes left, they equalise. The whole ground fell silent but I still believed we could win and was telling the lads to calm down and they'd be alright. Five minutes from time Matty Lockwood gets down the flank, crosses in a perfect ball and Hayles heads home his 25th of the season. The place erupted and the other results had gone our way so we were in the play-offs. From zeroes to heroes and the transformation had been satisfying to say the least

We had a real chance of going up and were up against Northampton Town, who'd gone up the year before. In the first leg of the semi-final at the Memorial we raced into a 3-0 lead with just 46 minutes gone. Then Hayles goes through and hits the post – it could have been four – but my lads look like they're celebrating getting to the final already when they pull one back to make it 3-1. That goal knocked the stuffing out of me, personally, but everyone else seemed to think we'd done it. I didn't because I knew it was only half-time, and as I was coming out I bumped into their manager Ian Atkins. He could see I was carrying a tape and said, "Is that today's game?" I said it was and he asked if he could have it. I said yes and handed over my copy without question, but he went away and showed it to his team. He told me in later years that he said to them, "That wasn't fair. That wasn't a goal. That was just luck." They beat us 3-0 in the second leg. We lost the plot and I couldn't get them re-focused and it was the worst night of my career. I was absolutely gutted because I knew we had them at one point, but I remembered the dignity Joe Jordan had showed in defeat several years earlier and wanted to conduct myself in the same way. I went in their dressing room and it was horrendous because they were cock-a-hoop. I shook hands and then got out of there. It was a crap, humiliating night and the Northampton fans had given me dog's abuse so I just wanted to get home and forget about football for a few weeks. I'd bought a suit especially for the game – it was only a Marks and Sparks three-piece thing, but I took great pleasure in stuffing it in the bin after I'd taken it off. Basically, I was still a rotten loser. Now I had to figure out how to get the lads' chins up again in time for next season. It was going to be the first real test of my managerial skills.

Chapter 15

Stack 'em and Rack 'em

Barry Hayles was presented with the Golden Boot for finishing top scorer in our division and had begun to attract interest from a number of Premiership clubs. I didn't want to sell him because he was my best player and I wanted to build a team that could win us promotion. I strengthened the team by bringing in a Swedish lad called Marcus Andreasson and Jamie Shore, the latter being another Bristolian marooned at Norwich. Jamie was a genius of a player and my scout Richard Everson put me on to him. He'd been at Lilleshall and they were convinced he was going to be one of the best players they'd ever had there. He was even tipped to be the next Paul Gascoigne and Man United had wanted to sign him, but he'd chosen to go to Gordon Bennett at Carrow Road. Norwich were reluctantly releasing him because he had terrible problems with his knee. We reckoned if we could get his knee right, we'd have a gem of a player on our hands, so we took a chance and signed him on a free in the summer. I took him pre-season training with me to build his fitness up and I could see there was something special about the kid. He was a winner and was unbelievably determined in everything he did. Time would tell whether or not the gamble would pay off, but it was a risk I thought was well worth taking. We'd taken another kid from Norwich who was being released because he was deemed not to be good enough. He came for a trial with the youth team and Phil Bater ran in and said, "You've got to sign this kid on, Oll!" Phil didn't get so excited that often, so we did. His name? Bobby Zamora. We also brought Guy Ipoua, who'd come from nowhere and impressed during a trial, so with two new lads to challenge up front and, having kept Hayles for the time being, I was hopeful that we could give it a good go for the 1998/99 season.

One player I did lose was Pete Beadle, who'd been scoring for fun for me. Geoff Dunford had called me and told me he needed £150,000 to put in the bank fairly quickly and with Beadle's contract running out, he was looking like the most obvious way of bringing the money in. Beadle had given me a list of demands for a new deal at Rovers and when I showed it to the board they all started laughing, asking me if he was serious. "Yeah, he is serious because he scored all those goals for us and he'll walk away for nothing if we don't agree a new deal with him. It's either that or we sell him." We were due to play Port Vale in a friendly and their manager John Rudge called me up and asked about his availability. I said I didn't want to sell him, but would for £300,000 – not a penny less – and it all had to be up front. I told Pete that Rovers weren't going to give him a new contract and that Vale wanted him, so he'd better play well in the friendly against them. He had a blinder and as we walked off John Rudge said, "I'll give you that."

"Give me what?"

"£300,000 up front."

"Alright, then."

If only every transfer was that simple. That was it – the deal was done, but I'd lost a good striker and needed a replacement. I spoke with Pen about possible replacements and he suggested looking at a lad called Jason Roberts, whom we'd tried to buy a couple of years earlier and was now at Wolves. We'd looked at him around the same time we'd been watching Barry Hayles and offered Hayes £100,000 for him, but they turned it down and Wolves came in and paid them £250,000. I looked at his appearances and goals since the move and in 18 months he'd hardly played. Mark McGhee was manager at Wolves and I called him up and asked if Roberts was available. He said, "Yeah he is, I just need my money back."

I asked if he'd accept the money in instalments and he was happy so long as he recouped the £250k. Our plan was to put £125,000 down straight away with the rest split over the next two years. That meant I could give Geoff Dunford the money he needed, plus a bit more, and bring in Roberts as well. I told him what I'd set up and he said, "What, you can do that?" He'd been trying to sell my captain Andy Tillson who was also our highest paid player for £50,000 to keep the bank manager happy.

I said, "What's the point in selling Andy for that when I'm going to need another £100,000 to replace him? No, you're not selling him." We had a bit of an argument about that, probably the first we'd had, but I had to stand firm because Andy was a bloody good player, a fans' favourite and a gentleman as well. Eventually we agreed that if the Beadle and Roberts deals went through without a hitch, I'd keep my captain. We got Roberts and his agent down and I had my doubts as to whether it would all go through. It was all about desire and Barry Hayles had plenty of it because he actually took a pay cut to join us from Stevenage and I needed Jason Roberts to do the same. I said, "I don't care what you're on now, I'm going to pay you less. You won't be the worst paid, but there are some who are being paid more. If you want to come here for the right reasons, Gary Penrice will get you playing again."

His agent, Johnny Mack said. "Shut up Ollie, we're going." But Jason said, "No, wait a minute. I want to come here and play." That was what I'd wanted to hear. Jason thought he'd be replacing Barry Hayles and so would be the main man. He didn't know it was Pete Beadle who was leaving. We had some great young strikers on our books already and if we could work out how to push Roberts' buttons, we'd have strength in depth most Premiership sides would envy. Pen's saying was 'stack 'em and rack 'em' because we both believed you could never have too many good strikers knocking around. He was my striker coach whereas I took the defence and midfielders and worked them in units. Pen would take two strikers at a time and work one-on-one with them every day of the week. He gave them the TLC they needed and it was working really well. Then, in November 1998, we played Fulham away and things started to get interesting. I'd told Barry that a lot of clubs were showing interest and Fulham might have been one of them, so if his heart was set on a big money move, he'd better impress. We lost 1-0 and he had an absolute stinker and I told him maybe he wasn't ready to move on yet. Geoff Dunford travelled back on the coach with us, which was unusual to say the least. He said he'd been to a business meeting in London and I thought no more about it. The following day I got a call from Kevin Keegan telling me he was going to "buy my striker". I told him he wasn't for sale and he said, "Well I'm sorry, he is."

"Who do you mean?" I asked, hoping he meant someone else.

"Barry Hayles."

"Yeah? Well he's not for sale."

"Yes he is. I spoke to your chairman yesterday afternoon and he was more or less begging us to sign him."

I finished the call, and seething, called up Geoff and started shouting and bawling at him and he agreed to meet me at the training ground where things got a bit nasty. He'd never lost his temper before, but he swore at me, so I knew I'd got to him. He told me we'd be getting £2m, all guaranteed in four payments of £500,000. I'd just signed Jason Roberts, had Guy Ipoua and Jamie Cureton and Pen could still play up front if I needed him to, so I had no real choice in the matter. Those are the facts of life at a lower league club and there's nothing anybody can do about it. The club needed money to survive and at that stage of my managerial career, I had to take it on the chin. There was no way I'd wanted to sell him, but I couldn't stand in the lad's way. Before he signed for Keegan I actually called David Pleat at Spurs because Barry's dream had been to play for them one day, but he didn't think he was a big enough name for Tottenham. I said, "Well actually, I think you're wrong about that. The lad's a winner and he'd help your club because he's desperate to play for you." As it was, he ended up signing for Fulham and went on to form a great partnership with Geoff Horsfield. I was sorry to see him go because from day one of him arriving at Rovers he'd been our best player, and he wasn't far off being one of the best players I'd ever worked with. He could do the lot and his attitude was always spot-on. He asked one day if we could switch from attackers v defenders so the strikers could have a go at defending against the defenders. Hayles was winning tackles and headers like a seasoned full-back and nobody could get past him! All I'd done at Rovers was give him a stage and within two years he'd gone for £2m, and though the majority of money went to run the club, I got some of it and decided to buy Nathan 'Duke' Ellington to give us another option up front.

Pen had spoken with Kenny Jackett, one of his good mates from his days at Watford, and he'd tipped him off about Nathan who was playing for Walton and Hersham at the time. The rumour was QPR had already signed him, but I called up Walton's vice-chairman and he said that wasn't true, so I went along with Pen to watch him play. I took Kim along too, because almost every decent signing I'd made had happened after Kim had come along to watch with me. He didn't play that well in the first half, but my God, the kid had some raw pace and power. I went into the boardroom at half-time and saw the Walton chairman and told him I wanted to do a deal. He told me he would cost £150,000 which was fine and I knew QPR wouldn't pay that much. I said before I did the deal, I wanted him to come to Bristol with his family and have a look around because he was only a young lad. I called Geoff Dunford and said, "I think we've got you another one, but he's only 17 and will cost £150,000." As I walked back to my seat for the second half I saw a head pop up from the paddock below. It was Pen, climbing up to sit with us and he said, "Ollie, you've gotta sign him! You've gotta sign him!"

I said, "Pen, I already have."

"Have you? Great!"

His enthusiasm for Ellington was frightening and I knew we'd got a great prospect on our books just by the way Pen was. Nathan's arrival was harsh on Bobby Zamora who'd been progressing well in the youth team. It meant he'd probably stepped a place down on the ladder and considering what he's gone on to do, that was a misjudgement on our part. Bob was skinny and tall whereas Nathan was stronger, and I think that probably swung it, though I do think I treated Bob unfairly in some ways. I should have brought him into the first team squad along with Duke.

I met Nathan and showed him around our training centre at The Beeches. It was very relaxed and informal and I told him what Pen could do for him and what he had done with some of the other strikers, and he basically bought into us and agreed a contract, turning down QPR's offer.

Jason Roberts was having a hard time settling in at Rovers and had only scored once in 14 games for us. Pen had sussed out what he thought the problem was, which I believe sums up what Pen is all about. It was annoying Pen who felt Jason could do a hell of a lot better. He came up to me one day after training had ended and said, "You've got to come out with me this afternoon, Oll, because I've realised what I've got to do with this kid. He's potentially got what it takes, but if I can't get him to focus, he's never going to be the striker we want him to be."

I told him no problem, and he added that it wasn't going to be very pleasant, but I said I didn't want to know what he had in mind and he should just go ahead and do it.

The Illustrated Ollie – my Publisher commissioned this caricature – what can I say?!

Pictured chuffed as a badger with my grandparents, mum and brother and sister.

Parkwall School Team 1972/73, the shield was almost bigger than I was!

On the shoulders of giants – pre-season training with dad for Saltford, aged 11.

It looks like a scene from Kes! This may have been one of my first TV appearances.

My dad Bill
and me.

Signing to Bristol Rovers as a 14-year-old schoolboy alongside Kevin Westaway,
as our delighted dads look on.

Signing for
Rovers, 1980

Playing for Rovers. In the left background is Keith Curle, long-time friend and then
team-mate – and no, that guy next to me is not my Mexican double!

PORTSMOUTH

FOOTBALL COMPANY LIMITED

Registered Office:
FRATTON PARK, PORTSMOUTH, HANTS. PO4 8RA

Tel: 731204

Dear Ian,

Thanks for your card, it was great to hear from you, and I'm glad to see you doing well this season. Keep playing the old one touch and you can't go wrong. Have a happy Christmas and be a great player.

Bally.

P.S. Loved the goal at Bournemouth!!

Alan Ball pictured during his Rovers career and Happy Christmas letter. What a class act on and off the pitch!

Wimbledon 1985/86 team line-up, I'm front row, second from left.

Kim and me tying the knot.

Rovers return:
back home.

A proud moment,
the birth of
my twins.

Mr Consistent — that's Holloway

Ian Holloway has been named Bristol Rovers Supporters' Club player of the year, a week after receiving a similar award from the President's Club.

He received the trophy at Twerton Park after pipping Steve Yates (the young player of the year), Devon White and Ian Alexander in a poll of members. Picture: Charles Breton

Mr Consistent!

Celebrating, during the Championship season at Rovers.

Wolves v Rovers, 1990 – back when shorts were shorts!

Mum – AKA 'Short One' presenting me with the Bill Holloway Trophy.

In a tussle with Ray Parlour, during a QPR-Arsenal clash.

Gerry Francis, my manager at Rovers & QPR and my mentor.

Pen (Gary Penrice) in action for QPR.

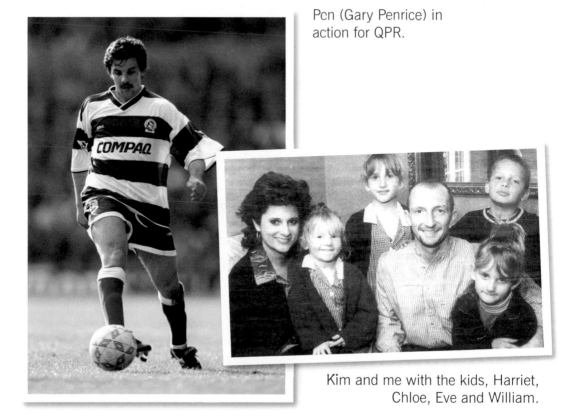

Kim and me with the kids, Harriet, Chloe, Eve and William.

As manager of Bristol Rovers, 1998

The infamous Captain Gas!

The pressure is on – and never off – as I take on the manager's job at QPR.

Woof Day! Barking instructions from the touchline!

Celebrating victory over Oldham Athletic in the Division Two play-off semi-final at Loftus Road in 2003.

UP ON THE WOOF

BARKING . . . Ian Holloway with Marc Bircham

Ollie boys play with spirit

...nd Furlong   FLYING . . . the Rangers squad start to par...

Promotion at last as we (QPR) beat Sheffield Wednesday 3-1, 2004.

This is my sister Sue and brother John.

My new Home...
Home Park,
Plymouth Argyle.

Still barking instructions from the touchline – this time with the Green Army.

Plymouth Argyle v Watford – FA Cup quarter-final, 2007.

Who'd be a feckin' manager?

"I've got to do it, Oll and I want you to witness it."

So we took out a few balls, our goalie, Andy Collett, who didn't get along too well with Jason anyway and was very chirpy and self-opinionated, and it turned out to be one of the most inspired sessions I've ever taken part in. Pen said to Jason as we stopped in front of a goal, "Your trouble is you can't focus, son."

Andy Collett piped up, "Yeah, that's right. I'll save whatever you've got." Jason wasn't having any of it and told him it'd be no problem. I started laying the ball off to him and he was hitting shots all over the place.

Pen said: "Oh, you can focus then, can you? That's rubbish, useless." Jason soon lost his temper and Pen called a halt to the session. He came up to Jason and said, "I'm telling you now you've got no focus. Your technique is fine but you just can't concentrate and I'm going to prove it. I'm going to shout some things at you and if you're focused, as you claim to be, you'll put most of the balls in the back of the net."

We began again and Pen stood behind the goal and began. "You're useless Roberts you fucking tosser!" Jason continued to shank his shots wide and Pen told him not to listen to him and ignore everything. "I was out with your mum last weekend" Eventually he blocked him out and started scoring, and scoring, and scoring. "Go on, that's it," said Pen. "Get your head over it, well done, that's it, that's focused!" By the end of the session, Jason was invigorated and looked a changed kid. From that moment on, he believed in himself once again and the difference in him from that day to this was amazing, and it's all down to Pen's expertise and it is also, as far as I'm concerned, the mark of his genius because I don't believe there are many around like him.

I recalled Jason to the starting line-up for the FA Cup First Round tie with Welling and he scored all our goals in a 3-0 win. He then scored in a 1-1 draw at Millwall and got another in the next game at home to Oldham. He'd end the season with 23 goals from 37 starts – not bad for a player who'd got one in 14 before that.

To give Bobby Zamora the experience he needed I loaned him out to Bath City and he scored a hatful of goals for them and from there, Brighton took him on loan and again, he did extremely well. The board were, around this time, trying to set up a structure whereby we paid a fixed wage to any youth or reserve player under a certain age who was up for a new deal. Bob wouldn't sign for the amount they'd decided on, which you can probably guess wasn't a great deal and I couldn't really blame him because he'd done a lot more than anyone else his age at Rovers at the time. He continued to score goals elsewhere while on loan with Brighton and I feared we'd end up losing him because the board wouldn't budge. We had some memorable days in 1998/99 and the two draws with Manchester City, who had slipped into our league for a year, were terrific results for us. We drew 0-0 at Maine Road and fielded the youngest ever Rovers team with an average of just 21. We also beat Reading 6-0 away, with all our goals coming after half-time – the 'Madejski Massacre' our fans called it – with Curo scoring four and Roberts two. So the promise was definitely there and on our day, we could be as good as anyone.

We finished 13th that season and I think losing Barry Hayles hit us harder than I'd imagined. Jamie Cureton at least walked off with the Golden Boot for our division after scoring 29 goals in 54 appearances – the second successive year a Rovers player had finished top scorer in the division. I knew I had the firepower, but we had to harness it to help us win matches, and with 12 games left of the season after that, of the 1999/2000 campaign, I thought we had. We were four points clear at the top and just had to keep doing what we'd being doing all season but with 10 games left, we hit a bad patch to end them all and we ended up even missing out on the play-offs on the last day of the season. It was the ultimate 'what happened next?' and people wanted answers. Why had we fallen away so badly? Why had we gone from first to seventh in 10 games? I'm not entirely sure, to be honest, but injuries to key players in key games cost us dearly, but I got blamed for the poor run and, as manager, you put yourself up there to be shot at and my ass had been peppered with buckshot.

We'd been on fire from the start of the season and I'd added Ronnie Mauge, Robbie Pethick, Andy Thomson, David Hillier and former Liverpool midfielder Mark Walters, who came about a third of the way through, and he was superb for us, a really class player. We needed a strong midfield because my forwards weren't that good at retaining the ball from back to front and I needed one or two wily heads in there to make sure they acted like a net so the ball didn't keep coming back at our defenders. Roberts and Curo were magnificent at running on to slotted balls from midfield. Hillier was, in effect, my replacement because I didn't really want to play anymore. Pen was also nearing the end of his playing days so it was the end of an era for us both, but I found it an easy decision to make.

Marcus Andreasson, whose contract I tore up when he told me he was homesick for Sweden, asked if he could come back and play for me, and because I believed in him I paid £120,000 to bring him back to Rovers. He told me he'd be fine this time and I was convinced he'd want to do his best to repay the faith I'd shown in him, but he didn't. He let me and himself down because he had the heart of a pea. The other lads could see it, but I couldn't and I got that one wrong I'm afraid. You live and learn, don't you?

So while we had a stronger, more experienced squad, it was my inexperience in management that cost us that season. We'd trained hard during the summer on certain moves that played to our strengths and it paid off for a while. All my lads could play a bit and pass it and we had one or two players with flair, and the fans were loving it. We were banging in goals left, right and centre and my team were getting a lot of plaudits, which was nice – it was Total Football Rovers-style. Then we had a few distractions and injuries that meant the formation options I'd had became more limited. I lost Pritchard for the season through injury – an injury that would mean he'd never play for us again. I also lost Simon Bryant, a brilliant combative midfielder who was only 17, for the season, with bone bruising to his knee. Then Ronnie Mauge was called up for Trinidad and Tobago, and he'd earned his moment in the sun, so to speak. Then Grenada wanted Jason Roberts to represent them and though I'd have preferred they stayed put, I wasn't going to stand in their way. How could I? It was unlikely these lads would ever play for England so how could I deny them a chance to maybe even play at the World Cup one day? But the lads going away backfired on me in a number of ways, none more so when Mauge broke his leg while with Trinidad. Jason's situation was entirely different. He missed one game, away to Oxford, so I put Nathan Ellington up front in his place, and he was superb. We won 5-0, a hell of a result, but Jason was back home in time for the next game. Instead of keeping the same team, which I should have done – and would most definitely do today – I put him straight back in. He should have been sub. When my lads were looking for me to make a stand against him and be strong I didn't, which was a mistake. There was a lot of political stuff surrounding Jason as we entered the final strait of the campaign. I think his family wanted him to move on because he was scoring goals and he and Cureton were constantly being talked about and linked with moves away. An old Rovers player had also unsettled them by coming to our training ground to tell them how much he was now on, which left me seething at the time. Pete Beadle was rumoured to be going to Bristol City, so I called him up and asked if he wanted to come back to Rovers, knowing full well I couldn't match the wage City would pay him but hoping the success he'd enjoyed with us previously might just swing it. Besides, we had to match City's offer because our fans wouldn't have been too happy if we'd not even made the effort to bring him back. As it was, in his infinite wisdom he chose to go to Aston Gate.

The following day I arrived for training to find Beadle in out kit room talking to Curo and Jason Roberts. I said, "What are you doing here? Get out you stinking shit head pig! You're not welcome round here anymore, get back to bloody Ashton Gate." He thought I was joking, but I wasn't. I was pissed off at him and I later found out he'd been telling Curo and Jason how much money he was on, which was considerably more than they were being paid. Unbelievable! I know it happens and players talk amongst each other, comparing wages and bonuses, but I wasn't happy that someone had actually come to my training ground to seek out two young lads and tell them they were on rubbish money. From that day on, I think I lost a piece of both players and something changed. It was hard for them when they were playing at the top of their game and were being paid what they were. Then, when somebody who isn't playing that well signs for your neighbours and gets three times as much, you're not going to put up with it for very long are you? The other lads were getting a bit cheesed off with us being labelled a two-man team, anyway, and after a 0-0 draw away to Bristol City, I was left spitting fire again. I read the match report in the evening paper and I couldn't believe what this guy had written. We hadn't played well, had drawn 0-0, but my defenders had been magnificent, and then I see a line along the lines of "if only City had Cureton and Roberts up front, then Bristol would have a team to be proud of." What? Was he having a laugh or something? I was livid and called the bloke up and asked him to come to the ground, which to be fair, he did. I got the whole squad together and asked him to explain his comments to them. I stood by Curo and Jason Roberts and said, "How dare you! I'm trying educate these two and they don't play well, but you say they did in your match report and you don't mention my backline or how well they played. These two were useless on the day and you're telling them they're great and by the way, when you're making a statement about my home town, be careful what you say. I'm already very proud of my team so how dare you insult my club by saying 'the town could have a team to be proud of.' Aren't you proud of us when we're working on the budget we are and still wiping the floor with you lot over there? How can you give him eight out of ten and him five? Because that's what you did. Are you watching the same game? Are you watching the right game?"

I know I shouldn't have done it and was bang out of order, but sometimes I think people should be held accountable for what they say or do. My lads loved it because I'd stood up for them and they were having me all day long because of the way I was with them. I just wanted to treat them the way I would want to be treated and I'd give my all for someone who believed in me when I was a player. After my rant, I said thanks to the reporter for having the bottle to come over and he went on his way. I was a stroppy little shite with the media and got it totally wrong at the time, but it's not always wise to play and manage the club you support because sometimes you just let your emotions run wild.

So I've got a number of distractions, half my team missing and nearly all the midfield safety net I'd brought in to support my strikers, and with the transfer deadline gone, I was having to play players out of position and totally change the complexity of my team. Mauge's loss hit us hard because he'd been one of the lads who'd been playing out of his skin, so it was a massive blow. Hillier picked up a few injuries and missed vital games and I was forced to play fancy-dan forwards and wingers across the middle – it was a disaster. The defence was constantly being put under pressure again and the team that had been flying in the early part of the season never played together again, and in the run in, I just couldn't stop the lads wobbling. With four games to go, Preston beat us 2-0 at home and went above us. Burnley had come up with a stroke of genius by signing Ian Wright and they came galloping up behind us and eventually took the final promotion place. We'd taken just two points from a possible 18 – a bloody awful run – and despite beating Bristol City 2-0, we picked up just one more point from our last three games and after losing 1-0 to relegated Cardiff on the last day of the season, ended in seventh. A win and we'd have been in the play-offs, but our abysmal form had caught up with us in the cruellest way possible and I take full responsibility for that. I think we all wondered how we could pick ourselves up after that, me more than anyone I imagine. My dreams and hopes shattered for the club that was in my blood, I had to face the fact that I'd let the Rovers fans down that season. It broke my heart, to be honest.

Chapter 16

Dead Man Walking

I wasn't a nice man to be around after we'd blown promotion and the house I'd built at Rovers began to fall in around me. Jamie Cureton came to see me moaning about his wages and ended up asking for a transfer. He'd finished one goal behind joint-top scorer with Jason Roberts who had won the Golden Boot for our division and it doesn't take a genius to work out that he wanted more money, which I couldn't really hold against him. Then Jason Roberts came round to my house with his girlfriend and we shared a nice bottle of wine. He said thanks for what I'd done for him and the next day he comes into my office, a totally different person and hands in a transfer request telling me he was never going to play for me again. Upset doesn't quite adequately describe how I felt about that little episode. I'd had meeting after meeting with his dad, his uncle Cyril and his uncle Otis and they were talking about his future and his affairs. Jason had two years to go and Curo had three years left on his contract so Geoff Dunford tells me that he has no intention of giving Curo a rise, but he was prepared to try and sort something out for Roberts. We made him an offer which would have made him easily the best paid player we'd ever had, but he turned it down flat. We had a pre-season trip to Ireland coming up so I called in Curo and Roberts separately and told them they weren't going on tour with us. I took Nathan Ellington and Bobby Zamora instead and I was fully intending to work with those two because I didn't want anyone who wanted away near the other lads. Bobby Zamora was tripped in our first friendly, fell awkwardly and –

unbeknown to us – he'd broken a bone in his wrist and consequently didn't do very well because he couldn't hold people off. On my return, the chairman asked how Bobby had done because he'd heard he was "rubbish", which annoyed me no end because he'd obviously been fed misleading information by a board member on tour with us. Bobby still wanted more money, too, which the board would never sanction and as he was out of contract, Brighton came back in for him and offered £100,000, which the club predictably accepted. I could see his potential but the chairman was worried about the Bosman ruling and so Bobby was allowed to move on with a 35% sell-on clause.

Two clubs were fighting over Jason Roberts and he was adamant he wouldn't play for us again to the point of arrogance. It wasn't the same young man I'd got to know quite well during the previous two years but I felt he was being influenced by outside parties. Eventually he left for West Brom who paid £2m for him. I didn't feel he was mentally ready to leave us, but he did. I told the board with the money they'd just got that they should reward Jamie Cureton for the goals he'd scored and I'd go and look for another striker as well as a younger forward to replace Zamora. To my Curo suggestion the chairman categorically said, "No, he's got a three-year deal, I'm not doing that."

I said, "Then I suggest you sell him because I can't motivate him if you won't pay him more." He asked what I thought we could get for him and I said it would be what we paid, because nobody would pay more. He eventually went to Reading after the first game of the season for £250,000, the fee we'd paid when bringing him over from Norwich. We'd raised £2.35m from the sale of three of my best strikers and when I went to say I'd be signing replacements I was told that the club had no money and I'd have to bring in loan players instead! I should have known the writing was on the wall for me and that I was being blamed – or not forgiven – for the previous season's failure. I was being set up to fail while cash was put aside for a new man to spend – that's how it looked to me, anyway. I never smelt the coffee and didn't even realise the kettle was on. I kept going, even though I was being set up. Pen said, "For Christ sake, Oll, can't you see what's happening?" But this was Bristol Rovers, my club and I didn't think they'd treat me anything but fairly. So I managed to bring in Mickey Evans on loan from West Brom and we started with two draws and a 6-2 win at Brentford. We were still unbeaten as we prepared for only our second home game of the season against Wigan and as I walked towards the ground, an old adversary of mine, a local reporter called Richard Latham walked towards me and I thought, 'here we go – he's going to slaughter me for losing my best strikers.' He was quite openly a Bristol City fan and we'd had some quite playful banter over the years about our club rivalry. When he got to me he shook my hand quite vigorously. I asked him what he was up to and he said, "I have to say that's the best bit of management I've ever seen. To sell all those players, get all that money in the bank and still carry on winning is amazing – I thought you'd had it." Little did I know I was the dreaded 'dead man walking' because you can't sell three players of that standard and not expect to struggle. I reckoned I was 72 goals down with the loss of Roberts, Zamora and Cureton, but finally the board bowed to fan pressure and signed Mickey Evans on for £250,000 and I felt with a couple more faces we'd be OK. I was more concerned that we'd not won at home and after we'd failed to win any of our 11 games at the Memorial Ground going into the New Year, the fans were getting a bit restless. I took off Andy Thomson and then I was treated to a chorus of "You don't know what you're doing!" Cheers, lads! There's an old saying in football that if you stay at one club too long, you end up smelling of fish and there was a definite waft of a trawlerman's gloves about old Ollie by that point. Captain Birdseye couldn't hold a candle to me! Their patience was starting to wear thin and after a narrow 1-0 defeat at Reading, I called the board and asked them to sort out my contract because I didn't feel they felt I was the right man to take the club forward anymore. They had wanted stability and given me a five-year deal so I told them to write their own pay-off because I didn't think that length of time was fair on the club and they came back with an offer which I accepted and within two or three days my Rovers management career was over. I wasn't a happy bunny. Could I hold my head up in the town that I loved or with the people I loved? Had I done enough to get another job in football? Who knew the answers? I wasn't good company, yet again, and I sat in my house, utterly gutted, wondering what was next for me. I thought it was going to be like the old adage, 'when one door closes, another one slams shut in your face', but, thankfully, somebody put their foot in before the door closed. A new chapter was waiting to be written within just three weeks and it was at somewhere I was already very familiar with.

I was a physical wreck towards the end of my time at Rovers, thanks to a cold sore virus I've inherited off my mum. Whenever I'm run down I get cold sores everywhere, but I'm the only person I know who gets them on his bugle or, in this case, on my eye. I wasn't permitted to talk about the deal I'd cut with Rovers at the time so, needing a total break from everything, I went with Kim and the kids to Lyme Regis to stay at my sister's place and it was one of the best weeks I'd had in years. I discovered myself again as well as my wife and kids and I started to feel human again. On the day of our return, my phone rang and it was Gerry Francis. It was weird because I hadn't really spoken to him for a while and he said, "You alright? You're not feeling sorry for yourself are you? You've got to get back in it – do you want to be a manager again? What's up with you?" I wondered what the matter with him was and then he said, "Well you'd better get yourself sorted out and come and have an interview here."

Gerry was QPR manager at that time, but he'd already told everyone he was going to leave at the end of the year. So he got me an interview and it was odd in a way because while I'd been on holiday I'd read a report in the paper where Iain Dowie said he wanted Gerry's job. I read it thinking 'Gerry won't like that,' and though Dowie was his assistant, I knew after working with Gerry as long as I had that he wouldn't be happy with Iain saying that when he had. I agreed to go up and met Chris Wright the QPR chairman, but he was the opposite of the man I'd imagined him to be. Being the head of Chrysalis Records, I'd expected a big go-getter, in-your-face-type but he wasn't – he was so quiet and introverted, but still a fantastic bloke. In fact, I liked him all the more for the way he was. A few days later I was asked back for another interview with Chris at a different location but I felt he wasn't really looking at my CV or listening to what I had to say. I felt he was thinking 'how can you help me get out of the trouble I'm in with the QPR fans? You ain't big enough, mate.' He basically pointed out that I'd managed a club in a division lower than QPR. I told him to read the CV, look at my record in more detail and see how I'd had to continually sell my best players. As it was, I went back for a third interview and he still wasn't paying much attention so I said, "You're not listening. Have a look at my CV and get back to me if you want." I think Chris just thought 'to hell with it' went along with Gerry's recommendation in the end and I was offered the manager's job, which I was delighted to take.

It's funny how things work out, especially for my family, because the schooling back in Bristol hadn't been right for the girls and we weren't happy with the arrangements for their secondary education. Because of their needs, there were only a few schools in the country that suited them, so we had looked at every possibility and, while I was still Rovers manager, had been up to a deaf school in St Albans. It was perfect and we decided that was the school for them. We set the wheels in motion but the education authority told us that because of funding issues, they wouldn't be able to help and instead they would make arrangements at a school in Bristol. That wasn't good enough and we let them know. Like any parents, we wanted the best education they could possibly have. We believed St Albans was right for them because the school they were already attending had no secondary department and the girls wouldn't have access to a full national curriculum with just one teacher for all the subjects. Then, by fate or otherwise, I get the QPR job and we move within just one mile from the school in St Albans! The education authorities could have no issue with the girls attending what was now their local school so things fell perfectly for once. It makes you wonder if there are bigger things happening that us mere mortals aren't privy to, doesn't it? They started in September and Hattie tagged along and went to a new deaf school, too, but poor old William had it tough. He was 13 and had to leave his mates and all the security and family that he'd had in Bristol and it's typical of what happens to a footballer's or manager's family. I liken it to being part of a travelling circus in that you bed down in one area for a while and then it's time to pack up all your things and move on again, and the kids have no choice in the matter. It worked out brilliant for the girls but terrible for Will. It was hard on Kim, too, having to deal with the small print of our numerous upheavals as ever. She'd also left behind the support network of her and my family, which again shifted the onus entirely on her shoulders. So on I went, ready to face a new challenge, lovely jubbly and all that, but what about my family again? The move suited some of them, but not all. Again, I didn't get the balance right and just sailed on into the next chapter.

To get a job like QPR was a bit surreal but a huge honour. They didn't even tell Iain Dowie he'd failed the interview so it was a bit awkward when I bowled into the club on my first day and I had to do a press conference and then meet the players. As I went into the press call, Iain Dowie said, "Obviously it's not your problem, but I had an interview for this job and they haven't even told me how I've gone on so obviously you're the manager are you?" He was totally respectful and fantastic about it so I asked him to call a meeting with the squad. I went in to see them and I looked around and there must have been about 25 lads sat down and as I was about to start, Dowie says, "We've just got to wait for the injured ones, Ollie." I expected three or four but another 27 people walked or hobbled in! The room was packed and I thought 'bloody hell – no wonder this place is in such a mess with finances.' We had 51 pros and a squad within a squad. There was a youth team section that was running itself and they wouldn't pass up their best players because they were trying to win the Under-19 league. They had an Academy, too – everything Bristol Rovers hadn't had, in fact. All the staff were out of contract, which was how Gerry had wanted things to be left until I came in. He told me that, as Director of Football, he was still going to be around and would do any bits of scouting that I needed, but then added that I had to do this, that and the other and I had to say, "Gerry, with the greatest respect, I'm the manager, I can't have you undermining me. Let me do it my way."

It must have been hard for him, because he was QPR through and through and was desperate to keep us up. To his credit, he said, "Okay, but I'm not going to let you see any of the wages."

I told him I needed to, but he said, "No, just try and keep us up because you'll only get angry."

I let Iain Dowie go, because I wanted my own coaching set-up and he handled things superbly and was very dignified throughout. Later, he'd tell me I'd done him a massive favour because he went into management after that and revelled in it. I'd had a wage budget of about £1m at Rovers and when I did eventually find out, I knew Gerry was right to keep it from me because I would have got angry at £5.3m worth of wages. As it was, I took over in February and I couldn't stop the rot. I'd watched QPR lose 5-0 to Wimbledon the week before and for my first game in charge, I kept the same team. We were home to Neil Warnock's Sheffield United and we were 1-0 up at half-time. Gerry told me I should have their midfielder George Santos man-marked but I said I didn't want to do that. "You never taught me to do that, I'm not going to do it," I told him. Santos scored twice in the second half and we lost 3-1! I hadn't made a fantastic start but Gerry then left me to it and I decided to go back to the things he'd taught me as a player. I had to ask him not to come to training anymore because I needed him out of the way but the truth was, I only had 13 games to save us from relegation and we ended up winning just one of those games. We were too far gone, no matter what we did. I just wanted them to work hard and get stuck in, which they sort of did. I didn't know exactly how our finances were or what the restrictions were so I called a meeting with Chris Wright to talk about the possibility of signing Marlon Harewood from Nottingham Forest. He wasn't getting a regular game at the City Ground and he was my type of forward and at around £600,000, the price wasn't bad either, so I asked Chris if there was any chance and there was a bloke stood behind him and he said, "No Chris, no more."

Chris said, "I know, but I'd like to help Ian."

"I'm telling you no means no – this has gone far enough and you're not doing it any more."

Chris turned around and looked at a painting on the wall. "What about that? How much is that worth?"

"The painting is valued at £800,000, but I'm not allowing you to do it."

That impressed the hell out of me because he was willing to do anything – even sell a prized possession – just to help me and the club out. That told me all I needed to know about Chris Wright, who was being blamed by the supporters for all kinds of things which wasn't fair because virtually everything he'd ever touched had been a success and it must have been killing him to see his beloved Rangers in that kind of trouble. We lost 1-0 to relegation rivals Grimsby Town at home and if it had been a boxing match, the game would have been stopped long before because we were all over them but just couldn't score – then they nicked one in the 86th minute to win the game. Their manager, Lennie Lawrence, had a girlfriend who worked at Loftus Road and after the game, he came into my office and started giving me advice on what I should do. I said, "Len, do me a favour mate. We just pissed all over you there, how dare you come in my office when you've been so spawny." I was a bit put out to say the least. The following Monday morning we had a really good positive session. We then went back to the dressing room and Nick Blackburn, our vice chairman was stood there with two blokes either side of him. He said I needed to get all the players into the food hall, which I did and then Nick said, "These two gentlemen are administrators. They have come in and we've got to listen to what they have to say."

One of the blokes said, "This company has gone into administration. All the debts the company owe have been frozen and what that means is we are now the people who make the decisions. Are there any questions?"

The players looked shocked and I put my hand up and said, "Yes, could you just explain to us ordinary people what administration means? It's a nice fancy word but what does it actually mean?"

One of them said, "Yes, I can. What it means is I'm in charge." He pointed at Gavin Peacock and said, "You, young fella. I can send you home and say I'm not going to pay you because you're on too much money. When we come out of administration, you'll get every penny owed to you, but I can send you home and you're not allowed to work, if I do."

Gavin was my most senior pro and also the highest paid and I swear he went white as a sheet and took a couple of steps backwards till he hit the wall. He was also our PFA rep and he said, "You can't do that."

"Yes I can."

"Actually," I said, "I don't think you can. You don't understand football do you?"

He snapped back, "Well you don't understand administration, do you?"

"Actually, I do and our PFA will not let you do that – have you spoken to them yet? The PFA have a union and you won't get away with doing what you say you can do."

I told Gavin that he had my permission to leave the room and go and call Gordon Taylor from the PFA. Gordon came down to see the administrators and informed us they couldn't do what they'd threatened. A deal was cut whereby we got our wages, but not our bonuses. The good thing that came out of it was the lads knew I had known nothing about it and we gelled straight away because of that, I think. It didn't make any difference to me because I was floating on air that I'd got the job and the fact of the matter was I'd had to work with little or no money for five years at Rovers anyway.

We had a meeting and I told the lads, "Look, we're still going to get paid but we're not earning any bonuses anyway at the moment so let's win a few games and you'll get your money at the end of the season. Let's ban the word administration, it's all about our product and we have to do well, because if this lot go bust you're going to need another job anyway."

We'd managed to get everything out of the way and in the open in one fell swoop. It turned out Chris had been losing £100,000 per week of his own money so it was inevitable that something would have to give eventually because one man can't sustain that kind of financial loss on a continued basis.

We never gave up hope of beating the drop but one game on the run-in illustrated perfectly how fate was conspiring against us. We were 2-0 up away to Crewe and seemingly cruising. I have to take my hat off to Dario Gradi at this point because he is very clever at coaching his side to work within the laws of the game to gain an advantage and I think we were suckered in on this occasion. As Peter Crouch ran past to get in a defensive position, one of their lads booted it up Crouchy's backside and then held his hands out to the ref to suggest it must have been intentional. He'd already been booked and the ref, showing wisdom and common sense beyond the call of duty, gives him a second yellow. A couple of minutes later Karl Reddy is sent off, so we're down to nine men and end up just about clinging on to a 2-2 draw. I also had to take Andy Thomson off because a ball hit him in the back of the head and knocked out a contact lens. We were all grovelling around trying to find it in the mud but it was lost and as he had no spare with him that day, he had to come off. With luck like that, we were doomed! We beat Tranmere 2-0 at home but we took a few risks at Huddersfield with the game balanced at 1-1 and we threw caution to the wind because we needed a win, but in going for it, we left gaps and lost to a late Delroy Facey goal – that was the final nail in our coffin and we were down. There were tears in the dressing room but I told the lads they should be proud of their effort and that it would be different the next season. I came out to face the press and as I'm being interviewed in the tunnel, a bloke sticks his head out of a corporate box and starts laughing, "Ha, ha, ha! Holloway's going down. Bye-bye QPR!" The only thing I was happy about at the end of that season was that Huddersfield went down, too, and I swear it was down to that one bloke, because sometimes, what goes around comes around. I don't want to upset any Huddersfield fans but that bloke doomed you.

So with our relegation finally confirmed, I started having meetings with my staff as the big sort-out began in earnest. I called in Warren Neill, Chris Geeler and Gary Waddock from our youth set-up and I said, "Alright, lads. What have you got for me that might help me out a bit?" Warren says, "None of them. This will damage them in the situation we're in."

I said, "Excuse me?" Normally I'd expect at least two or three youngsters to be ready to join the senior squad and that took me back a little. It turned out they had some 19-year-olds in their Under-19 team and I'd always been of the opinion that as the lads got older, you tested them out at a higher level to see if they had what it took, but they wanted to keep them all. They were doing well in their league and had reached the play-off final in their division, but lost to Nottingham Forest. It was like having a club within a club and if the reserves needed cover, they'd send their worst player up, usually the subs who couldn't get in the Under-19 team.

I threw about three or four teenagers in for our last home game against Stockport and we lost 3-0 – the kids weren't good enough after all, but the situation with the Academy would need to be addressed in the summer.

As we walked around the pitch applauding our fans at the end of the game, I was getting patted on the back by Rangers fans who were saying things like, "Thanks for giving us the spirit back, at least we played with passion" or "It's not your fault and we're looking forward to next season."

That was pleasing and exactly what I'd hoped I'd hear. The QPR fans understood our predicament and all they'd wanted to see was a bit of passion and players playing for their shirt, which was the very least I demanded of my lads. I had a busy summer ahead and had to get a squad together capable of taking Rangers back to where they deserved to be.

I was also about to learn why Gerry had been so keen for me not to see what some of the players had been earning…

Chapter 17

A Bag of Chips

I sat down and started to sift through all the contracts of the players with my chief Executive and discovered that four or five of the young players had been given four-year contracts – or more – because the Bosman ruling had been due to come in at that time and they didn't want to lose some of the Academy's brighter hopes. The club were paying them gross amounts of money – and they weren't good enough! What really stuck in my craw was these five young lads were all on double what my best player had been on at Bristol Rovers. I'd had a fantastic pro at Rovers called Andy Tilson who'd worked hard all his career to get where he'd got to and these kids were already on more money than he was and they didn't give a monkey's about the club. We'd bred these people and they were like lost souls because they had all the trappings of success but hadn't had to earn it. It was unbelievable.

During the summer, the administrators didn't so much as prune my squad – they butchered it with a chainsaw, leaving me seven fit players and two long-term casualties in Clarke Carlisle and Richard Langley who'd both done their cruciates. I didn't even know if they'd ever come back and play again. There had been people out of contract but I was instructed that I couldn't re-sign any of them – they all had to go. Some of the lads with longer deals were offered a pay-off to cancel their contract and I had to sit there with my chief executive David Davies, who had helped me greatly since I'd been at the club and was a gentlemen who cared about people, while he spoke to every one of them. They told them the club couldn't honour their agreements because they'd go bust if they did and would they please accept 25% of what they were owed and then they could go and find another club for nothing. It was heartbreaking to see young lads be told the future they thought they had wasn't going to happen, at least not at QPR, and it was horrendous. We were both devastated for the lads and it was the worst day of my managerial career up to that point or since.

I had no staff, no squad and David Davies and I had to go to the administrators and say that we needed to keep functioning and fulfil our fixtures or they'd never sell the club. We needed another striker and we had to prove what we needed and do it one case at a time. We had to keep going so they okayed a player called Mohammed Barr on a free from non-league and Leroy Griffiths from Hampton and Richmond – we were trying to find a few bargains here and there and I could only select from the local populace because I couldn't pay a relocation allowance. Steve Palmer came on a free from Watford and I brought Kenny Jackett in as my assistant on Pen's recommendation. Ken was vastly experienced, good at his job and Pen reckoned I'd get on with him like a house on fire. He'd recently lost his job, lived in the area and despite all the problems we had, he agreed to come and work with me.

Tim Breacker had been helping Gerry with one or two things and Gerry recommended I let him take the reserves, which I was happy to do. It was a fantastic learning curve for me but coming from Bristol Rovers, who'd been run as though they were in administration anyway, it was probably the perfect grounding.

Sometimes as a manager it's like you've got a tree and some of the branches are fine and some are ugly and need taking off so new shoots can come through. We were dealing with a virtually pollarded tree. I had a trunk and nine short branches and I needed to start building again from scratch.

Kenny Jackett was proving to be invaluable because he had so much experience and I tried to add Pen to my staff but Bristol Rovers wouldn't let me touch anybody. Our running costs went from around £5.3m to £2.2m and our skeleton squad returned for pre-season training probably feeling like the survivors of an air crash. Despite everything, we got off to a flyer by beating Chelsea 3-1 at Loftus Road and were using a load of trialists by that time. Then we beat Steve Bruce's Birmingham City 1-0 and made nine changes after the break – five of whom I'd never seen in my life! Steve Bruce asked after,

"How the hell did you manage that?"

We had a great pre-season and the lads were working really hard and we took that into the 2001/02 season by beating Stoke City 1-0 in our first game. Stoke were one of the favourites to go up, so it was a confidence booster for everyone and we followed that up by beating Bury 2-1 away. I couldn't have asked for more, but we were never going to run away with the league because my squad was so small. When we did get beaten, a few of our fans were still a bit whingey and some were demanding to go back at the first attempt, which I understood, but I needed to get a message across to them that we were where we were and we couldn't think of ourselves as the famous QPR anymore – we needed to forget that for the time being.

I couldn't believe the level of interest there was in QPR from the media compared to Bristol Rovers and it was round this time I started having a little bit of fun with them, I suppose. Having lost my job at Rovers and feeling mentally scarred from the experience, I knew it wasn't healthy for me to give the job that much emotion any more, so I tried different tactics. Anyone who knows me knows I have to get thoroughly immersed in whatever I do but I couldn't live it as I had been doing, so basically I was much more relaxed with the press and I wasn't taking everything as a personal affront. I also had the best excuse in the world – administration – it took the pressure right off in a funny sort of way. I wasn't in control of what was happening behind the scenes. I needed to galvanise everybody into the same mindset if we were to move forward, but if we lost a couple of players, it weakened us severely. What I now know is that, as a manager, you're only as good as your weakest link and while I had a team, there was nothing else around it, no support network and we were very inconsistent throughout that season. Injuries meant we could bring players in on loan and after losing one of my centre-halves, I brought in Danny Shittu from Charlton. He met us on the coach on the way to Peterborough, but it turned out to be a debut from hell because we lost 4-1 and while Peterborough were absolutely fantastic on the night, I won't ever forget their fans goading the R's supporters by singing "You're not famous anymore! You're not famous anymore!" It was ringing round the ground and it broke my heart to hear it. While it was awful to hear, it was also reality and what I needed to do was get our supporters to realise that and all our players, too, but we weren't quite there yet. The hard work ethic was there and we'd lost the losing mentality I think we had when I first arrived which was important, because we could have kept going down like Bristol City had done in the past. Sometimes you can't stop the rot, but what we managed to do was ban the 'A' word because I thought people might try and use it as an excuse, given the opportunity.

Danny Shittu was starting to look fantastic at the back for us and one of our supporters, Harold Winton, wanted to buy him for the club. It was a huge bonus for me and we bought the lad for £250,000. One significant game that year was an FA Cup tie at Swansea that we lost 4-0. I knew our fans would be spitting venom because they were in a division below us but we'd had Leroy Griffiths and a French lad called Dudu, who was a two-foot nothing Frenchman whereas they had Paul Williams and Kevin Nugent and they were the difference on the night. I said in the post-match interview that it was alright saying Swansea were a lower league club, but our strikers were inexperienced and we were desperately short of attacking options, and I said, "So if there's any strikers out there, why don't you come and sign for us? The boys who played today are great lads, but they need to get more experience. They shouldn't be playing for QPR at the moment."

I'd advertised our plight and everyone thought it was very funny and what have you, but the next day I get a call from Kevin Gallen's agent, Phil Morrison, asking if I was serious about wanting players. I said I was and he said, "Good, because Kevin's available." I went to see Nick Blackburn and David Davies and said, "I know we're in administration but we need to win promotion. I strongly recommend you bring Kevin Gallen back to this football club." They agreed and Kevin came in time for our home game against Swindon three days later and if you've ever needed an example of an instant impact, it was his debut, because he scored one and made three, giving the fans a massive lift with 'Super Kevin Gallen' echoing round the ground throughout the game. That helped me, too, because I'd given the fans one of their heroes back – I couldn't get them Les Ferdinand, because he was well out of reach, but Kevin Gallen was back. I tried to bring in players and people who cared about the club, and I think that got us through some tough times over the years. We finished eighth in the table, which wasn't a bad effort considering everything that had happened.

Nick Blackburn and David Davies were trying get enough money together to buy the club and they managed to do it, paying off all the club's debts and everyone we'd ever owed a penny to was sorted out in time for the 2001/02 season. We wouldn't have been allowed to operate in administration again so it had to be done if QPR were going to continue and it was good to have a board and a chairman again. The budget they gave me was nowhere near enough to get us in with a chance of getting out of the division and I said as much, so they managed to find a bit more. I brought in Mark Bircham and Brett Angel to strengthen the team. Kev Gallen's agent called me again and said another of his players, Paul Furlong was interested in signing for QPR. I told Phil that at this rate he could take over as my striker guru, but I wasn't complaining. I was uncertain about signing Furlong, though, and Kim, being a spiritual type, just happened to have her Tarot cards out one evening so I jokingly asked her to do a reading regarding bringing the player to QPR. He'd been at Loftus Road before on loan, but hadn't done that well or been very popular with the fans. Steve Bruce told me he was a great bloke and wouldn't be a problem and that he could be a useful signing for me. So I asked Kim some specific questions about Furlong – was he still hungry for instance? She dealt the cards and I have to admit, it was unnervingly accurate of his situation! The cards summed him up as being someone who had money around him and played at a higher level, but his main card showed an unbelievable desire to prove himself and Kim said, "If I was going on these cards, I should sign him."

I called Phil and said I wanted to speak with Paul before anything else and arranged a meeting. I asked him a series of questions and he gave me all the answers I was looking for. He was exactly the type of player we needed, but I knew I'd have to be patient because it'd been quite a while since he'd played regularly.

I promised him we'd get him fit and also get his mind right and he was more than happy to join us on that premise alone. I now had Furlong and Gallen as my preferred strike pairing – a proper partnership – but when one of them was out, we'd be back to square one, so I was continually on the look out for more forwards.

We were more consistent that season and also had a bit more about us and were up in the mix going into autumn and then injuries and suspensions started to hit us hard and we began to fall away quite badly. We were losing league games and then we went into the FA Cup First Round tie with non-league Vauxhall Motors with just a bare eleven, and we were very lucky to come back with a 0-0 draw. There were grumblings after that and because of our poor league form, I was starting to feel under a bit of pressure. I was six games without a win and then we had the replay with Vauxhall and go 1-0 up after six minutes through Andy Thomson. The relief around Loftus Road was tangible, but the forward momentum we should have had from that goal never came. We stopped playing and Vauxhall started playing, and when they equalised, it was no real surprise. With our confidence non-existent, the last scenario I'd wanted was a penalty shoot-out, but that's what we got and they beat us, fair and square. Furlong missed one of the penalties, and try as he might, things just weren't going for him. If he fell in a barrel of boobs he'd have come out sucking his thumb. The following day there were major ructions – I was hopeless, everything was rubbish – so much so that the day after that, a taxi driver I'd got to know really well as a player and as a manager, phoned me. He was one of the most ardent QPR fans you could ever meet in your life – QPR were tattooed on his heart, so to speak, and he called me up and started having a real go about the way things were going, so I invited him to the training ground because what he was saying didn't make sense. I couldn't pick the team he'd wanted, so I took two hours to talk to him, showed him around and went into great detail as to why certain players weren't available and suchlike. I said, "Vauxhall Motors – it's embarrassing! But at the moment, we haven't got a strong enough squad to even beat them. We should have won with the side we put out, but we didn't – so get on with it. You go to work and you're going to take some stick and get ribbed on occasion, but so what? I still need you with us. We still need your support. Are you still with us?" He left having calmed down and I think he could see why we were struggling the way we were. Our next home game, against Cardiff, we were drawing 0-0 with 75 minutes gone and we ended up losing 4-0 after collapsing like a pack of cards. Rob Earnshaw scored a hat-trick inside 15 minutes and I'm stood there watching all this in my technical area as a woman comes up to me from the side. As she approached, I thought back to a few nights before when I'd spoken with Kim about handling any personal abuse that might come my way, and she just said, "Why don't you just reply, 'I'm all of that plus a bag of chips.' It'll diffuse any situation." God bless her for that! It made me laugh, so I rehearsed it at home and this woman is now right up to me and she says, "You're a fucking wanker, Holloway!" and then threw her season-ticket at me. I just looked at her and said, "I tell you what love, I'm all of that and a bag of chips." I wasn't worried about her reaction to me saying that, just that

I got the delivery right! She told me to "fuck off" before walking back the way she'd come and I turned to my bench who were all laughing. My physio wanted to go after her when he heard what she'd said, but she was just another frustrated QPR fan at that time. It was a horrendous experience, in all honesty because who needs that? Then we lost 3-0 at Notts County and then Iain Dowie's Oldham beat us – it was a run from hell and I was up shit creek not only with no paddle but with no boat. Even Robert Shaw would have had trouble rescuing me at that point.

Paul Furlong continued to miss chances and he failed to put a free header home in one game and did it again a couple of games later. He said, "Don't worry Oll, I'll put them away, I've done it all my career and at least I'm getting in the right positions. I'll finish them, don't worry."

But the pressure was beginning to tell after his latest miss and when he said, he'd start scoring, I said, "It's about time you took responsibility Furs and any chance of fucking heading it in the fucking net? God isn't gonna make it go in, you should with your focus, that's what you used to do. If you don't, I ain't gonna support you anymore. You put it where it needs to go because you're good enough."

I'd lost it because I thought I was going to lose my job at any moment. Then quite a large section of the Rangers fans start chanting "Chelsea reject" at him and, bear in mind I was on a sticky wicket anyway, I had at go at the boo-boys in the press and said, "How dare you. You ain't helping me and you're slaughtering someone because he used to play for Chelsea? How childish is that? If he's missed a couple of chances give him some stick about that – but I need you to encourage him and if anybody wants to dish out unfair stick, come round to my house in St Albans and I'll fight you on the lawn. Any chance of you lot doing your job and supporting my team? They're the ones we've got, I can't change them, let's get on with it." I meant it, too and felt good for saying exactly what I'd wanted to. So after yet another soul-destroying defeat, I thought I'd be sacked any time, but the next day I met with Nick Blackburn and David Davies and they were superb to me, going over the game and saying we'd been unlucky and that we probably needed to strengthen our defence – Nick especially gave me all sorts of support and I wasn't getting blamed by the board, despite the beast of a run we were in. We were in it together – they needed to have success so the club could move on. I reckoned if we had a decent left-winger, Furs would start knocking them in so I went with Kenny Jackett to see David Davies and ask if we could sign Lee Cook from Watford. Nick had apparently never heard of him so David said no on the strength of that. I said, "Don't say no to me. I need a left-winger and he's the one I want."

He said, "Well if you two don't sort it out, it won't be your call."

"Just get me the winger, will you?!" I then rang Nick and said, "What's this you don't know who Lee Cook is? Just let me get him. I'm telling you he's a bloody good winger and he's available, so just do it."

They relented and Lee Cook signs and on his debut he waltzes down the wing, crosses it for Mark Bircham to score. We drew 1-1 and stopped the rot. Cook was just what we'd needed and he made a monumental difference to our season – plus he was a QPR fan, which fitted into the type of person I wanted at the club. We beat Wycombe 2-1 away and he set up the winner. We set off on a hell of a charge up the table after that and all because we'd been desperate for a quality wide man to supply our quality forwards. Another factor in our sudden improvement in form was Pen's arrival as my striker coach. He took Furs for one-on-one sessions and he soon started scoring the goals he'd promised. We'd bottomed out against Vauxhall Motors – how much worse could it have got? The shit hit the fan and we all got a bit of a coating, but we showered and were looking – and smelling – half decent again.

Chapter 18

Let's Have Coffee

The optimism was returning to Loftus Road. You could feel an expectancy from the supporters, but a positive one, rather than the negative, impatient vibe some of them had been giving out. Make no mistake, Loftus Road can be a scary place to be when things aren't going well and it's a stadium that can swallow you up if you allow it to. The long-term casualties, Clark Carlisle and Richard Langley were back, Lee Cook was on fire, Paul Furlong was on song and scoring and there was plenty to smile about. The impossible now seemed possible and somehow, we'd come from nowhere and were on the verge of cementing a play-off place. We'd been on an incredible run and wins over Huddersfield and Bristol City made it nine victories in the final 12 games and meant we'd finished fourth and would face Iain Dowie's Oldham in the play-off semi-final – a little ironic considering I'd sacked him after taking what he – understandably – must have thought was his job at Rangers. Bristol City would play Cardiff in the other game and with the final at the Millennium Stadium, we knew if we made it to the final, playing Bristol City was the preferred option because playing Cardiff in Cardiff would be a nightmare.

Oldham had finished in fifth place and had already beaten us once that season so we knew it'd be a tight game up at Boundary Park, but we took thousands up to Oldham and they were loving every minute of it. They'd suffered for the past few years, as we all had, and they were going to enjoy their moment in the sun. We went 1-0 down early on but kept our shape and didn't concede any more before half-time. I'd been on at Richard Langley to take a gamble on any far post crosses for a few months because he had a knack of doing it in training and I said to him to try it that day because the full-back looked half-asleep. I told the lads there were two games to play, so to keep calm because I felt we'd create one or two good chances before the end and, as if by magic as Mr Benn used to say, Langley ghosts in for what seemed like an over-hit cross and scores a great goal to make it 1-1 – and that's the way it stayed, with the balance only slightly in our favour.

What an occasion the second leg was, though! The moment you walked into Loftus Road you could feel it. It was usually fairly quiet and Gerry Francis always used to say, "Don't wait for this lot, you've got do something and then you'll get the atmosphere." Not that night, though. It was unreal and the hairs on the back of my neck stood up and the game had that extra edge because of Dowie. Nick Blackburn told me that at half-time during the first game, Iain Dowie's wife came up to him and said, "Oh actually, you've signed the wrong Ian." I didn't really like that, but Nick just laughed it off. I think he told me to spur me on. I was pumped up for the game anyway because the prize of a final at Cardiff was at stake. It was an even tussle and it wasn't until the last few moments of the game that we scored the winner – and who got it? Paul Furlong. He held off Fitz Hall as the ball came over the top and had enough nous to flick it past the goalie before rolling it home into the far corner. The noise as the ball crossed the line almost took the roof off Loftus Road. The atmosphere that our fans had created that night and that I walked into when I first arrived, made me very proud to be associated with the club. In the dying seconds, our keeper Chris Day made a Gordon Banks-type save, diving down low to his left to keep out a certain goal – it was a match-winning stop and our fans went mad when the final whistle went. We had our lap of honour at the end and then I went up on a microphone and said a few things, ending with, "This is a proper football club. See you all at Cardiff." I was especially pleased for Paul Furlong, who'd been through all sorts of things that year but kept trying his best and not allowing anything to ruin him and had now come through the other side of it.

I knew we still had a lot to do because we'd be playing Cardiff in Cardiff – the worst case scenario, but we were in with a 50-50 chance of going up.

We took 30,000 to the final – they must have had about 40,000 – but the game itself proved to be a huge let-down. Neither side played well or could even string two passes together but we went in 0-0 at the break. I told the lads to relax, just as we'd done at Oldham. We came out and were the better team and though we weren't streets ahead of Cardiff, it looked like there would be only one winner. I had a lad called Tommy Williams on the bench and he was in my ear all the time, "Go on, put me on, I'll win you this, I'll win you this…" In truth, it reminded me of how I would have been in his shoes so I decided to give him the chance to back his words. I'd left Andy Thomson on the bench and should have had him on from the start, so I got it all wrong, truthfully speaking. So Tommy comes on, gets the ball, beats one, two, three, four… he's in the box and Furs is on, begging for the ball because he's got to score, but Tommy shoots from an angle you wouldn't believe and misses the target. Then, 10 minutes from time, Lennie Lawrence makes one of the bravest substitutions I've ever seen, thinking it's heading for extra time, he takes off crowd favourite Rob Earnshaw and puts Stuart Campbell on in his place – and he scores the winner. My defence should have caught him offside or caught up with him, but it was their only mistake of the afternoon. We lost 1-0 and what still greatly bothers me is that I felt we were the better team on the day. If Tommy had squared it, it might have been us celebrating, but it wasn't. To this day the QPR fans sing a song about Tommy Williams with the line 'why didn't you pass to Paul Furlong?' It was horrific and it was more like a home game for Cardiff, but I was so proud of what we'd done, but the thought of having to do it again was hard. I wondered how long I was going to have to play the bridesmaid for, too, after losing another play-off final when I was with Rovers and we should have gone up but fell away and now it happened again with QPR. My CV wasn't looking so good, but we'd finished fourth and had made progress again. At the end of the game, I used the words Gerry Francis had said when we'd lost a play-off semi-final at Rovers and told them to take the pain of losing against Cardiff into next season and remember it so it doesn't happen again. I told them we were going up and to get their heads right for next season.

We'd done really well, but the mistake we made was not adding to the squad to consolidate the momentum we'd built. As ever, I needed more strikers and brought in Tony Thorpe from Luton – he'd fill in for Kevin Gallen or Paul Furlong if they were absent. I signed Jamie Cureton again and with Brett Angel coming at the end of the previous season, I felt I had a good complement of forwards at the club. We also brought Gareth Ainsworth, Richard Edgehill, Richard

Johnson, Lee Camp and Stephen Kelly in on loan. The board backed me again and instead of blaming me for losing the play-off final, they asked me, "How can we make things better?" and as a manager, you really can't ask for more than that.

We started the next season by beating Blackpool 5-0 at home – off to a flyer – but I think it raised expectation levels unrealistically high and made the rest of the division more wary of us. I wasn't complaining, though. All the new lads I'd brought in were looking solid, and away to Rushden & Diamonds, we were 2-1 up when mad Tommy Williams – I always think of him as 'Clunk' from the kids' cartoon Whacky Races – was running down the left wing and he pings a ball across to the other wing to an unmarked Gareth Ainsworth, and as I'm up saying, "What are you doing?" the ball falls over Gareth's right shoulder and I can see he's shaping to hit it on the volley, 35 yards out. I shout, "Gareth no...YES! Get in there!" He caught it perfectly and it flew in like a rocket. A fantastic goal but it was spoiled by conceding two late goals. And drawing 3-3.

I was having problems with Clarke Carlisle, that I'd rather not go into in this book, but he was missing training and failing to turn up for games so I disciplined him until we eventually got to the root of the problem. Meanwhile, we beat Chesterfield 3-0 and were different class in the first half – Queens Park Power Rangers, in fact – but after the break Chesterfield had four great chances, missed them all and the score stayed the same. I wasn't happy because we'd thrown the lead away at Rushden and it could've happened again, so I let the lads know it because I thought they'd taken their foot off the gas. I said, "I ain't so sure about you lot. I've got people not turning up, I've got you thinking you've won games when you've not – have you forgotten last season? Have you forgotten what it felt like losing against Cardiff?" I went upstairs, still in a bit of a mood, to talk with the press. The first 10 questions were about Clark Carlisle and why he'd been dropped, so I said it was an internal matter and I wouldn't be answering any questions about him. I managed to bat them all off without getting angry and then one bloke said, "You must have been delighted with that – what a fantastic performance." So, typical me, moving off without checking my rear view mirrors, I start waffling on about a bird in a taxi, not dreaming in a million years it would result in changing my life and how the vast majority of football fans viewed me. I said I was pleased with the result, but not the performance so I thought about how I could get the point across in a sentence and came out with, "It's like when you meet a bird who's not the best looking. You talk, things go well and she gets in a taxi with you, get her back home and lovely jubbly, let's have coffee." They were all sniggering away and I thought, 'hang on, what's going on?' I'd said it before to my lads, but because I was a manager talking about a high-profile club and comparing it to a night out on the pull, they couldn't believe it. The following day, I get a call from Clark Carlisle at 7pm on the Sunday evening, and I said, "Where the hell have you been?"

He said, "Ollie, can I come and see you?"

I told him to come and see me at my house and I wrote everything down we spoke of because it was now a very serious club matter. The lad needed help and because he'd asked for it, I believed we could help him. What the 'let's have coffee' quote had done, was diffuse a difficult situation and shifted the spotlight away from him at what was a difficult time. I knew the press would be calling me mad old Ian Holloway again, but the real reason I'd said what I had was to help a player who needed it. Tim Lovejoy off Soccer AM must have been intrigued by the quote and invited me on to the show, the first of many memorable visits. I'd laughed at myself all my life and the truth was it was usually part of a more serious scenario, but I didn't anticipate it causing such interest and I certainly didn't mean it to be derogatory to any young ladies because I thought they'd do the same thing. If they go out and all the best ones have gone, I think they too might go, "OK, let's have another look at him."

Things went barmy after that and though there were one or two 'Ollie-isms' already out there, this was the one that really took off, if you like. A few people called me mad after that, which is unfair and that's something I can't say I was overly happy with. I'd never describe myself as 'mad' or 'madcap', because I'm not. I just use humour in my life and I grew up with it – my dad had a wonderful sense of humour, my best mate is Pen – say no more – and my wife has a quirky sense of humour, too. I've always used that in my life and my thinking is, if you can't laugh at yourself, what sort of person are you? I don't laugh at people, I laugh with them and if that involves me, so what? I think that cuts through an awful lot of problems.

I want to be as reliable as a manager as I tried to be as a player, but if you don't have empathy with your players and try and understand their feelings and try and help them out when they need it, you'll struggle to survive. If I can't personally help, I'll find someone who will. Alleviating problems as best I can and taking the worry away is what I think being a manager is all about.

Not all the portrayals in the press about me after that were complimentary and one bloke turned everything completely around and pretty much slaughtered me, which I couldn't understand. Nothing I've ever said was to draw the focus in on Ian Holloway and I don't do it on purpose, but when I think about the way my dad was and the things he used to come out with, the old saying 'an apple never falls very far from the tree' springs to mind. My tree is my old man and I think like him and according to my sister, I talk like him, too. All I know is that the world is a sadder place without laughter and I'm not going to change and will keep on saying whatever comes into my head, no matter what is written about me.

But back to the important stuff. On the pitch, we were looking good going in to the run-in. I was still full of doubt about myself and angry at home and after the Chesterfield match, a lot of people seemed to be interested in me and I was being asked to do all kinds of things, one of which was a programme for the BBC called 'Stress Test'. I was 41 and didn't want to behave like a five-year-old when I didn't get my own way anymore because Kim was suffering. I'd cried and whinged to my mum to get my own way as a kid and I didn't want to do the same at 41 and I actually don't agree with Bill Shankly's quote, 'Some say football is about life and death – it's much more important than that.' It's not to me – I love football and all the people connected with the game but nothing is more important than your health and your family. So when the BBC asked if I'd take part, I said, "Why should I take part?" They told me there was no money, but they could make me a better person, which was good enough for me, so I agreed to do it. It was pretty invasive and they followed me around for months, but ultimately they put their finger on what was causing me to be like a bear with a sore head every day. It was one of the hardest things I've ever done because you have to lay yourself bare and how you believe you behave and talk to people is actually totally different to reality and you don't always see things you like. The psychologist I'd been assigned pinpointed my problem to me believing nothing I ever did was good enough. He said, "It wouldn't matter if you won 20 games in a row at the moment if you lost the next one, would it? Some people have a perfectionist scenario and no matter what they do, it's never good enough. Arsène Wenger isn't like you – you're destructive because what it comes back to is nothing you ever do, in your eyes, is good enough. You're two people – I've seen it. When someone needs your help at work, you do everything you can to help them out, but when you talk to yourself in your self-talk, you beat yourself up. If you could be just one person and look in that mirror and say 'warts and all, I'm good enough', you'd be fine." Then he asked Kim, "Kim, what would you do if Ian lost his job and didn't get promoted?"

She said, "I'd live in a cardboard box in the middle of a motorway with him if he's the person he should be."

He said so many things that made sense and ended with, "Your determination is fantastic – your anger is a problem. As far as I'm concerned, you've gone through about four months of counselling in four days."

It was enlightening, yet exhausting but I believed the things that happened in the next few months wouldn't have happened if I hadn't changed. The team were doing great and, ironically, it was us, Plymouth and Bristol City who looked most likely to go up going into spring. Both Kenny Jackett and I were out of contract at the end of the season and Ken said to me, "Something's going on here, Oll. We're doing what we're doing and we've not been offered new contracts. I'm not happy about this."

So I went to see Nick Blackburn and I said, "I am strongly recommending to you that you need to get him a new deal because he's asking me about it and because he's bloody good at what he does."

He said, "I can't offer any new contracts out at the moment."

"Fine, then Ken's going to look for another job, then and I don't want you to stand in his way."

I didn't want to lose Ken, but I understood his thinking so I recommended him to Bristol Rovers, which he appreciated, but they didn't take him on. I said, "Look Ken, we've just got to get on with this regardless of what's going on because I need a promotion on my CV and you need one on yours and I'll try and help you as best I can."

We had a bit of a wobble in the last few games, including a 1-0 defeat to promotion rivals Bristol City, which also turned out to be Ken's last game before he went to take over at Swansea. We'd gone from three points clear of City to none, but with a game in hand which was Tranmere away. It proved to be an unforgettable game. We should have got a free-kick on the halfway line, but didn't get it. I was leaping around and screaming for that foul and then they pump the ball forward and their striker is offside, but that's not given so when he's fouled in the box, they get a penalty and we're down to 10 men because my lad is sent off, I'm not the happiest man, am I? Talk about a travesty of justice! They score, but the ref orders a re-take. This time he hits the post and Lee Camp makes a fantastic save from the rebound and we come away with a 0-0 draw, which puts us a point ahead of City. I looked back at the game later and wondered, 'did something happen there that day?' The luck I was bemoaning had changed and we were back above City by a point. Then it was away to Plymouth at a packed Home Park and it was during this game that my anger management therapy really kicked in. We were probably slightly the better team and it was 0-0 when Mark Bircham suffered a nasty head injury. My physio went on and told me I had to bring him off because he was suffering from double vision so I brought Steve Palmer on. Mark didn't want to come off and was giving me stick as he came off and our fans didn't know why I've taken him off so when they go ahead a few minutes later, it looks like a terrible substitution. Not long after that, they make it 2-0 and it's game over. Their fans are celebrating because that win was enough to make them the champions and it's going to be that much harder to go up automatically now. Then, on the coach going home, I get a text on my mobile from a QPR fan who hadn't put his name on the message, saying 'Yet another inept performance, why don't you fuck off? You're ruining QPR.' His number was displayed so I call it and this guy answers.

"Who's this?" he asked.

"It's Ian Holloway and you know it is, too, because my number will have displayed on your phone. Thanks for your criticism, but I actually don't agree with you because I still believe we are going to do it, but thanks for making me stronger in my belief." Even if we didn't go up, I would have still believed we'd made progress from the previous season, but we still had two games left and a great chance of going up. Bristol City had also lost that day, so two wins would be enough to win promotion. I kept the same team from the Plymouth game, something I would have never done prior to the stress test experience, and Martin Rowlands scored in the first minute – enough for us to win 1-0 against Swindon Town. City had won, too, so it was all on the final game against Sheffield Wednesday at Hillsborough. I'd already decided I was going to tell the lads how well they'd done regardless of whether we went up or not but I was struggling for something to say, so I decided to dig out my old Bristol Rovers league champions medal and put it in my top pocket. It's always difficult to know what to say in a pressure situation like that, but I had an idea and just before we got on the coach at our Sheffield hotel, we were waiting in the reception among quite a few Rangers fans who were coming up and wishing us luck. I sat down with our lads and invited the fans to come and sit with and among us as I did what I hoped would be my pep talk. Steve Palmer had asked if I thought it would be OK because the fans were there and I just told him not to worry because I knew what I was doing. We'd been over our tactics in training so this was purely aimed at getting something in their hearts and minds that might just edge things our way. So the lads and some of the Rangers fans were all sat around in front of me and I began. "I've had some special times in my life and it was the people I was with at Bristol Rovers that helped me win this medal – my team-mates. I don't know if we're going to get promoted today, but I just wanted you to hear what these supporters think of you regardless of what happens."

I asked a young kid to step up and say something to the lads and he smiled, took a deep breath and said, "You've been brilliant! Absolutely brilliant!" I asked a bloke to step up and he said how proud he was of how hard we'd battled. I said, "As long as we come off that pitch today and we couldn't have done any more, I won't have a problem. I've cherished this medal all my life, and I hope you have the chance to cherish something with a group of people because for me, you've earned the right to do that and you couldn't fail me if you tried today because you're already a success." It was emotional stuff, I admit and I had no idea whether it would help or not. It hadn't been about football, it had been about people and I wanted them to understand how everyone felt, no matter what.

So we start the game and after 10 minutes their scoreboard flashes up that Bristol City are 1-0 up. I couldn't believe it and felt it was absolutely scandalous to do that while my lads were still playing. I couldn't give a monkey's what happened at half-time, but that wasn't right. Then, a few minutes later, it flashed up that Bristol City are 2-0 up, so as it stands, we're not going up automatically. I got up and told Steve Palmer to calm everyone down and it took another 10 minutes for us to stop wobbling. Their fans were singing that we weren't going up and I was fuming inside, though outwardly calm. Then, finally, Kevin Gallen puts us 1-0 up and my lot finally settle down. There wasn't much that needed saying at the break and in the second half Furs, born again bad, makes it 2-0 –

but Wednesday pull one back and we're all on pins again. That's when I went into slow-motion mode and when I get nervous I need the toilet so I end up going back and forth three times in the last 10 minutes and just as I go back out for the last time, Martin Rowlands hits a ball across and it takes a deflection, wrong foots the keeper and we go 3-1 up. Time seemed to go backwards and I thought there were still a few minutes left when my keeper coach Tony Roberts grabs me and I tell him to get off because it's not finished. He says, "We've done it! He's gonna blow any second!" And then he grabs me again because the ref actually blew and four or five others joined in, jumping on top. I'd been told by officials we had to get back in the tunnel in case of a pitch invasion so, still in some kind of weird mental haze or disbelief and denial, I break free and trot down towards the dressing rooms and as I do, I glance up at a scoreboard that says 'Owls 1, QPR 3' and it starts to sink in. I couldn't believe it. We pipped Bristol City by a point and their manager Danny Wilson called me up to say well done and shortly after he gets the sack. He'd progressed them four seasons in a row but was shown the door, which is ludicrous. He goes, I get offered a new deal. That's football, and it could have been the other way around. I feel that if I'd had an anger management course when I was at Rovers, I swear I would have taken them up, too. I'd finally put things right because when we'd gone down, I'd told myself that I was going to get them back up again and now we'd achieved that. We'd been through administration, had 51 pros and chopped it down to nine and now built it all back up again and most of the players and fans had all gone through it together and we all took memories from that season that will remain with us forever. The comment that the press picked up afterwards was when I'd been asked how I felt, I replied, "Every dog has his day and today is Woof Day and I just want to go off and bark somewhere." The following day we held a party at my fitness coach's pub – a fitness coach with a bloody pub! Ha! We let the supporters know about the party and where and when it was being held through various outlets, and we had an absolutely fantastic time. It didn't get much better than that but it was to be the beginning of yet another turbulent period at QPR.

Chapter 19

The Italian Job

Six games from the end of the 2003/04 season vice chairman Nick Blackburn had called me up and asked would I mind if he came down and introduced somebody to me and that was the first time I met Gianni Paladini. Nick said he was a new board member and I knew nothing whatsoever about him. It turned out that we'd been on the verge of going bust again and as we wouldn't have been allowed to under FA rules, Gianni, who fronted a Monaco-based consortium, joined the board after paying £500,000 to save us from going under. We needed the money and I don't think Nick and David were that particular where it came from and had no idea they were in fact sealing their own fate. The board that had backed me fantastically well by helping me reinforce the squad were effectively penniless – to such an extent they'd almost bankrupted themselves. I don't think they realised just how involved the consortium wanted to be and it wasn't long before Gianni was asking questions about bills and suchlike and was obviously intent on a hands-on role. He wanted to know everything and the consortium wanted to control the club's finances because they weren't happy with the way the club was being run.

For my part, I had a great day-to-day working relationship with David and Nick. We made a great team and if things could have carried on like that, we'd have gone from strength to strength, I believe.

We'd won promotion with the same board and Gianni was now a member, but I was still only offered a one-year deal. My agent, Robert Segal, told me as I was out of contract, in his opinion he thought it would be better if I found another club. he'd arranged for me to speak with the Burnley board, and after two interviews, their chairman Barry Kilby told Robert it was between me and another manager for the job, which carried a minimum of a three–year contract. On hearing this, Kim and I sat down and discussed the implications for our entire family, should I actually get the job, in particular the girls' special educational needs, because the nearest deaf school would have been two hours away in Doncaster. Having weighed everything up, I decided to withdraw from the running to be Burnley's manager, impressed though I'd been, and re-sign a one-year deal at QPR. I felt that I could build on the strong relationships we'd forged at Rangers during the previous three years battling adversity, administration and God what knows else. I could only see us getting better and stronger and I didn't want to just throw all that away,. I believed in my team and I believed in the people who were behind me. Little did I know that before the new season had even started, the whole structure of the board would change again.

Gianni had a massive row with David Davies who was very popular with the staff and basically everybody's boss and it rocked the club's foundations to the core.

Gianni, a hot-headed Latino when he had a ruck with somebody came out of his office one day shouting, "I'll have you fucking killed you bastard. I'll bloody kill you." If Gianni fell out with somebody or didn't trust them, he'd be totally unprofessional and let everyone know about anything he was unhappy with. It's a Latin thing and of course it was all hot air, but for people who'd worked at Loftus Road for 20 years or more, and there were quite a few, it was incredibly unsettling to see and hear things like that. Everyone was comfortable behind the scenes and didn't want things to change, and for Gianni to undermine the man they respected and trusted in such a way left them rocking and wondering what was going to happen next.

Afterwards, Gianni palled up with Bill Power, another board member, while David Davies, Nick Blackburn and chairman Ross Jones were all forced to leave the club. So in hindsight maybe my agent had been right, because I was in effect back to square one with a new board in place – again!

Within three weeks of the new season, my job was under threat. I'd got to know Gianni really well because I'd been travelling all over the place with him looking at various players, and he was terrific company, but I think the consortium probably wanted their own man. My advice to any board taking over at a club is, put in place the man you want whether the fans have a go at you or not. Have some balls and do the right thing for all concerned – it's the only way to move forward.

Mark Devlin, who'd been at the club a few years before was brought back as the new chief executive. I knew Mark and thought he was a terrific bloke and had no problem with his appointment at all, but the fact was I'd lost not one, but two points of contact on the board, and as a manager you need at least one point of contact. Nick Blackburn, David Davies and I had made a hell of a team, and had I known they would be leaving, I'm not sure I would have signed the contract. All that I had done before had been smashed with a mallet and I now had to start building new relationships, and that's why, after just six games of the re-start, my job was under threat and I'm expecting the sack at any moment. That's how fickle football is!

Danny Shittu and Mark Bircham were injured and were missing for the first few weeks of the 2004/05 season and both were vital members of my team. I'd hardly added any new faces to the squad, but the momentum we'd been promoted with had gone and we took just two points out of 18 before we won away to Gillingham, but then lost at home to Sheffield Wednesday. It was the worst start imaginable and with Gianni's extensive contacts in the game, there were rumours linking John Gregory and Jim Smith with my job. Something was beginning to build – I could feel it, and it wasn't good. I'd somehow become Public Enemy No 1 in the press who seemed desperate for a new man to be brought in, and the speculation was almost unbearable. It was big news at the time and rarely a day passed without some story or other. Then a quote appeared in the Press after the Sheffield Wednesday match from a 'QPR insider', saying that the football was awful and had been for the past two years. It wasn't in the tradition of QPR and the consortium weren't happy with the football being produced by the manager. It was obvious to me who said those words, though I can't prove it. The next day I asked my chief executive Mark Devlin to come to the training ground – I had a meeting in front of him with the lads and I asked him to explain what had been written and I was unhappy with his answer, so I demanded an immediate meeting with the board which he arranged. Tim Breacker took training and I went to meet the board with my agent within the hour, by which time I was absolutely fuming. There were also rumours that Ramon Diaz was coming to QPR to take over my job, along with John Gregory and a few others, all rumours started, in my eyes, by the comments of 'the club insider'. Whether they were true or not, I didn't know, but I got my agent to come along as well because I could smell a rat. Gianni represented the consortium and I think the owners picked up on a couple of whingers on the websites, blew it all out of proportion and rubbished everything we'd done over the past few years – at least that's how it seemed from where I was standing. Bill Power and Mark Devlin denied the club had made those comments, but Gianni had been quiet until the end when he said in his Italian accent, "Well I don't understand. If you are a manager and your team isn't winning, do you expect to keep your job?"

I said, "Yeah, if I'm not able to pick my strongest team, if they're all injured. You haven't even seen them play yet and you've rubbished everything we've done, and you only saw the last six games of last season. You'll see that we're good enough, just admit you said it." But he wouldn't. The thing was, I liked Gianni a hell of a lot because he was such a likeable bloke. Charming, generous and terrific company – I just wasn't sure I wanted him as my boss! He blew hot and cold and I never really knew where I actually stood with him. So I carried on and turned up for work the next day and the lads seemed quite relieved. We managed to win our first home game of the season against Plymouth in our next game, coming from behind to win 3-2 and I said to the lads afterwards, "You lot have ponced around worrying whether you're good enough for this level and these people have rubbished everything you've done." The fear I think the lads had been carrying with them, the self-doubts and lack of belief, had gone. They'd shown what they thought of me and paid me back for the way I'd backed them. Shittu and Bircham were back and the team had a totally different look about it, just as I'd thought it would. Then we beat Crewe and Brighton.

On the pitch, I'm awarded manager of the month thanks to our seven wins on the bounce and we go from almost bottom to almost top and it was very gratifying. The lads were now calling Gianni 'Zorro' by this point because they all thought it was him that had been quoted in that article and they felt it was him that had stabbed them in the back. There had been so much speculation about my job that during an interview around that time I said, "Possession is nine-tenths of the law so if someone out there wants my job, come and get it."

I told the board I was fed up with all the speculation – why was it there at all? I said I'd done nothing wrong, my lads had done nothing wrong and I didn't deserve it. It was a joke and in my eyes, there was no smoke without fire and I wasn't having it anymore. I forced the board's hand and they relented, giving me a new three-and-a-half-year deal. It meant I could settle down again and plan in earnest for our future. Shortly after signing the new contract, Kim and I were invited to Monaco to meet Antonio Caliendo, head of the Monaco-based consortium. Gianni came too and, as ever, was the life and soul of the party. He was terrific company and reminded me of a cartoon character called Bert Raccoon who'd wanted to help everybody but had ended up letting everyone down, though not intentionally. He just couldn't say no to anybody and that was probably his Achilles heel. We had an amazing trip and didn't pay for a thing and finally, I get to meet Antonio, the main man behind the consortium, and after a minute in his company, I was thinking, 'thank God!' He could barely speak a word of English and Gianni had to interpret for him, but what he did was grab my arm and say, "I wanted my own coach, but I like how strong you are and how your players play for you. That's why we've given you a new contract."

I asked if his coach was Ramon Diaz and he just smiled. We went to a casino a bit later and Antonio was playing roulette and had amassed a stack of chips and Gianni comes up, grabs a load of them, places them here, there and everywhere and loses the lot! That was Gianni in a nut-shell. Antonio went ballistic at Gianni and then walks off to play blackjack and slowly but surely, gets all his chips back. Just by watching him do that told me he was the brains behind the operation. Gianni was no fool and his rise had been meteoric. He actually was a former waiter who'd got friendly with several Aston Villa players while working in Birmingham and eventually he'd gone back to Italy as an interpreter when Gordon Cowans moved there from Villa. He was later involved in the transfer that brought Fabrizio Ravenelli to England and, I believe, made a substantial amount of money on the deal. After the Monaco trip, I almost felt in the circle of trust and with a solid coaching staff of Tim Breacker, Pen and Mel Johnson. Mel had been a huge part of what we were doing because if ever we needed someone bringing in to cover an injury, I'd just ask Mel to find me someone and I'd leave it to him because he never let me down, but he'd done so well for me that Tottenham heard about his talents and made him an offer he couldn't refuse. I spoke to our board about keeping him, but they didn't even try and looking back, with Gianni being an ex-agent and Antonio being an agent, they wanted to bring their own players in. It was an Italian way of thinking, but not one I was happy about. Worse still, they never replaced Mel. We were operating without a chief scout, which no club should ever do, and I had to get Pen to do some of the scouting work as well as his coaching job. We finished eleventh that season and during the summer I went all over the world with Gianni watching players he felt we should sign or had been tipped off about, and said no every time. By the time we started pre-season training, there were players turning up for trials that I'd never even heard of! I felt under pressure because the consortium wanted to show the supporters they were moving the club forward, but I couldn't sanction any deals without seeing the players first. The fans were starting to question the consortium's long term intentions and they in turn wanted to fend them off with some impressive new signings. The fans wanted to know who Antonio was and what he did, so Bill Power who regularly read the supporters' internet site forums started promising big name signings on the net! I said, 'Bill, you can't do that – we're not signing anyone.' I called a board meeting so I could tell them what I was thinking. Pen had been working his socks off and I took a huge flip chart in with me and showed them exactly where we needed strengthening and had a list of strikers as long as my arm. At the top, were Marlon King, then Leroy Lita, Barry Hayles, Steven Howard and Stefan Moore of Aston Villa. I also had Ian Evatt on the list because we needed a central defender but some of the reports on him had been a little indifferent, so I finished by saying that we didn't need to do anything immediately. I was going away on holiday and told them I'd pick up where I left off on my return, but while I'm away, I get a call from my physio telling me we'd signed two players. I wanted Steven Howard because he was big and strong before we got anyone else, but Gianni had brought in Luke Moore instead – and Ian Evatt – without any agents being involved or having a medical! Then Gianni rings me and cheerily says, "We've got Evatt , he's going to sign for us."

I said, "For crying out loud, what are you doing? We don't need to do anything." When I got back off holiday there were other players Gianni had promised were on the way, so I came out to speak to the press and said, "Well I don't know what's going on at my football club because I've haven't signed these players." You are judged as a manager by the players you bring in and it was being taken out of my hands. I had to come out and say how I felt and whether that was professional or not, I don't know, but I felt I had to keep the supporters in the picture. Gianni, and chairman Bill Power, had also been in the papers while I'd been away saying we were going to sign a really big name – I thought it might be Arnold Schwarzenegger – that's a big name.

Then I get a call from Dennis Wise. He said, "Ollie, I'm supposed to be having a meeting with you."

I said, "What's all this about then, Den?"

He said, "Well if you don't know about it, I'm not too happy about it, then."

I told him to let me have a think about it and he said that he was due to have a meal with Bill Power and Gianni, and was I going? I told him I didn't have a clue about it so I called Gianni and he said, "Oh yeah, he's a bloody good player."

I said, "Gianni, let me have a think about it. He's 38, ex-Chelsea – our fans hate Chelsea – and do I even need a midfield player? I don't know about this at the minute."

Then I called Dennis, who might have made a great addition if I needed a player of his ilk, and said I wasn't sure about all this and he said, "Well I'm pissed off at your chairman, Ollie and I'm going to tell him."

I think they'd even promised him a contract. I put it all down to over-exuberance and inexperience on Gianni's and Bill's part – no more than that – but it was starting to cause me major headaches and seriously undermined my position as the manager. There also seemed to be some kind of power struggle behind the scenes and I felt Mark Devlin and Bill Power weren't getting along with Gianni and the cracks were beginning to show. We could have been great if Gianni and Bill had stayed together because they got along like a house on fire, but Bill and Mark Devlin tried to set up a potential investor without Gianni's knowledge, and when he found out he wanted Mark out. We went on tour to Ibiza to take part in a tournament and Gianni was telling everyone he was going to get rid of Mark. Bill told him that would happen over his dead body and if Mark went, he was going to go, too. They stopped talking to each other and yet again the club was thrown into turmoil – it never seemed to end. Mistrust, suspicion – it was all happening, and when we lined up for our team photo just before the season started, Bill, the club chairman was missing, which pretty much summed up the whole situation, and everything came to a head when we took on Sheffield United three games into the new campaign.

We'd taken four points from our games with Hull and Ipswich and I'd been enjoying my usual touchline banter with my old mate Neil Warnock. It was the first time in all the years we'd had matches against each other that I'd let him get to me, because I usually just laughed at whatever he said. He was going on at me throughout the game, which we ended up winning, and whenever I questioned a decision, he'd shout to the referee, "Don't let Ian Holloway run the game!" I laughed it off, but later on he did it again after I said something to a linesman, and said, "Don't let him run the game!"

"Do me a favour, Neil" I said to him. "What the fuck are you on about? He's running the game for you – he's made two bad decisions in your favour."

"Fuck off!" he said back.

"What?" I asked. Then I let rip. "Everyone else in the game is right, you know. You really are a wanker!" "You what?"

"For years I've stood up for you because everyone reckons you're a wanker and I totally agree with them now. You fucking idiot!"

Neil's name, famously, is an anagram of Colin Wanker, just for the record, but I shouldn't have let him get to me. I've no beef with Neil whatsoever, never have, never will. He just knows how to wind people up, and the bugger had finally managed to press my buttons that day, although after the match we were back to our old selves again.

Then, as I'm walking down the tunnel our press officer comes up to me and say, "Ollie, there's been an altercation in the boardroom and Gianni's been rushed off to hospital, and an alleged shooting has taken place."

After talking with the team, I went into my little room and Bill Power walks in, looking as white as a sheet. "Bill, what's wrong?"

"I don't know, I don't know," he almost whispered.

"Is Gianni alright?"

"Yeah, yeah... don't say anything will you?"

"About what? I don't know anything about anything."

So I go upstairs for the post-match press conference and not one question was about the game. I told them I didn't know what they were on about and did anyone want to ask a question about the match that had just put us joint top? One or two did and then I left, but before I did, I said, "By the way, this is about football. This club has been rocking for years and we've managed to keep our focus on the football so if you want to ask me a question about football, do it, otherwise, piss off!"

Gianni, it turned out, was OK and the events of that day have been well-documented and not really something I want to recount in my book, but eventually Gianni and the consortium took complete control of the club and Bill Power and Mark Devlin left Loftus Road. It wasn't long before the rumours over my job started to resurface, but I had three years of my contract to run so I wasn't overly concerned. I even got a dreaded vote of confidence! I wasn't having any of that crap so I turned the tables and when I was asked about it, I said, "I'd like to give the board a vote of confidence instead. They're inexperienced, but I'll give them time to get it right."

I believe I'm still the only manager to have given the board the confidence vote. They weren't too impressed. My lads were still with me but they'd been horrified to read an article in The Sun prior to our match with Stoke City where club president Harold Winton slaughtered me saying I was useless, and my time was up. When Gianni came into the dressing room after we'd won and said, "Ha, ha, Ollie. Every time you get criticised you win. Maybe you should get criticised every week," Martin Rowlands said, "Why don't you just fuck off?"

That pretty much summed up the mood of my players who were still one hundred per cent with me. One thing was for certain – the situation had to come to a conclusion one way or another.

Chapter 20

"We're Gonna Need a Bigger Garden"

My job as QPR manager was getting harder by the day. Gianni's business partner, Antonio Caliendo, changed the way the club did its business. All of a sudden none of the cheques the club had issued recently were being paid. Instead accounts were being settled at the end of the month, as most big companies do, I'm told. The staff, who'd done things differently for 20 years, were horrified. It was like the equivalent of having a monthly shop at the supermarket but not saving any money for anything in between so if you needed more bread or milk, tough luck, there's no money available. It just wasn't working and the staff could see it wouldn't work and kept coming to me to say as much, but I told them, "Look, this is the way they are going to do it, so just get on with your job."

It was a really unsettling period and everything was coming back to me all the time and most of the problems had nothing to do with football, but it was spreading down to the players. The butcher wasn't being paid on time for the meat he supplied to the club, the groundsman told the players we had to be out of our training complex by the following Wednesday – it was madness and the players were getting fed up with it all. It felt like we were slipping back towards administration again.

I arranged a meeting with Gianni to try and clarify everything but he just said, "Ah, that's rubbish!" or "That's not true," but the problems didn't go away.

I decided to get the lads together and told them they couldn't use the current situation as an excuse and that they were being paid to win matches and if anyone didn't like it, they could go, just as I'd done a couple of years before.

We were due to play Leicester the next night so I phoned Gianni to try and see if we could sort anything out. I said to him, "Gianni, this is pathetic. Today, the groundsman told my players to empty their lockers and be out in two days because you haven't paid your bills."

He waved his arms and said, "Ah, no worry Ollie. It's a no problem, I will pay the bill and everything is okay again."

"It is a problem," I countered. "The lads are all over the place and if we're not careful, they are going to be hopeless against Leicester tomorrow. I need to speak with Antonio and tell him there are major problems at this football club with the way he's paying people. I'm having too many problems to be your manager, so tell him I need to see him before tomorrow's game."

At half-eleven that night, I get a call from Antonio saying, "Ian, don't worry. Don't you trust me to run a big business?"

I said. "Yes, Antonio, but at the moment, this isn't working. Everybody's worried because they're used to doing things one way and these are problems that I don't need to be getting. I'll see you at the game tomorrow."

His English wasn't brilliant so whether he understood me properly, I don't know. Instead of preparing properly for the game with Leicester, I'd had the lads wobbling everywhere and it was a joke. I went up to Gianni's office before the match and Antonio was there and they were on about taking me out for a meal the next day and sorting out a new deal because of, as they put it, 'how wonderful I was.' Do me a favour!

I said, "Look, these issues cannot carry on because it keeps coming back to me and the lads and it isn't good for the team's morale." I needed to know Antonio understood what I was saying but I wasn't sure he did. I left them there and went down to prepare for the game. We lost to Leicester, who were struggling at the time and we were absolutely horrific, though we still only lost 3-2. They didn't look the same group of players and we thoroughly deserved to lose the game. Gianni insisted he wanted to take me out the next day, but I told him I couldn't because I had to have a piece of skin cancer removed at hospital.

I felt very apprehensive on my way for my appointment because I didn't know how much skin they needed to remove or where from. I was on my own because Kim was off with the girls and the doctor ended up taking a lump out of my back and a piece off my face, just under my left eye. I was fortunate that I didn't need a skin graft and probably just got away with it and was left feeling both relieved and unnerved by the whole experience.

As I was driving home, I got a phone call from Rob, my agent, whom I'd told about the mention of a new contract from Antonio. Rob said, "Really? Well, I've had a weird experience today. The conversation you had last night looks a little different today."

"What do you mean?"

"Well Leicester have called Gianni to ask for permission to speak with you and he's given the go-ahead."

I said, "What does that mean, then?"

"It means he doesn't want you. He's granted permission for you to talk to them."

I asked why Gianni hadn't called me? Rob said Gianni told him he'd tried but couldn't get hold of me, which to be fair, was probably true because I switched my phone off at the hospital. I said I would call Gianni, but Rob said, "No I wouldn't. I'd go and see Leicester. Son, wake up and smell the coffee – they don't want you. I'm telling you, you should go up and speak with Leicester."

"When do they want me to do that?" "This evening. Get your suit on, I've got directions. Get up there."

So bear in mind I have a lump missing from my back with three stitches in it, and a lump out of my face so I wasn't looking the best. I was worried about the skin cancer, pissed off about the previous night's performance and I was going somewhere because my agent was telling me to, which I wasn't sure about so I wasn't travelling north in the best of moods, in all honesty. Kim had asked me how I felt about it all and I said that I was pretty angry about the whole situation.

It was one of the most surreal days of my life but I met up with a director from Leicester at his house in the country and he was a nice guy. I sat down, feeling a bit weary and looking a little worse for wear and had a cup of tea. I was asked about how I felt about things and I said, "I'm a bit shell-shocked in truth because I wouldn't have expected Gianni to give you permission to talk with me. Why am I here?"

They told me I was one of eight people being interviewed for their job and I just laughed. I said, "You do realise I'll get the sack, now?" I knew my meeting Leicester would put me in an untenable position because it would give the board the opportunity to claim that I didn't want to be manager of QPR, which was completely untrue. I left knowing nothing would come of it and I was never asked to go for a second interview. In fact, they never spoke with me again and I felt they'd been a little flippant towards me. The whole affair left a bad taste in my mouth, but I had to carry on unless told otherwise, and the next morning I was driving into work when my phone went. It was someone asking about taking one of my players, Ian Evatt, on loan. He needed some games and I'd been thinking of sending him out anyway so I called Gianni to discuss it with him and I said, "Gianni, I've got a bit of a problem…"

"Ah, Ollie. I'm sorry I didn't ring you. I suppose you'll be taking your staff with you."

"Taking them where?" I said. "To the training ground? I'm driving into work. They were interviewing eight different people and why you said I could speak to Leicester I don't know. Why I went up there, I don't know, so I'm coming into work today." He sounded utterly shocked by all that. I added that I was calling because somebody wanted to take Ian Evatt on loan and he said, "No, no, you can't. We'll talk when you get here."

I started to wonder whether I was manager anymore so I called Rob and said, "Does he want me to take this game on Saturday or what?" Rob told me I had to be careful and I said, "Well I've just spoken to him and it's as though I'm not the manager anymore."

Rob called Gianni and got back to me to say that I was in fact still the manager. I still felt I had to sort things out with Gianni so I phoned him and said, "Gianni, what's going on?"

"Well in Italy when a club calls to speak to the manager, the deal is already done. I thought this was the case…"

"Well you thought wrong, Gianni" I said. "And I don't like the fact that you let me go for an interview in the first place."

I didn't see him again that week and just got on with things. Then we had a problem with our goalie Simon Royce and we didn't have any back-up so I called Gianni telling him we needed a keeper for the weekend but he kept knocking me back saying we couldn't afford anyone. Then he tells me he could get Carlo

Cudicini on loan from Chelsea and I said, "No you can't. You wouldn't be able to get him to come here." I got hold of Pen and asked him to gather some targets together and we tried absolutely everybody without success and eventually Chris Coleman said we could have Paul Jones on a free, but he'd broken his finger and wouldn't be fit until the week after and I needed somebody there and then. I started to get the feeling something was going on because everything we tried failed. We were on a coach travelling up to Leeds by which time I was frantic. I had a young kid on the bus but it would have been too much for him when I get a call from Pen saying, "I've got a belting idea, Oll. I think this is a total stitch-up. They want you to go with an untried kid and get beaten tomorrow. Why don't you call Neil Warnock? He never has a goalie as sub – he'll want you to beat Leeds and I guarantee he'll let you have him for nothing."

I managed to get hold of Neil and he said, "Yep, you can have Barnsey."

I told him we needed him today so he could sign before the deadline and play him, and the deal went through at noon on the dot, just hours before kick-off. I called Gianni and told him I'd managed to get someone and he said, "I told you we got no money, you can't do that."

I said, "Yes I can – he's free." He couldn't say anything to that but things were still not right. As I walked into Elland Road, Sam Ellis, Leeds' No 2 looked at me and looked like he'd seen a ghost. He said, "Ollie, I didn't expect to see you here." I laughed and said that the Leicester thing was all rubbish but he said, "No, not because of that. Come in here a minute." I walked into Kevin Blackwell's office with Sam and he said, "Hang on a minute, I'll just get Kevin."

Kevin arrived a moment later and said, "Ollie, I didn't think I'd see you today, listen to this." With that he put his mobile phone on loud speaker and played a message he'd received. It went, "Hello Kevin, it's Ken Bates. I've got some information here. Just talking to Paladini upstairs. He said he's sacked Holloway and they've got Barnes in goal from Sheffield United. See you later."

As far as I'm aware, Ken Bates knew something only me, Neil Warnock, his secretary, my secretary and Gianni knew. I've no beef with Ken Bates because he was doing what any chairman would do if he felt it benefited his club, and was merely passing on info that his manager might have been able to use. Kevin was only doing what I believe he would hope I'd do for him if I was in a similar situation – which of course I would because it was the right thing to do. Talk about undermining me before a game!

I did the team talk and made a few changes – in fact it was more like Queens Park Strangers than Queen Park Rangers and though we did reasonably well, we still lost 2-0. Pen called on the way home and I told him what had happened and he said, "That's an absolute fucking disgrace, mate – an absolute disgrace."

I decided I wasn't going to have this anymore. I had a terrible night's sleep and woke up early and called my agent and went over in detail what had happened the previous day and he asked me how I felt about it all. I told him it was a disgrace and he said, "Well you'd better call Gianni up and tell him, then and be professional about it. Whatever you do, don't shout." So I had a coffee, tried to compose myself as best I could and called him.

"Gianni…"

"Ah, don't you listen to he say what she say what he say what she say."

"Listen to me and listen to what I have to say. There's only one person who could have said this. Ken Bates told Kevin Blackwell we'd signed the Sheffield United goalkeeper and that you told him you'd sacked Ian Holloway. Just for once, tell me what the hell's going on."

He went quiet and then said the board wanted a change.

"Great. Talk to my agent."

I put the phone down and later Rob spoke with him. The next morning, thinking I was going to be sacked, I was placed on gardening leave, which basically means you stay at home on full pay but that they don't want you in because you're a bad influence. I'll never forget what Gianni said regarding my interview at Leicester. He said, "Why, if you're happily married, would you go and see another woman?" The fact is I was told by my wife to go and see another woman, not the other way round, so why hadn't he said it that way instead? I believe the whole thing had been manufactured to get me out and because I didn't want the players they had wanted to bring in but didn't want the fans to turn on them because most of them were on my side. It was a sad end to my time as manager, which contractually it wasn't, because I still had two years to run on my contract, it seemed I wouldn't ever work for the club again.

So I was no longer the manager of QPR, which hadn't been what I'd wanted at all. I still believed in my team and think with the right backing I could have taken the club forward and think my players still believed in me, too.

Gianni called me to tell me that I would get my wages every week paid into my bank account, but my world had stopped. Apparently I had a bad attitude and a negative input on the football club and was to stay away. This was my reward after working that hard to keep things together. That didn't sit well with me at all, I can assure you.

My staff and I had been on a long hard road together and we'd given everything to QPR and after plunging into administration and having just seven players on the books at one stage, no goalkeeper and two long-term injuries. Then we win promotion two years later, despite everything, and were well-placed in the table in our first year back up. I felt that was a major achievement, not a bad influence.

My agent told me to chill out but three weeks later I picked up three points for speeding and lost my license. My ego was in tatters – I'd lost my job, my car and my right to drive – three things that no man wants to lose. I felt a part of my manhood was gone, and I was reduced to a fit of pique in a supermarket when I trashed a shopping basket into a fruit stall. I wasn't a nice person to be around – again – poor old Kim. My agent told me not to go to any games anywhere for a while, and he then started to get me loads of work on TV. I did some work on Sky News as a kind of resident pundit for the day and I really enjoyed it. Things went well and they offered me different types of jobs after that. The more I did it, the easier it got and I was covering a few different sports and because of that, I got asked by ITV to do around three 'World Cup Cuppas' with Steve Bunce off Capital Radio and it was a good laugh. Then I got a 10-match deal to appear on a World Cup programme for ITV2. I met some fascinating characters, including a hero of mine from Blackadder, Brian Blessed, and he was an inspirational bloke in many ways. I asked him about his many adventures, including climbing Everest. "I'm going to do it again and this time I'm not going to use any oxygen," he bellowed in that incredible voice. "My doctor said I shouldn't but I'm bloody well going to do it." I asked him how he still had so much enthusiasm and he said, "Well I wake up each morning and I need a new challenge and I keep looking forward to my new Everest. Some people's Everest might be picking a finger up off a bed because they've been paralysed for however many years, but if you don't want that challenge each time you wake up, you're wasting your life young fella." He was an outstanding human being and sometimes you imagine how certain people are and put them on pedestals and they let you down when you actually meet them – Brian

Blessed was exactly the opposite. All the while, I had to keep my mouth shut regarding my situation, because if I'd have said one derogatory comment about my job at QPR, I could have been sacked.

I was doing all sorts of things and having a bit of a laugh, too. Meanwhile, Gianni was doing interviews saying, "Oh we're never going to have him back," which totally contradicts what gardening leave is meant to be, which is being sent away for a little while and then going back to your job at a later date. It was all a bit weird.

I got a stack of wonderful letters from the Rangers fans saying some really lovely things and I'll be eternally thankful for that, but none of them really made me feel any better. I read them all and sent a hand-written reply to each and every one and it took me a long time. It was a very emotional time for me, because I never go into any relationship without being fully committed so it was the equivalent of bereavement for me. It wasn't a nice time for Kim, either, because we should have enjoyed the extra time we had together and gone places and generally chilled out, but I was angry and not much fun to be around, if I'm honest. I actually tried a bit of gardening but ended up pulling a lot of Kim's expensive plants out and leaving a fair amount of weeds, so that was the end of my active gardening service! We then decided we were going to sell the house we'd bought in St Albans, so I painted the whole place from top to bottom, which took me about three weeks. In between shopping and doing the school runs, I was finding it hard to occupy the time and I was desperate to do something constructive again. I'd gone from telling everyone what to do and being the most important figure in my workplace to being at home where everything I said didn't actually mean that much! I was treading water and it was driving me mad – could I really do this for two years, which was when my QPR contract was up? With the TV work I was doing, I even wondered whether I could be bothered going back into management again and when interviews came up, I asked myself if I really wanted the jobs. I had some serious thinking to do and I mulled over the events over the past few months and things just didn't add up.

It made me think back to about three months before the contact from Leicester, when I was receiving phone calls from somebody claiming to be a senior official at the Nigerian FA, telling me they wanted me to manage Nigeria at the 2006 World Cup.

"To be honest," I said, "I'm very worried how you've got my number. I don't know who you are…"

"I am the president of the Nigerian Football Association and this is a great honour to manage our country…"

I had to intervene with, "Look, you're actually breaking the laws of my contract. I've got a wonderful job and I'm very happy at QPR and I can't help you. Sorry."

I called Rob and told him about it and he told me it was bullshit and that I should get the number when it came up on my mobile. Each time it read 'number withheld' and this guy called twice more and I told him the same thing each time.

Was I being tested? Who knows. I asked Danny Shittu, who is Nigerian, about the calls and he said, "Just take no notice Ollie – nobody knows who's doing what."

The bottom line to the whole affair is that I don't believe the consortium ever wanted me to run their club. They wanted their own man in, someone they could manipulate so they could control who was coming in and out of the club. Instead of telling me the truth to my face because they thought I was popular, they resorted to underhand tactics in my view. They used to read the fans' websites and because there were no dissenters at first, they left me alone. After a few poor results, however, there were a few whingers coming on, and I think they saw a chink in the armour and went for it.

Later I found out my replacement, Gary Waddock, had sent out youth coach Joe Gallen and his chief youth team scout, to do some match reports on our next two opponents – and this was the Saturday when we played Leeds United, when Ian Holloway is still manager of QPR. Should I believe that he had no idea that he would be the next manager, then? I think the evidence is as damning as the phone call Ken Bates made to Kevin Blackwell. All I know is that Waddock, Joe or the scout didn't say one word to me about researching those two games, and they could have mentioned it anytime that week because I was still the manager. Had I been in their shoes, I'd have said, "Well actually, Oll, I was approached when you went for that interview." But nobody said a word to me. Waddock got the job and the first thing he says is, "I'm going to change the style of football. We're Queens Park Rangers and we have a tradition of playing a certain style of football and I'm going to change things overnight."

I think that hurt me more than anything else did. As a manager, you cannot be undermined and the minute your chairman undermines you, you might as well walk, because nobody is going to believe you're in charge ever again. Too many chairmen do that and it was happening to me all the time towards the end so perhaps I should have seen all this coming. Being a chairman or owning a club means you take on an awful lot of responsibility and power. I often wonder if they realise that they are carrying the hopes, dreams and aspirations of every fan who would run through brick walls for their club and give up time with their family to watch you play at the other end of the country through wind, snow and rain. The QPR fans had that passion and loyalty, but I'm not sure the men at the top recognised that.

I couldn't have asked any more from my players who were incredibly loyal to me, but even they couldn't do anything in the end. Had Chris Wright stayed, I think I might have still been at Loftus Road today and we might have even been in the Premiership. I'm incredibly proud of my time as QPR manager and what my staff, my players and I achieved, and nobody can take that away from me. Nobody.

Chapter 21

The Pig of Plymouth

Gianni had told my agent that I had to apply for new jobs while on gardening leave because obviously the sooner I found a new position the better for him because they wouldn't be paying me for doing sod all. I was contacted by Tranmere and Brentford, but the money wasn't anywhere near what I was looking for and then I went to speak with Millwall, who impressed me but I'd already promised I would go and speak with Milton Keynes Dons. Millwall chairman Stewart Till tried to put me on the spot asking me for an immediate answer to their offer but I told them I'd given MK Dons my word and I didn't break that for anybody. I told them that if they couldn't be bothered to let me be a man of my principles, I wasn't going to work for them. I actually really liked the Millwall chairman and think I could have worked with him.

I'd met him at a hotel in London and they answered my queries – and I had a lot – very well. I asked them questions related to whether or not there was likely to be a power struggle because I wasn't about to go through that again. It also proved I knew about business and was an experienced manager and it showed I wasn't desperate for a job. I had the best part of two years' wages to come so money wasn't an issue and with all the media work I was doing, I was actually earning more than I'd ever done before and I wasn't going to give that up easily. I'd been taught not to be pushed around and I think if you looked at my CV, if I wasn't forced to sell my best players, I could take teams up and I also believe I can manage in the Premiership. Things went well, but Millwall were itching to make an announcement of who their new manager was so they could get moving and planning for the season ahead, but I knew MK Dons were building a new stadium and I was keen to speak with their chairman Peter Winkleman. I told Millwall that I couldn't commit to anything and if their terms were answer now or no deal, I told them to take me out of the running. They came back with an improved offer, but it wasn't about that and more money wasn't going to change anything because I wanted to meet Peter in Milton Keynes. When I actually did go, I found Peter a fascinating man and I'd never met anyone who had such a burning desire to make a town and a football club mould together and work. I was only with him a couple of hours but I learned a lot from him in that time, though I was disappointed not to at least get a call to say that they'd eventually given the job to Martin Allen.

Ipswich then came on the phone and wanted to interview me, but Millwall were still pressing for an answer, but I wanted to hear what Ipswich had to say. I'd met their chairman David Sheepshanks a few times in the past and I went over to Suffolk for a pre-interview, which I thoroughly enjoyed.

I kept thinking of Millwall, but something was nagging away at me – something that made me wonder if problems might lie ahead in the future. They'd told me they were very keen to redevelop the ground, so much in fact that I wondered if it would be at the expense of the team. One of the Millwall directors had spoken about Barry Hayles needing to be sold on and that also set the alarm bells ringing because I thought he was miles away from being a good judge and if he was voicing concerns to me like that in an interview, chances are he would want an input in team affairs if I did take over. If we couldn't agree on the basic issue of how good Barry Hayles was, then I doubted we'd be able to agree on a number of things. I told him that if I was offered the job, the first thing I'd do would be to sit down with Barry and say, 'What the hell's the matter with you? What the hell are you doing playing at this level and not scoring goals?' I believed in Barry and I would use that knowledge that he was considered surplus to requirements at Millwall to my advantage in the months ahead. I wasn't prepared to catapult myself into anything that I thought might be a nightmare scenario and ultimately Millwall wasn't right for me at that time.

I spoke with David Sheepshanks again after I'd turned down Millwall's offer and he said, "Look, Ian. We're not going to interview you again. We've already decided on who we're going to have as our next manager but I thought you were absolutely terrific and I'm delighted I met you, so thank you very much." I appreciated the call and while I was disappointed that things hadn't gone further because Ipswich have a fantastic tradition and I liked Mr Sheepshanks' attitude, I felt very positive about everything. I decided to take Kim to watch Spurs play Fulham at White Hart Lane, but before I did, I called him back and left a message. I said, "I'm on a crusade and a learning curve and it would be helpful if you could tell me why I didn't get the job – what aren't I good at and what do I need to improve?"

He called me back and said I needed to get my badges. That was roughly it. He said they were employing somebody from within the club, which turned out to be Jim Magilton. He also said, "Basically, what we wanted was someone who talked about Ipswich with the same passion you talked about QPR to us. On your next interview, make sure you just talk about their club because they don't want to hear about your last one." It was very good of him to impart that information to me and it meant that I could take something from the experience and learn from it. The problem, I think, was that I'd been effectively gagged about speaking about QPR and after he'd fed me a bit of Trill I sang like a canary! Since then, I've taken my UEFA C and B badges and will complete my A badge shortly and after that I'll take my pro-licence. So five jobs had come and gone and I probably could have had at least three of them if I'd really wanted, but something was keeping me back. Kim was her usual laid-back self and because of a dream she'd had about a year before, she said, "Oh don't worry, you'll end up as Plymouth manager." She never lost faith in that dream and in her mum's house there are lots of different pictures of animals, one of which is Caesar the pig and Kim told me, "You'll be the pig of Plymouth, just wait and see."

There were rumours Tony Pulis would be leaving Plymouth and going to Stoke City. When that became a fact, I was contacted by the Plymouth board, after they'd been given permission by Gianni, and wondered if Kim's prophecy might be about to come true. I could smell it in my snout!

Argyle chairman, Paul Stapleton, invited me to drive down and meet club officials in Taunton for an interview – and after two years in Plymouth, I now know why – every taxi driver is an Argyle fan and there'd be no way they could have kept the interview quiet! I sat down and Paul Stapleton said thanks for coming down and that's when I got my list of questions out! I said, "Well actually I've got some questions I'd like to ask you gentlemen."

Paul said, "Well, that's a bit unusual, but on you go – fire away."

So I began and after a couple of answers from Paul, my general feeling of not really wanting the job and being happy receiving my wage each month and doing media work changed to, 'Well hang on a minute, I could work for this fella.' That's when I became nervous and apparently I started swearing, though I wasn't aware I was doing it at the time. I'd started out feeling relaxed and in control but the minute I realised I really wanted to be Plymouth's manager, I changed and later Paul told me they nearly didn't take me because of my bad language! That could only happen to me! Kim was waiting for me outside having doubled as my chauffeur – she hadn't felt it was right to be in on the interview, plus I was banned from driving for six months after picking up too many points for speeding. She asked me how I'd got on and I told her I really wanted the job. She said, "Oh I told you you'd find somebody one day and I told you you'd be the Pig of Plymouth."

Kim said moving to the south west would be great for our family because there was a very good deaf school in Exeter, so other aspects about taking the job were appealing, too. Then Paul Stapleton finally called me himself, after a few days of tricky negotiations between him and my agent Robert. The deal was done and he said I needed to come down to Plymouth and start work the next day.

So I agreed to be announced as Plymouth manager the following day, travelled down on the train and was blown away by the beautiful landscape and coastal resorts as I approached Plymouth. Everything felt right and I met up with Paul Stapleton and his family, watched the World Cup final at his house, slept like a baby at the Astor Hotel in town and awoke to the sound of seagulls. For a moment I thought, 'that's not right – where the hell am I?' Then it dawned on me. I was the Plymouth Argyle manager and I thought that any job where seagulls wake you up in the morning can't be half bad, can it?

I was unveiled the following day and the players reported back the next day! It's fair to say I had to get cracking immediately but in hindsight, I should have let the chairman get rid of Tony Pulis's remaining coaching staff so I could bring my own people in but they were desperate to announce me to probably quell supporters' concerns about going into the new season without anybody at the helm. Instead I was forced to start on my own with somebody else's staff and no chief scout because the one we had was going to go with Pulis to Stoke and

I couldn't ask him to do anything because then Stoke would've known who we were after – it was a bloody nightmare. I was in the deep end and I either sank or swam and even the media attention threw me back a little. They'd got the Argyle carpet out and in the boardroom I had to field my first press conference which was packed with journalists, reporters and TV crews and that's probably the first time it struck me how big this football club is. They'd handled everything fantastically well and seemed to be professionally run from top to bottom and I couldn't help but be impressed by everything and they came across to me like a mini-Man United. I had tingles down my spine because I felt excited by what I was seeing and experiencing and I couldn't wait to begin the job of putting Argyle where they belong – in the Premiership.

I had to hit the ground running and I hadn't had time to think of anything, but I was back in management again, batteries fully recharged and raring to go, but as ever, there were casualties of sorts. Moving across the country would be good for the twins, bad for Hattie and Will, who'd had enough by that point. Relocating to Plymouth was a major upheaval and stressful for everybody, as moves generally are. Prior to taking the Argyle job, Chloe and Eve had already been accepted at Exeter Royal College for the deaf where they'd be taking equine studies and also be boarding there, too, all funded by Hertfordshire Education Authority, but within three weeks of starting my new job I had to move my wife, three kids and four horses and a dog to Devon. For Will, who by now was 18, this was one move too far and he refused to move with us. He wanted to stay in St Albans, but it just wasn't possible so he said, "I want to go back to Bristol. How do you know how long you're going to be manager of Plymouth? I'm 18 now and I want to live and work in Bristol and be with my family and mates and I'm not coming with you this time." He just couldn't take another move and within four weeks we'd helped move him back to Bristol, and he started working with my old mate Paul Lewton. Will wasn't the only one with their world in bits. Hattie, now 14, had to leave a school she loved, her best friend Ellie and her boyfriend Tommy. She was broken-hearted and absolutely hated me because of it – I was not flavour of the month as you can imagine, and living up to my tag of 'The Pig of Plymouth'. The consequences for my family were again quite shocking. It was also a very difficult year for Kim because the girls were all boarding which they absolutely hated, but were committed to do. She was left to deal with all the family angst and disagreements while I scooted off to work. It all comes with the territory, of course, but sometimes the terrain is rough and inhospitable, full of pot-holes and ditches.

In general, life was on the up, though, and Plymouth felt like the ideal place to lay down our roots. Isn't it funny how clever people in life can sometimes see things coming long before you can yourself? My agent Robert and my wife Kim were telling me other things were on the horizon and, as usual, they were both absolutely spot on. Still, those bloody seagulls will take some getting used to!

Chapter 22

Bring on Los Galácticos

With Tim Breacker and Pen still on gardening leave at QPR, I was having to play the role of manager, coach and chief scout. I had coaches David Kemp and Mark O'Connor preparing to leave for Stoke but I had no other choice but utilise them so I met the lads and said, "Now you can either have me out there with you taking the training sessions, or you can work with these two lads while I go and try and get some new players in." I trusted Mark and Dave to look after the lads and to a man they all said I should go and try to bring new players in. I was only adding to the squad and nobody was being replaced, so nobody was worried for their future. The physio and fitness coach Paul Maxwell – 'Maxi' – was out of contract and also looking to swap Home Park for the Britannia Stadium. It wasn't the best way to start my managerial career with Plymouth but that had been my own fault so there was no point complaining. After two days of assessing the lads, I decided my first job was to keep Maxi at the club because, frankly, he was too good to lose. I had to convince him that we could really go places, despite Tony Pulis saying that it was all about money and we were really going to struggle to get out of the division we were in without a major investment of funds. There is some truth in what he said, but I felt differently about the situation and I told Maxi my thoughts and ambition for the club. I told him that I felt we could compete with the right training facilities and gymnasium work, which was his bag, and I told him that I thought we'd actually do very well.

I revealed the names of players I was hoping to bring in, one of which was Barry Hayles. I said that I felt I could talk those players into coming to Plymouth and Maxi said, "Well nobody ever has before," and I said, "Well I think I can. I believe I can because I believe in the club and I also believe in you and I want to keep you here." I proved as much by negotiating a deal that brought his money up to what I thought it should be at Championship level and Maxi signed a new contract, which I was delighted by.

Then I had the small matter of convincing our Player of the Year, David Norris, to commit to a new deal because he was out of contract at the end of the 2005/06 season and there was no way I could let a player of his quality walk away from the club on a free transfer. I talked with him about my plans for the future and though it was by no means straightforward, I managed to get his money up to what I thought a player of his ilk at that level should be getting and he signed a new deal. It was like wham, bam! – 2-0 to Holloway with not even two weeks on the calendar.

Next, I called Sir Alex Ferguson because Pen had given me a list of strikers he felt were worth pursuing during our time at QPR. I'd kept the list and one of those players was Manchester United youngster Sylvan Ebanks-Blake and Pen had suggested a loan deal for him. There was also a kid called Campbell and Pen had suggested United might be willing to sell him and it was worth trying. So I spoke with Sir Alex and asked him about Ebanks-Blake – he'd already said no to loaning the player a year before, but there was no harm in trying. While we were chatting, I also asked him about the availability of Campbell, John Evans and another youngster and Sir Alex said, "My God. Who's telling you about those lads?" I told him it was Gary Penrice and he said, "Well tell him he's got a good eye." Then he proceeded to say no to the lot! I wasn't going to give up so I said, "Well you've got this lad called Campbell coming through and you're bound to want to play him in the reserves, why can't I buy Sylvan?"

It went quiet at the other end, and then he said, "Er, well how much are you thinking?"

"So you would think about selling him, then? I don't know, how much were you thinking?"

"About £200,000?"

I said, "What, £200,000 guaranteed?"

"Well there'd have to be a few bits and bobs if he does things..."

I agreed, depending on how it was paid and he said, "Well I might, then."
"I think you should…"
"Well I might." I told him I needed to speak with my chairman and that he should think about the bits and bobs he wanted attaching to the deal and I'd think about ours and then we could try and meet somewhere in the middle.

I felt excited about the deal and then left the fine print of the deal to Michael Dunford and got back to Sir Alex to say why we couldn't agree to some of the things he'd wanted including, but we ended by agreeing the deal in the most amicable way imaginable. I then said that while it was all well and good us agreeing his transfer, I needed to actually speak with the lad because he might want to remain a Manchester United player or might not fancy moving to Plymouth. I knew Sylvan's agent was keen for him to play for me and Pen because of the reputation we had with strikers, which was half the battle, and Sylvan wanted to learn, too. He wanted a piece of what Bobby Zamora, Nathan Ellington, Jason Roberts, Barry Hayles and Jamie Cureton had had, so I arranged a meeting with Sylvan and his agent Paul Martin near St Albans and I thought the lad was fantastic. I can always tell by the eyes and he looked straight back at me and he was strong and he said the right things so I told him I liked him and I wanted to sort the deal out.

I began talking with his agent and while we were chatting, his phone rang and it was Watford and after speaking with Sir Alex, they also had an option to speak with the kid. They had been promoted and were now a Premiership side and had matched the offer we'd made so his agent told me Sylvan would want to talk with them. I cursed my luck, but asked Paul to make sure he didn't make a decision without at least coming down to see us in Plymouth and he more or less guaranteed he'd do that.

I called the chairman to tell him how things had gone and that Sylvan would be coming to have a look around. I said, "Look, all we've got to do is make sure that he gets the same kind of reception I got on my first visit to the club and told him we needed to pull out all the stops – put him in a top hotel and show him around the city and what Plymouth was all about. I added that I would sort out one or two other things but I'd leave it to the chairman to show him around and look after him.

I got a Plymouth shirt with Ebanks-Blake and No 9 on the back and put it in a frame and presented it to him when he arrived at Home Park and said, "There you go, son. How do you fancy wearing the No 9 shirt, then?"

I'd briefed all the staff what his name was and to address him accordingly so he'd feel straight at home and people were saying things like, "I've heard a lot about you, Sylvan, I hope you sign for us," and I think it all worked a treat because he did sign for us over Watford. Several other clubs came on the scene at the death, all of them bigger than us, but he wanted to work with us and learn more about being a striker.

Scoring is a special skill but it is something you can learn. It's about technique and focus, but most of it's in your mind and because Pen had lived through his own barren patches and lived through it, he has empathy with strikers and though they might not always like the way he gets his point across, they accept it because they know he cares about them by the encouragement he gives out.

I think Sylvan was keen to work with Pen, too, who wasn't even with us at the time, but he is my centre-forward guru and I wouldn't have considered taking the Plymouth job if I hadn't been able to bring him with me at some point.

Basically, strikers need their self-esteem building and they need to be boosted, moulded and given assurances. A striker is always worried about his place and whether he's scoring or not but I don't know what that feels like, as Pen took pleasure in telling me once after I'd made a throwaway comment about a striker we had and he went for my throat.

"Don't you say that," he said. "You've not got the balls to play up front. It's alright for you, Oll. You can run around for two years and not score a goal and everybody pats you on the back and says, 'Well done Oll.' But if you were a striker and didn't score for two years you'd be out of the game – you haven't a clue about the pressure." He was right, too and that's what I love about Pen – he cares so much about the strikers and the lads all know it and that's why they respond to him.

So Paul Martin called me a day or so later to say that Sylvan would be joining Plymouth, and that was a belting call to receive. Then I received another piece of news that was as surreal as it was unbelievable.

Argyle's chief executive Michael Dunford was a little concerned about the numbers travelling to Austria. He was organising the trip and we had several places reserved for new arrivals but I had no idea who exactly they would be. The accommodation was sorted and we would play a couple of games while we were there, too. Obviously Sylvan would be one of the players but with only 10 days to go before we left, the pressure was on and the clock was ticking. Then Michael calls me up and says, "I've just had a strange call from Real Madrid asking if we'd move from our hotel." I asked him what he meant. He continued: "Well, we've booked the castle hotel that they love because it's always been lucky for them and they want us to move out."

"No – who do they think they are?" I said and Michael went, "Well there's more to it than that – I haven't finished. If we move out, they'll play us in a friendly while we're out there and they'll pay for all our accommodation while we're in Austria, too."

I said, "Well yeah! Of course we'll move out!" We couldn't fail – we were taking 36 people for 10 days and I'd say that would have cost Argyle quite a lot of money, and to have a once in a lifetime chance to play Real Madrid was just too good to turn down. Michael said he was asking out of courtesy because he thought it was a great deal.

"Great? It's unbelievable!"

"OK, I'll announce it, then." I'd just been preparing to go out training with the lads, because I'd not had much of a chance up to that point and before we started I gathered everyone around. I went through what we were going to do then said, "Oh, and have a guess what else I've got for you then? We're going to play Real Madrid while we're over in Austria. They smiled and shook their heads because they thought I was joking but when they realised it wasn't a wind-up, they were chuffed at the prospect, as was the whole city.

After the session I had to go in and do a press conference as I always did on that particular day and the Madrid game was big news for the club. I sat at a desk, still feeling the day's events were a little unreal and the first question I'm asked is, "Can you tell us your reaction about the Real Madrid game?"

It was music to my ears – for Ian Holloway to be presented with a chance like that, I had to take it so I just fell off my chair on to the floor. Des Bulpin was chuckling away at the back and I just told the reporters, "I told you you'd have some laughs with me, didn't I? What a bloody stupid question – what reaction do you think I'm going to have to playing Real Madrid? I was stunned and amazed."

My first real meeting with the Plymouth fans was a few days before our first pre-season friendly. It was an 'ask the manager' evening at Home Park and I was gobsmacked to see about 600 Argyle fans behind the goal at one end. I had a microphone and I had a compère to help field the questions and it turned out to be a very successful evening and it was good to hear what they were thinking and for me to able to get a few points across. We then travelled to Tiverton for my first game as Plymouth manager and I quite enjoyed that, too. We played some nice stuff and it was a good exercise for us for a number of reasons. Tiverton had set a defensive stall out, and their forwards split to mark our full-backs, which is quite unusual – an idea they must have got off Trinidad & Tobago manager Leo Beenhakker, because they'd narrowly lost to England 2-0 not long before. It was bloody effective, too. I played one team in the first half and a different eleven in the second and we went in 1-0 up at the break. I changed things around tactically and we scored another three in the second half and the lads did what I'd asked them to really well and I could see they were enjoying themselves, but there were a couple of things I wasn't happy with. There was too much bickering among the lads and instead of it being about wanting the ball, it was all about them as individuals rather than the team and one lad in particular, Bojan Djordic, got shouted at by Lilian Nalis and I didn't think Bojan liked that. Bojan had given the ball away and Tiverton went through and nearly scored and it was only because Nalis managed to get back and clear the danger that they didn't. Nalis then looked back to Bojan, who was still on the halfway line moaning, and had a go at him. I'd noticed one or two things about Bojan's performance that night that I wasn't happy with so when everyone came in at the end, I think they all thought I'd be happy with the performance and scoreline, but of course, I wasn't. This was my first game and I needed to nail down anything I didn't feel was right and I could see they weren't encouraging each other and that had to change. I said, "Lil, why did you moan at Bo?" and Bo said, "Ah, he always moans at me."

"Shut up, I haven't asked you a question yet," I told him. I asked Lilian again and I said, "Tell him why you moaned at him because I don't quite think he understands."

Bo said, "That's easy, he moaned at me because I gave the ball away."

"No, hang on, why did you moan at him, Lil?"

Lil said, "No, I didn't moan at you because you gave the ball away, I moaned because you didn't run back and try and tackle the fella – you let me do that."

I turned to Bo and said, "When you play for me you're allowed to give the ball away, but you are not allowed not to chase back and correct your error because that's what we all have to do, here. Lil, will you moan at him if he chases back?"

Lil said, "Well, no, I won't."

I turned back to Bo and said, "OK, Bo, make sure you understand why people are having a go at you. We want you to express yourself and pass the ball but we don't want you to stand still when you've not got it and then expect someone else to win it back for you!"

I'd been able to nail down one of my most important points in my first game in charge and it was perfect.

Then I turned my attention to Barry Hayles at Millwall and having spoken to Peter De Savary when I was interviewed for the Millwall job I knew that he didn't rate Barry, so I tested the water and was proved right. Their manager didn't want to sell him but I knew their board would and I was determined to bring him to Home Park. I agreed a fee for him but what I still had to do was talk him into taking quite a hefty cut in his pay. I knew Barry was a winner and would have hated the season he'd just had at Millwall and while it might have been good to be back with his family in London, it hadn't been happening for him on the pitch. I felt he was with Millwall for the wrong reasons and the person I knew he was, meant that I had to ask him some honest and straight questions. If he gave me the answers I thought the old Barry would, I knew he'd want to come and play for me and prove me right. I said to him, "You have to care about what you're doing – I've got some winners at my club, what the hell's happened to you? What the hell are you doing? You've never just taken money, your heart's got to be in things so why don't you come here and help me with this lot because I think I've got a bunch of winners, here."

Barry just smiled and said, "Yeah, I'll do that."

You have to know the essence of the man to talk like that and though he cost me £100,000, I told the chairman, "Look, you might not get your money back, but you will on the pitch." I added that we couldn't go into the Championship with inexperienced strikers and even if Nick Chadwick had been fully fit, he'd only scored six goals the previous season and I needed a proven goalscorer. The chairman said, "Well Hayles only scored four last year."

I said, "Yeah, but his heart wasn't in it." I managed to talk him into it and he signed a two-year deal. It wasn't in time for our next friendly, away to Grays, which would be the last match before we set off for Austria the following day. I took a squad of 24 and had both Sylvan and Nick Chadwick available for that match. Things were going along nicely and we were 3-0 up against Grays at half-time and Nick scored all three. I think he thought that because Sylvan had arrived, he'd begin on the bench but I decided to play him in the first half and he responded accordingly. The pressure was now on Sylvan and though there were no more goals after the break, I was pleased with the way the lads played and I liked their calmness on the ball and because we'd not had much time to work on any formations as such, they were just playing for me.

I managed to get Des Bulpin who I'd been considering for the position of head of the youth set-up before I'd actually got the job. Des had trained me at Bristol Rovers and had gone everywhere Gerry had been, including QPR and Tottenham, and I trusted him and respected him.

I wasn't sure if I'd ever get Pen or Tim Breacker, so Des became my first addition to my coaching staff and joined me at first team level. I decided to leave the youth team as it was. Des took to the role straight away and the lads liked him from the word go, which was fantastic. In fact it was better than I'd imagined it might be. Mark O'Connor then left and handled himself with great dignity. He'd told me he wanted to go but wanted paying by Plymouth first but despite his future lying elsewhere, he worked his socks off for me, planning the training from start to finish and he was different class. David Kemp was a bit longer in the tooth and though he was very polite to me, he didn't do much in all honesty, it had all been down to Mark, or 'Des' as the lads had nicknamed him after Des O'Connor. So Mark went off to Stoke and I told Kemp that I had no intention of getting involved in his dispute with the club, which was now escalating slightly. The board wanted to send him, here, there and everywhere, but I told him I just wanted him to do a bit of scouting for me and that I wasn't taking him to Austria. I wanted to start my training regime at this training camp and I now had Des Bulpin, Maxi and Geoff Crudgington, our goalkeeper coach, along with me for the trip and our kit man Jacko, whose real name is Ian Pearce, but who is an absolute ringer for Jack Nicholson – he's even signed autographs from people mistaking him for Jack in the past. We were ready to go and with Barry Hayles to come, I liked the way things were shaping up. It was just me, my new coaching team and my squad from here on in.

Chapter 23

Storm Clouds Gathering

I couldn't have been any happier with the way my first few weeks at Home Park had gone and I flew out to Austria in a fantastic frame of mind. Maxi did impressions of Elvis and we had a great laugh on the plane journey. I was so excited to get back to work again and everything was going as well as I could have hoped, but perhaps I should have realised, in hindsight that they were probably going too well.

We travelled by coach from the airport and I started asking the driver "Are we there yet?" because it took me back to being a kid when dad drove us all to Cornwall and I drove him mad by asking "Are we there yet?" all the way, even when we were only at the top of our road. I continued asking until we reached the hotel, which seemed to be carved out of the side of a mountain. It was peaceful and picturesque and exactly what we needed, and the facilities were superb. We were very professional about everything, as we had to be because I was trying to impress my staff and players. I'd had six months off so I was able to reel off everything I wanted clearly and in exactly the way I needed to. The lads were positive and everything was going my way and I was a bit hyper because I was absolutely loving it. The training facilities were the best I'd ever seen and were just 10 minutes down the road and we had two days to settle in before our first match of the tour, against FC Graz who'd beaten Stoke 2-1 recently. I'd put my footprint on the way the team were training and how we would play, which was something I had to do and the lads were responding fantastically well. I managed to get a lad who wrote for the club website to get me information on all the Graz squad as well as a head and shoulders shot of each player and we put them up on a board in the dressing room before the match. I think the lads were shocked when they saw it because it wasn't something that was expected in a friendly overseas. I doubt anyone thought I'd know anything about the Graz side but I was doing my best Jose Mourinho impression by being so informed about the opposition. We had a match report from their game with Stoke so along with the club doctor, we copied all the details of the Graz squad off their website and each player had his own profile, including details non-football related. Doc and I decided to embellish on those facts and we added something by each player. On one lad we put 'Likes wearing high heels and an apron and good at Origami.' It took us about an hour to put together and as well as the funny stuff, there was genuine information about style and tactics they used. Nobody but the doc and I knew about it so you can imagine everyone's faces when I unveiled it before the game.

I began with the keeper, "Good on crosses, good handling and comes from a long line of ostrich farmers," and it all went down an absolute storm. The lads were happy and relaxed and it showed, too, as we beat Graz 5-1, watched by Barry Hayles, who had flown over to join us, just prior to finally signing his contract. We'd scored 12 goals in our first three games, conceding one and while the standard of opposition might have made people think that we should have been winning by comfortable margins, things don't always work out that way in reality. Some Argyle fans had travelled over to watch us and they were buzzing about everything and I don't think things could have gone any better for us.

A couple of days later we set off to play Real Madrid. We had to drive about an hour to the venue but it was blue skies and sunshine all the way until we reached a long tunnel and came out into dark clouds and drizzle. It was like the tunnel from hell and I thought it didn't bode well for the game ahead, envisaging a drubbing. We had reckoned there probably wouldn't be too many regulars in their team due to the World Cup having ended not that long before, but to their eternal credit, there were eight first-teamers in their starting eleven including the likes of Jonathan Woodgate, Thomas Gravesen, Guti, Julio Baptista and Ivan Helguera. I was still going to play two teams, one in each half, so I could assess all my squad and make sure all the lads had a chance to play Madrid because they might never get the chance again. Fabio Cappello had just got the manager's job for Madrid and he's sat a few yards away from little old me, but there were paparazzi all over him so I didn't really get the chance to speak to him. The lads were so excited and we acquitted ourselves brilliantly and had a few chances to score in the first half, as they did but we went in 0-0 at half-time. We changed the team and our tactics round a bit at the break and held out until the 75th minute when Julio Baptista scored for Madrid from the spot to win the game 1-0. I said in the interview afterwards that I thought we had a hell of a chance of going through in the return leg at Home Park – well, you just can't miss chances like that, can you?

The next day we had one of the best training sessions I've ever had as a manager and I decided to let the lads have a night out after that. And then it all went wrong. Horribly wrong.

The key to success, I believe, is team spirit, and for a few days I'd been going on about having a singing competition – players versus the staff – on our last evening in Austria. We had been looking forward to a wonderful meal and it ended the night and the tour on an incredible downer that could quite easily have ended with the death of one of the lads at the hands of another. We hadn't had a drink, so alcohol wasn't to blame for what happened. The cause was nothing more than teasing, and it had been building up for quite some time over the singing competition I'd suggested. I'd made it clear that if anyone didn't want to join in, they wouldn't be forced to do something they weren't comfortable with, but one player had been bottling things up for around two years unbeknown to anyone. A few of the other lads had been winding him up, joking that they were going to force him to have to sing a solo number and they all started laughing. The player concerned had a voice that some of the lads would impersonate during the past couple of years. After the latest wind-up about his voice, he stood up, grabbed a glass jug and smashed it into face of another lad who'd been laughing a few chairs down. It was violent and awful and it shook everyone who witnessed it and for a time, we thought the lad was a goner – thank god we had a trained nurse and the club doctor on hand to administer immediate treatment.

The player was rushed to hospital to have emergency surgery on the back of his ear which had been almost hanging off. An inch either way and his artery would have been severed and we'd have been looking at something along the lines of manslaughter. It was the worst injury I'd ever seen and it sickened everyone because it had been so shocking and it goes without saying that nobody had seen it coming because we'd have made sure it hadn't, had that been the case. I tried to help both players out as best I could but it was a huge test of my managerial skills. The positive atmosphere and energy that we had all been carried along on had gone and there was an uneasy feel about the place. It showed, too, in our next game which was a friendly at Bristol Rovers, where we played badly and lost 1-0. The shock was still reverberating amongst the team and with only a fortnight to go before the season started, I had to figure out what I could do to get things back on track, but then I had another problem to sort out.

After the Rovers game, one of the lads asked if he could get off and go with his family, which of course I said was fine, but on the coach going home I learned that he'd gone back to Plymouth with a club director because he wanted to get home quicker than the rest of us, which I was fuming about. I called the director on his mobile and asked if the lad was in his car and he said he was. I told him, "Don't you ever do that again. Tell him he's lied to me and I'll see him in my office in the morning. What gives him the right to get back sooner than the rest of us? Plus we've just lost so what will you be talking about on your way back? He shouldn't be party to anything like that – he's one of us and he should be on our bus."

I saw the lad the next day and we exchanged words and shortly after I had an assessment of the squad I had to present before the board. At the meeting, I told the directors that they couldn't be that close with the players and they couldn't have favourites, either. It was incredible how events had dictated a complete U-turn during that first month and there were all kinds of strange things happening. One minute we're playing Real Madrid in one of Plymouth's most high profile games ever, the next I'm at a police station wondering if one of my lads is going to prison or I'm arguing with a director – who'd be a bloody manager, eh? I had to get us winning football matches again and our next game was at Home Park against Yeovil and a semblance of normality returned as we won the game 2-0. Barry Hayles scored his first goal for us which was another bonus and I felt we were just about ready for the new season, a week away. I released the player who'd been involved from his contract, after he'd been at the Sporting Chance clinic.

I felt a lot of guilt about the incident in Austria. The dressing room is a tough place at times and you have to earn respect from other players – I knew that from my own experiences at Wimbledon and Bristol Rovers where I got stick about my nose, but I gave it back. I could laugh at my problems but how can anybody know things are going too far if there are no outward signs whatsoever? As a teenager breaking into the first team, you have to expect to be given stick by senior pros and you've got to give as good as you get or you'll never survive. But nobody knew how badly the mimicking was affecting him until he snapped. It was a new experience for me and one I never want to go through again. I did consider resigning at one point, the whole episode had been that horrific and I still can't get my head around how someone can bottle up so much and react so violently.

It had all been going too well and I had to pay for it somewhere down the line – life's like that, isn't it? There's always a price to pay and that's just the way things are.

We started to come out of the collective daze we'd be in and by the time we kicked off our new season, I think we'd just about returned to somewhere approaching normality and all that stood between us and a morale-boosting start, was Wolves at home. Happily, the injured party was fit in time for this game and was in my starting line-up. It was a tough game with more than 16,000 inside Home Park and I was pleased enough with our performance in a 1-1 draw. We had a ridiculous fixture at Colchester the following Tuesday night and we flew to that game. Layer Road is always a horrible place to go, but it was good to see my old mate, Colchester manager Geraint Williams, again and I was more than happy to leave with a 1-0 win, thanks to young Luke Summerfield's spectacular goal. It didn't get any easier and our next match was away to Sunderland who were wobbling badly and had lost their first two games under Niall Quinn and in hindsight, we couldn't have played them at a better time. Before the match I told the lads they had to have the constitution of a police horse. For me, horses are amazing beasts as they are trained to deal with stress or noises and bangs which are against their nature, because they are naturally flight animals. My thinking was, if they can do that with a horse, why couldn't I do the same with a group of footballers? A lot of that team talk was about having the right mentality and keeping our focus no matter what was going on around us. Everyone knew what their jobs were and we'd prepared really well, but before my bum hit the bench at the start of the game, we went 1-0 down. My lads didn't flinch, however, kept their focus and we went in 2-1 up at half-time. In the second-half they equalised and suddenly their fans woke up and went from being against their own team to being behind them – and my God that was scary! Then I had a choice to make and I decided to stick two strikers on because I wanted us to attack them whenever we had the chance because I didn't think we were good enough to keep them out for the remainder of the game. The bench thought I was mad but I made two attacking substitutions, one being Nick Chadwick, who goes and scores me the winner in the 87th minute. It was just a fantastic feeling. After the game I said I'd like to buy a drink for every one of our fans who travelled to watch us. I'd thought they'd been amazing and there must have been five or six hundred and they never stopped singing from start to finish, though they'd outdo themselves around a month later. I added another striker, Cherno Samba to the squad after that match and he was a kid who Des Bulpin had heard about and he'd been a bit of a wonderkid at Millwall a year or so before and Liverpool had been rumoured to have been on the verge of signing him for £1.5m. Millwall hadn't wanted to let him go, he couldn't handle it all so went back home to live with his parents in Spain. We got him over for a trial and I liked everything about the kid – he played with a smile on his face and did all the right things so we signed him.

Seven points from the first nine was exactly the start I'd hoped for, but we lost our Carling Cup match against Walsall, which brought everyone back down to earth. I had a few words with their manager Richard Money afterwards because I thought their lads over-celebrated in the tunnel after the game, considering the level we were playing. I said, "Well done, you played well but get them real, eh?" I actually wished I hadn't said it afterwards because the fact was they were two leagues below us and he was right when he said it was a great result for them. I looked at the next three games and thought, 'good God!' We were playing an ex-Plymouth manager, an ex-Plymouth manager and then QPR! You couldn't have scripted three more connected games. It was a very difficult phase for me, in all honesty and first up was Sheffield Wednesday and Paul Sturrock at home. The Argyle fans love Sturrock – or 'Luggy' as they call him – because of everything he achieved during his time there as manager and they gave him a great reception. In fact, my chairman called me the day before the game and told me he was having a meal with him after the match and asked me a) did I mind? and b) did I want to come? I said I didn't mind but I didn't want to go because however the result went it just wouldn't be right. As it turned out, we lost 2-1 to a late goal meaning we hadn't won any of our first three home games which wasn't ideal and I was angry at myself for over trying because 1-1 would have been fine but I went for the win and I think it may have cost us the game. But you can't always get what you want, can you?

Chapter 24

Coach Holloway!

Two home defeats in a row meant I had to think outside the box a little, and on the following Monday morning, I decided to do something completely different and not even my staff knew what I had planned. A guy had written to me – a performance coach, I think he described himself as. He said that he'd read some of the things I'd said and he thought I was very positive and added he'd really like to work with me. I'd let him come into the dressing room for one match so he could assess what I was doing. Afterwards, he suggested I should watch a movie called Coach Carter, because I reminded him of that character. I watched the film and was blown away by it and I have to say, likening me to Coach Carter was a hell of a compliment. I'd decided I'd show the lads this movie as soon as we got beat because I thought I'd sussed them out. We'd done well, done well, done well, lost and then lost again and I could have lost the lads myself at that point. So on the Monday morning, I said to them, "Alright, get your trainers on, we're going to do something a bit different today." We organised some pots of tea and coffee and mini pasties and we headed over to the education room at the Pilgrim Centre where a lot of school kids with learning difficulties often come to study. We closed all the curtains, got the lads around the screen and Des said, "What are you showing? The Sheffield Wednesday game?" and I said, "No, this is for you as well."

I think the lads were waiting to see how I reacted to two defeats in a row, so when everyone was settled, I said, "OK lads. This is our training for today. Have what you want to eat and drink and just watch this film." They looked around at each other and there were one or two comments so I said, "No seriously, I just want you to watch a movie, thank you. Play the film." I didn't tell them why, I just wanted them to watch it together. Next to the screen was a blank flip chart and everyone got really into the film, because you can't help but get involved. It's a brilliant movie, and when it finished, we put the lights up and bang! Off I went. "That's how you lot are to me," I said. "And now I've had enough time with you to know exactly who you all are and it's all about my judgement on you and what you are going to bring to my club." I then proceeded to link each character with one of my players because they either did something in a similar way or they had personality traits that were the same and I nailed everyone of them and the lads were laughing as I did it, because they couldn't argue with my assessment. There were two lads who I always thought seemed a little isolated from the rest of the group – Ákos Buzasaky and Bojan Djordjic – both foreign lads, but we had three French lads at the club now and they weren't ostracised from everyone else so I couldn't understand it. Argyle had been champions twice in the previous three years, so there was no reason not to feel part of everything so it was baffling me but after watching Coach Carter I woke about 4am and thought, 'My God, that's it!' it was like, Eureka! I got a pad and scribbled down my thoughts while they were still fresh and wrote 'My champions won't do their suicides.' And then went back to sleep. What that actually means is, there was one kid in that film who was thrown out of the team by the coach because of ill-discipline and the coach said, "If you want to get back on my team, basketball is a privilege and you have to earn the right to have the privilege and I want you to do one thousand suicide runs for me." Suicide runs are one length of a basketball court and back again, plus sit-ups and push-ups and he had to do them within five days. He went away and thought about it and he came back and told the coach he wanted to play on the team, to which he replies, "OK, but you still owe me those things you need to have completed them by Friday and you'll never be able to achieve it. What is your biggest fear?" The kid then started trying to do the runs and by the deadline on Friday, the coach told him that he was still 85 suicides short and to get out of his gym. Then, two or three of the team said that they'd do his runs and push-ups because they'd seen how much he'd wanted it and he got back in the team. So I associated Bojan and Ákos with that and reckoned they weren't prepared to do our version of the suicide runs, whatever that might have equated to and thought what Coach Carter would have done and it was simple – he'd have thrown them out. One didn't do it because he tried too hard and the other lads weren't very nice to him and the other was moaning and whinging all the time so he'd created an atmosphere around himself so I threw him out. I said to Bojan, "You're not playing with us anymore. I'd do Ákos's suicides but I wouldn't do yours and I'm not having it in my club." I asked Paul Wotton if he'd do Bojan's suicides and he said, "No, I wouldn't." I think I'd pinned down everyone's character and nobody could argue, because I think I got every one of them right. I told Bojan that if he wanted to come back, he'd seen the film and he knew what he had to do. I told him he had to do what we wanted because we weren't going to do what he wanted and that he wasn't welcome. He didn't moan, scored four goals in his first youth team game and three his next game and he kept looking over at me and was very respectful. Our training improved because they'd seen how strong I was and it wasn't until another four weeks that he came to see me and I let him rejoin the group. What a bloody film! Talk about inspirational – I decided after I'd seen that film that every day of my life, I was going to live the right way, I was going to do and say the right thing. If it was good enough for Coach Carter, it was good enough me, because he cared about his players in the same way I do and playing for QPR or Plymouth Argyle is an unbelievable privilege that you have to earn. Being given talent in your feet is not enough as far as I'm concerned and I could not have got my point over any better. It was a bit unusual and a bit weird, but I think it worked because our spirit was excellent afterwards. I believe all of us can shine and I think we're all good at something and if I have one talent, it's that I think I can spot that shining within people and I can get to it and encourage it and take away some of the worries and concerns so that they can go away and shine. I cried my eyes out at that film because the essence of the story was what I believed in my heart. It was an immense moment for me.

Next up was Tony Pulis's Stoke away and our fans were pretty derogatory towards him because he'd been quite negative about Plymouth's chances of promotion before he'd left. It was a bit of a weird atmosphere to be honest. We played some nice stuff and we came home with a 1-1 draw, which was no more than we deserved. We were unbeaten away from home, but couldn't buy a win at Home Park and our next game was massive for me because it was the first time I'd come up against QPR since leaving.

I could have just as easily been sat in the visiting team dugout at Home Park but for off the field activities at Loftus Road that had been none of my doing. It was an odd experience to say the least. I was angry, emotional and wanted to smash Gary Waddock off the face of the planet because I still wasn't happy with what he'd said after I left. I focused on my team winning the game, but we fell behind to an early goal before levelling matters and then proceeded to pass them off the pitch, and how we didn't win that game, I'll never know. The Rangers fans were a little strange with me, though it was understandable because we were neck and neck in the table and they wanted their side to win. I was desperate to win, too, and ram Waddock's words down his throat and I was very aggressive on the line, I have to admit and I let him know exactly how I felt at one point which I have to admit I sort of regretted later. It was the most one-sided 1-1 draw I'd ever witnessed and I was proud of my lads. Waddock's comments afterwards were that his side had "done a job," and I thought, 'Yeah? Well where's the overnight change of style that you promised on a manager's seat that was still warm?' I didn't get caught up in everything, though, and shook his hand at the end. I wanted to be as professional as I could and just got in and got out, not sticking around to speak with anyone. I would never want to hurt Rangers or their fans, but Waddock's words had hurt – no two ways about it. To label me as a long-ball merchant was absolute bullshit and, well, that's enough on the subject.

For all our good away form, I still hadn't given our fans anything to cheer about at Home Park. We were fine in the table but had to start winning at home if we wanted to kick on. My chairman kept asking "What about the fans? The gates are still down," and I told him that they wouldn't come back if we weren't winning home games. We were playing attractive football, which is my philosophy, and if truth be told, the Argyle fans wouldn't have allowed me to do anything else. So the style wasn't an issue and my philosophy is to attack anyway, but there was something else we needed to fill Home Park each week. Don't get me wrong, if we were first or second, there'd be no problem but to get to that level we need the Green Army behind us each week, frightening the visitors to death each week.

The first time I heard a few moans was when we played top-of-the-table Cardiff City in our next home match. We were 2-0 down at half-time and I could hear a few groans around the ground as we went in and I'd not experienced that at Home Park before. Worse was to follow when we went 3-0 down and that made my next decision easy. I'd been toying with changing formation from 4-4-2 to 4-3-3 for the last few games because I felt we'd become a more potent attacking force, but the only problem being we hadn't actually had time to practice it on the training pitch. The funny thing was, we were playing quite well despite the score and then Des says, "What do you think, Oll?"

I said, "I think I've got to change things around."

"You can't do it without practising it," Des said, not without good reason. But I thought now was the perfect opportunity. I had Lilian Nalis sat on the bench and I just thought 'why don't you make your own feckin' mind up and do something Holloway? There's nothing to lose.' It meant taking two senior players off to make it work, but I had to do what was right for the team so I took off my skipper Paul Wotton and left-back Anthony Barness and brought on Nalis and Nick Chadwick. I explained to Lil what I wanted us to do and I thought we'd be all right if he sat just in front of our centre-halves in a Claude Makelele kind of role and pushed my full-backs in. We started sending the ball long and then picking up the scraps because we had enough players forward to do that. Cardiff kept their formation and because of the timing of our substitutions, Dave Jones didn't really have time to envisage what we might do. It was a gamble, pure and simple but almost immediately we pulled it back to 3-1 with a bit of a scuffy goal. The lads kept plugging away and pulled it back to 3-2, though time was running out. Then, with five minutes left, we made it 3-3. I'd rolled my dice a different way and it'd paid off – this time. Des said, "Oh, well done genius," but he'd been quite right saying I shouldn't have tried 4-3-3 without trying it out first. The fans had loved it and even though we were still without a home win, it felt like we had won and I felt like a manager, too. That might sound odd, but there are plenty of times you don't feel like a manager, trust me. I told Dave Jones afterwards that all the reports I'd had back on his team said there were no weaknesses throughout the side and he thanked me for that, but the reports on our next opponents, Southampton, were the best I'd ever seen. I decided to start with 4-3-3 again to try and unsettle them but it turned out to be the most bizarre game I can ever remember. Three of my players were knocked out by head clashes and two had to be carried off on a stretcher. Our goalie hit his head on the post and had to come off for treatment, and I'd lost two players by half-time. The personnel we'd lost meant I couldn't switch back to 4-4-2 and that eventually cost us a goal but the one thing I did take from the game was pride. Our supporters, and there must have been around a thousand of them there at St Mary's that day, never stopped singing from the first minute till the last and it was the most amazing feeling I've ever had at a football match – and my team weren't even playing that well. "Green Army, Green Army, Green Army!" or "Ian Holloway's green and white army!" It was fantastic and sounded like a constant hum throughout the 90 minutes. Whether they'd carried on from the Cardiff game or whether they'd always been like that, I'll never know, but I'll never forget it or the professionalism my players showed in difficult circumstances – it's odd, but when I'm old and grey, that's one of the days I'll cherish – and we lost 1-0! I've bumped into one or two Southampton fans since and they've all said that they've never heard an away following sing like that before, not unless they were winning, so take a bow Green Army – that's another pint I owe you all.

Pen and Tim Breacker had eventually joined me with their gardening leave situation finally sorted out and I felt like all the pieces of the jigsaw were coming together. I'd also brought in a big centre-half in the form of Marcel Seip because we'd been after a big defender because height was something we'd missed at the back up to that point.

Better still, we then went on a seven-match unbeaten run and finally ended our home jinx by beating Norwich City in the next game. We beat Derby County 3-1 with 10 men live on Sky, which was unusual for Argyle because the club had a history of freezing in front of the cameras, and seeing Billy Davies again was good because I've got a load of time for him. It reminded me of a time Gordon Bennett brought him along to one of the youth games at Bristol Rovers and he played against my side – he was small, but what a player. He had three lads on him and the next thing he'd scooped the ball up over all of them and was away. He was the best player I ever saw at junior level and afterwards Gordon came around to my house and said, "What did you make of him, then?" I said I thought he was brilliant and he said, "Well he won't be playing for us. You're a different type, but, do you think he was good enough?" I said yes, of course and Gordon said, "What are you worried about your feckin' height for then? You've got a good foot on him."

I was happy with the way things were shaping up and when we did lose at home to Birmingham, we battered Steve Bruce's side but lost 1-0, and even Steve couldn't work out how we'd come away with nothing. If it had been a boxing match it would have been stopped in the first half. Prior to our away game at Southend a few weeks later, Bojan Djordjic came up to me and asked, "Why am I not I playing?"

I said, "Why haven't you been asking me about it? You seem happy playing where you are."

"No, I'm desperate to come back," he said.

"Well any chance of showing us a bit more? If you do, I'll put you back in." I don't believe for one minute that Bojan thought I'd ever play him again at first-team level but I picked him for Southend and he scored our goal in a 1-1 draw. Then I played him against Leeds and he scored a goal and he played in the next game against Luton and scored the winner so I was absolutely delighted with him.

It was around that time that the partner of the chief executive asked if I'd mind coming and giving and talk at the school she worked at because she had to do a talk about exams in front of all the kids. I'd done a few speeches at dinners and suchlike while I'd been on gardening leave so I said no problem. They were year 10 and 11 students, and she told them about the importance of taking exams and the various rules and regulations surrounding the actual exam itself. Then it was my turn because she thought that if I talked about how important taking your exams was, they might listen better to me because I was manager of Plymouth Argyle. The main problem the school was having were students not attending the exams so I tried to think how I could link taking exams back to my players. We did coursework of sorts through the week and then were tested on a Tuesday or a Saturday. Then we were marked on our performance – even though ours was in the paper – and I told all this to the kids and I thoroughly enjoyed it. All I basically was saying was that you have to set a goal on what you wanted to do and where you wanted to be. I told them we are all tested in whatever we did, every day. Whatever hairstyle you choose, the clothes you wear is all a test because you are putting yourself up for judgement against other kids, but it's what you want to do in the future that really matters because everyone needs to earn money and to do that you have to have a job. I asked them wouldn't it be better if, like me and my players, you earned money doing something you actually enjoyed? I asked them to imagine having to earn money doing something that you didn't like doing. I told them they were in control of their own futures and they had to think long and hard about how they were going to arrive at their goal – if they did that, all roads in their lives would lead to that destination. If they didn't, their lives would be like a roundabout going round in circles. I was lucky because I only ever wanted to do one thing and I had a focus. I told them they needed to look at exams differently because they could be the beginning of a fantastic journey.

I thoroughly enjoyed talking to the kids and I then got a call from the lady who'd asked me to do the talk in the first place. She said, "There's not been one absentee from the exams. It was a one hundred per cent turn out and it's a school record – everyone turned up." I was absolutely delighted about that and talking with those kids actually helped me in my job as a manager. It opened my eyes to different ways of getting a point across and how important it was to go out in the community and get the natives on your side, because without their support, I can't do anything. If the supporters aren't singing your name and don't believe in you, they won't cut you any slack and you won't make it. If I fail at Argyle, it won't be for the want of trying, I can assure everyone of that.

Chapter 25

The Trouble With Refs...

We were still fairly well placed in the table and definitely in with a chance of the play-offs going into 2007, but there were areas of the team I felt needed strengthening because whenever I had players ruled out with injury I was having to put younger and younger kids in to replace them as the squad became seriously stretched. I had a budget of around £200,000 to bring in new players and we needed another striker and a centre-half, but I didn't think the money I had would get me very far. Pen had been out on the road and was working ever so hard to find new talent that we could afford and he had one or two interesting ideas that might or might not bear fruit.

We played Southampton on New Year's Day and after a couple of blatant offside goals had been scored against us in previous matches, I was absolutely fuming and fit to burst by the time we played that game and by the end of it, I'd lost it completely. I'd never been a fan of the new offside laws so you can probably imagine how I felt when we were the victims of the new rule not once, but twice in the same bloody game! We should either have won the game 1-0 or 2-1 instead of the actual 1-1 scoreline it ended up. There were two identical incidents during the game and on the first occasion they scored one that was given and we scored one and it was disallowed, and the second instance with exactly the same circumstances, they scored and it was given. Southampton hit a ball over the top and one of their forwards was a mile offside so my keeper came out and cleared it but it went straight to the guy who'd been offside but when he rolled it into an empty net, the ref gave the goal. He'd been offside and gained an unfair advantage but they go 1-0 up regardless. We make it 1-1 and in the last couple of minutes, David Norris scores for us in similar circumstances only because the keeper is on his line, it's ruled out for offside. I took my video evidence into the officials' room at the end of the game but would they watch it? Would they hell! Later, I got a call from referee assessor Paul Durkin telling me I'd been right to protest, and the incidents would now be used to help train refs and show them how they sometimes get it wrong!" It didn't help us because we'd lost two points and that could have been the difference in the last few games between us challenging for a play-off spot or not. Maybe I'm clutching at straws but it would have made a difference and I'm still minging about that to this day.

Then came the Saturday all managers dread – FA Cup Third Round day. We'd drawn Peterborough away, which might not sound too daunting, but with the injury crisis we had by then, added to that fact that Peterborough were flying at home and had already knocked out Ipswich Town at London Road in the Carling Cup and they were right up for us that day. I could feel the cold steel on the back of my neck and it's a horrible time. We arrived with a really young side but were awarded a penalty which Hasney Aljofree took and missed. The ref wasn't happy, however, and ordered a re-take which Hansey tucked away, but they equalised and took the game to replay.

The board told me they were happy with the way things were going and I said that we needed a few new players in to up the ante, particularly if we wanted to have a crack at getting into the play-offs, and to be fair to them, the first time I asked for help, they gave it to me. I managed to sign Rory Fallon for £300,000 – a record fee paid by Argyle – and two Hungarian lads in Péter Halmosi and Krisztián Timár on loan, plus Kevin Gallen on loan and though I knew what a great signing Gallen could be, I knew absolutely bugger all about the Hungarians. All I knew was that Pen had recommended them and that was good enough for me. I'd called Pen up and said that I might need a few players in and he said, "Don't worry, come over because I think I've got a few players for you to look at."

I said, "What? Have you got them in your front room or something?"

"No, I've got some DVDs and I've done some homework on them and they're coming out as great characters." I went round, watched the DVDs and said, "I'll have them. I like that, they both look quality."

Pen told me to bring Timár over for a trial, which we did and I liked his attitude – another one who'd kick his grandma – and Hamolsi turned out to be a very accomplished midfielder and a totally professional footballer with stacks of ability, and I thought bringing those two lads in would get me another player, because Buzsáky had been homesick up to that point whereas now he had two compatriots to settle him down a little. I used some of the lads in our next game at Norwich and we won 3-1. I then added Chelsea reserve striker, Scott Sinclair, who had become a bit stale in the stiffs at Stamford Bridge. He was quick and Pen reckoned we could use him as an impact player. I was pleased with the new additions and we hadn't spent a fortune in doing so, either. I'd spent £1.2m in my first year – more than I'd ever done before as a manager, so the Argyle board are giving it a real go, aren't they?

We saw off Peterborough 2-1 in the replay but then I got hauled into the Mike Newell bungs controversy which broke in the second week of January. I'd made some statements when I'd been at QPR and my former chairman Nick Blackburn included them in a book he'd written not that long after. The incident had happened while Rangers were in administration and I'd been trying to sign a player on a free so I told the agent I was dealing with, "There's got to be no fee because we're in administration and we can't get any money to pay any fees." The agent said not to worry and everything was fine. We talked about a contract and the length of it and the agent calls me back the next day and says, "Well there is a fee, actually, because there's an agent's fee." I think it was £40,000 or something so I said, "Didn't you hear me yesterday? I've got no money, so there's no deal."

Then he said, "No, wait a minute, you don't understand. How much of it do you want?" I said, "Look, do me a favour, you idiot. I'm going to talk to my chairman because there's no deal now." I put the phone down, told Nick that I was sorry for wasting his time and asked if he'd call the agent to confirm the deal was dead because he'd now asked for money and even asked how much I wanted.

My quotes were out there, then when Mike came out with his statements on bungs and stuff, I think a journalist either recalled or was tipped off to the quotes attributed to me in Nick's book and this reporter said, "Well you've been offered bungs haven't you?"

I said, "No, not really. It was a conversation and that's all." I explained what had happened and that I didn't hate agents but the facts were that if a window of opportunity is presented in life, somebody will grab it. The problem is that there shouldn't be any loopholes which have been caused by the Bosman ruling because that would eliminate a lot of these windows of opportunity, and there wouldn't be so many grey areas surrounding transfers deals. As for Mike and his comments, I'm not sure what he was doing and couldn't believe what he was coming out with. He seemed to be trying to tar everyone with the same brush, but what I couldn't do at the time was leave him stood out on a limb so I wasn't denying what had happened to me, but nothing ever came of it so there was no problem. I got sort of sucked into that whole row whereas I wouldn't have actively been involved otherwise.

Back to action on the pitch and we were due to play Coventry City away when I heard that my old mate Mickey Adams had been sacked. He called me up and said, "Beat that lot for me, would you?" which was typical of Mickey's humour though I knew he was hurting badly after that. Adrian Heath was put in charge for the game, which was live on Sky, and we won 3-2 – we were getting a taste for live TV!

Our next FA Cup opponents were Barnet away and, just like Peterborough, it was a tricky tie and against a bloody good home side. They were probably a little bit better than us in the first half but after the break I decided to freshen things up by taking off Peter Halmosi and Akos Buzsáky and replacing them with Scott Sinclair and Luke Summerfield. We went 1-0 up through an Aljofree penalty and then Scott scored a goal that probably only he could have scored, taking on and beating half of the Barnet side before slotting it home, cool as a cucumber. That was his first senior goal and it gave all the lads a real boost. We knew what he could do because he'd done it in training and after turning two of our best players inside out during one run I remember Paul Connolly, a Liverpudlian right-back and wag of a lad saying, "Fuckin' hell! He's better than Aaron Lennon. Where the fuck did you get him from? Can you play him over the other side or what, gaffer?"

Scott had earned the respect of our lads straight away and that was nice for the kid, especially coming from a club like Chelsea and it could have been hard for him. I was also pleased on a personal level because I'd seen him as a 10-year-old when I was player-manager of Bristol Rovers and to see that boy becoming the player he is becoming – he's not there yet – is very pleasing for me. He hadn't changed a bit in that time, either, and was as solid as a rock – he doesn't drink and is never late and does everything properly – a lovely kid – and to see him score that goal was fantastic. It also put us in the fifth round of the FA Cup – a place I'd never been as a manager before.

Like everyone else, when the draw was about to be made we were hoping for a big tie at Home Park – but I'd have taken anyone at home. I watched it live and we drew Derby at home – and shortly after they showed all the Derby players' faces when they found out they had to go to Plymouth again, having already lost against us not that long ago and we'd only had 10 men. It was the last team they probably wanted to be drawn against, but for us it was great. They were top of the table so it'd be a decent test of how far we'd come and if we lost, there would be no disgrace but I used the Derby players' body language to our advantage because they'd made it so obvious they weren't relishing coming to us.

In between our Cup progress we still had League games to win and a trip to The Hawthorns to play West Brom had me jumping around on the line again because I thought the ref was treating the match as Big Club v Little Club and I wondered if I'd contributed to that by saying to him before the game by saying, "Great ground isn't it?" He seemed awe-struck and said, "What a club – it's amazing isn't it? Great atmosphere." It was unbelievable but I have to say he was right – I just didn't want to hear that from the man in charge of the game!

West Brom had Diomansy Kamara and Kevin Phillips and several other good attacking players but I wasn't happy with the way everything seemed to be going against us. The ball hit Akos Buzsáky's hand but it was a classic case of ball-to-hand and the ref gave a penalty. They went 2-0 up through a brilliant Kamara goal before big Rory Fallon scored his first goal for us to make it 2-1. Then Sylvan Ebanks-Blake broke through, lifted it over Dean Kielybut was felled by him as the ball rolled towards goal but was cleared by a defender. It was a stonewall penalty but the ref topped that by doing the same thing again when Tony Capaldi pushed it past a West Brom player in the box, only to be clattered by a two-footed challenge. I couldn't believe what I was seeing – it was the worst decision I'd ever seen up to that point. Incredible!

I rested a few players for our next game at Wolves, which was a bit of a gamble, but the young lads did really well, particularly 17-year-old Danny

Gosling, and we came away with a 2-2 draw. Next up were Roy Keane's Sunderland and I must admit that game was our most comprehensive defeat because Sunderland shackled us down and beat us 2-0 at Home Park and I was very impressed with them.

Then came the day we'd be waiting for – the FA Cup tie with Derby County. This was a huge game for us and boy oh boy – what a performance. There was a massive crowd and I had a virtually full strength team to pick from, though I had to decide if Barry Hayles was fit enough after just about recovering from a broken toe. I decided to go with Sylvan and Kevin Gallen, who can link up play fantastically well and was probably the perfect foil for Sylvan. Kev drops back and can ping the ball all over the place and plays a kind of Teddy Sheringham role for us. Things had started to improve for Sylvan by this point, because he'd been having a tough time up till then and was even booed off during one game – that seemed to snap him out of whatever it was that was stopping him playing to his full potential. The whole of Plymouth was talking about the game and a lot of people were saying that the last really great Cup run Argyle had been on saw them beat Derby before getting knocked out to Watford, who were, by coincidence, still in the last 16 this time around. I told a few journalists that mentioned it that it was alright for them to go on about it but it didn't mean much to me.

So Billy Davies brings his side to Home Park and we played as well as we'd done all season from the first whistle to the last. We competed for everything, we were disciplined we scored two goals and they had a man sent off. We were given two penalties as well in that game, though Kevin Gallen missed one, but that meant in two home games against Derby that season we'd been given four penalties, and Billy had moaned like hell about that, but I think we'd earned a bit of luck, and I'm a firm believer in what goes around comes around, even though Derby had done us no harm. We seemed destined for the quarter-finals and that was the best overall performance by any of the teams I've ever managed. We were in the quarter-final and the whole city was going crazy. Again, I just wanted a home draw and Chelsea and Manchester United were the teams we most wanted. I didn't care who it was, so long as we didn't have to travel and, just as everyone had predicted, we pulled Watford out of the hat. We were actually the last two sides out and I was just relieved that we came out first. We were just two wins from Wembley and if I could pull that one off, I really would be the Pig of Plymouth!

We played just as well against Colchester two days later and won 3-0 so the confidence seemed to be growing and we were on something of a roll – so I thought. I can't say I was looking forward to my next game, which was away to QPR.

Gary Waddock had gone and John Gregory had taken over and I'd called him to congratulate him on the appointment. He let us use QPR's training ground prior to the match, which was fantastic so for me, all the animosity was gone and all I wanted to do was win the game. I had no problem with Gianni Paladini, either. I felt very emotional the night before the game because I'd spent five years at Loftus Road but it had felt like ten after all the problems we'd had and for most of that time I felt like I'd been the cement trying to hold everything together. I hoped I'd get a good reception from the QPR fans but I didn't really care because I just wanted to focus on winning the game. I was too emotional and I went out of the tunnel just before the game kicked off because I didn't want to be the centre of attention but I think things will be easier next time because football is like a river flowing underneath a bridge and hopefully a lot more water will have gone under by then. In hindsight, I wished I'd not done what I did at Loftus Road that day and think I would have felt better if I'd at least gone out and clapped for some of the QPR fans. As for the game itself, we went in 1-0 up at the break and in the second half, our goalie is rammed sideways as he caught the ball, drops it and Lee Cook taps it home. My lads stopped, waiting for the foul to be given but instead the ref points to the centre circle. It had to have been a foul and Lilian Nalis, the most placid man on the face of the Earth, then chases the referee to argue the decision and gets booked and then five minutes later he gets booked again, still arguing about the goal. We held out for a draw but the whole day had been a bit surreal and had felt a bit like my dad's funeral where I'd felt like I'd not really been there. I'd needed to shut down to cope with the day and I think I ruined what should have been a pleasant experience because the QPR fans were very friendly and nice and I believe they were chanting my name before I came out. I felt like one thing might trigger me off and the last thing you want to do is blub in front of your bloody subs. I might not have applauded the Rangers fans that day, but I am now, so thanks for your support during those five years and thanks for the way you treated me on my return – it meant an awful lot.

Chapter 26

Life On the Ocean Waves

As the 2006/07 season drew towards its conclusion, it seemed every game had some kind of edge to it and our game after QPR was Stoke City at home and the return of my old Rovers team-mate Tony Pulis. Pu had done a brilliant job keeping Argyle up the previous year and it would be unfair to say everyone was gunning for him on his first return to Home Park. He'd alienated a lot of fans by his negative comments, but I think he just did what he had to do to keep Argyle up and I have to say he also left me with a great bunch of lads. I wanted to distance myself from any perceived Holloway v Pulis sideshow and instead sat in the stand initially, though I had to go down the moment I saw something I didn't like. We drew 1-1 which was a fair result, though I knew my directors had been desperate to win that one!

The talk was all about Watford and the build up to the game was hugely enjoyable. We still had business in the League to deal with first, though and our trip to Sheffield Wednesday left me absolutely bewildered. Remember I said the decision at West Brom where Capaldi was almost snapped in half was the worst I'd ever seen up to that point? Well that's because an incident at Hillsborough eclipsed even that. I changed the team around again in preparation for Watford and the referee that day was guilty of the worst decision I'd ever seen at any level as a kid, adult – anywhere. The score was 0-0 when a ball came across into our box and our goalie catches it and as he does, their striker stumbles – I think purposely after watching replays – and hits our keeper's legs as though he's been fired out of a cannon. It flattened our goalie and he drops the ball to one of their players who thought he was going through the motions of tapping the ball in regardless, a little embarrassed by his actions judging by his body language. Not dissimilar to the foul we'd been on the end of at QPR, our lads stop, look over to the linesman and he's only kept his flag down. I was watching it all in disbelief and I've got to say the Sheffield Wednesday fans were absolutely hilarious and I love them for their reaction. They were leaning over and apologising to me because they'd never seen anything like it, either. When Lilian Nalis had got sent off at QPR, I went mad at him for losing his rag and said referees would make mistakes and it was futile showing any dissent. With that in mind my lads calmly get on with it but it was me going ballistic on the side like a complete fruitcake. My lads then go and equalise and then dominate the remainder of the game. The Wednesday fans were telling me it was embarrassing. "Your reserves are twice as good as our first team Ollie!" was one shout I liked. We drew 1-1 but I was incensed and after watching the replay several times on my laptop I thought, 'Bugger it.' I went to the ref's room singing an old Eighties song, 'You're unbelievable,' as I banged on his door. I went in and started to say my piece. He said, "You're raising your voice."

"Raising my voice?" I turned to the linesman. "And what the hell were you doing?"

"Oh I couldn't see it from my angle." "Couldn't see it? Everyone in the ground saw it, what are you talking about? What's the matter with you?"

I was out of order but I needed to get that off my chest and I calmed down a bit after that. But it was another two points lost and when you look at our final total, it's heartbreaking that such clear-cut decisions didn't go our way because if they had, I believe we'd have sneaked into the play-offs.

Then – at last – the game was here – Watford at home in the FA Cup with the winner going into the semi-finals. I was stunned by the media interest in us but we managed to box them all off in one day and there were some fantastic interviews done. One bloke from The Sunday Times spent three hours with me and Kim and wrote a blinding article on our lives – apart from the fact he called me an unfashionable, scruffy, little Bristolian!

I got presented with a gift from FA Cup sponsors Eon because I'd made a comment about my teams being like a cheap tea bag – we didn't stay long in the cup – and Eon sent me an expensive box of tea bags with a letter saying, "You can't call yourself a cheap tea bag anymore, Mr Holloway." These were only small things, but they meant a lot to me.

The whole of Plymouth had gone mad, the lads were up for it and it was a relief that the game was finally here. The whole squad was fit and for the first time since I'd been at the club I had to leave some of the lads in the stand. It was live on the BBC on a Sunday evening – it was a huge occasion.

We prepared meticulously and went over and over Watford's main threat which was from set-pieces and blow me, what happens in the end? They score from a set-piece and we lose the game 1-0. We'd felt like we had half a chance but despite throwing everything at them, we just couldn't score on the night. I was incredibly proud of my team, who played without fear and gave me everything but young Mr Foster – in their goal – who didn't play in the bloody semi-final – was superb. Man United wouldn't let him play against them in the semi and how can that be fair? If you a loan a player out, he should be able to play against anyone, not who the club who own him choose.

So I was left bursting with pride but fuming as well. It felt like I was always the bridesmaid, never the bride. We had 10 league games left and I told the lads that if we could win nine of them, I thought we'd get in the play-offs, because we were good enough. We had a game two days later and came back down to earth with a bump, losing 4-2 to Barnsley, who had a terrific attitude in that match, but I think my lads tried to too hard to win it when it was 2-2, probably because of what I'd said about winning all our games. I think they tried too hard to make it happen and it cost us three points, so I'll never say anything like that again.

We bounced back with a win over Crystal Palace thanks to a wonder goal from Scott Sinclair and that win eased a little bit of the pressure I was feeling but all it did was precede what I now call The Week From Hell (TWFH). Because of the Cup run, we had to squeeze in a game with Burnley and I'd gone for the soonest possible free day because I thought we could take advantage of the rotten run they'd been on. Carole, the secretary at Plymouth said to me, "Do you think that's wise, Ollie, playing Ipswich, Burnley, and Leeds all away within a week?" I said, "Carole, Burnley are on a bad run, we need to get it in so let's do it." So we did, but boy did I learn to rue that day! TWFH began at Portman Road where I had every confidence we could do well, but I lose my centre-half in the first minute. My lad nudged the Ipswich player, who went over like he'd been shot and the ref waves play on. The linesman, meanwhile, puts his flag up, play stops and the ref speaks to the lino and then gives my lad a straight red – how can you go from waving play on and giving no foul whatsoever on to sending someone off? How could he not see a foul and still give someone their marching orders. I saw him afterwards and he said that it had been a goalscoring opportunity and I asked him if he'd had any idea how quick my centre-half was and that there was no way he'd have time to do that. We went in 2-0 down and then Sylvan Ebanks-Blake goes through after charging the ball down and scores a great goal. The same linesman kept his flag down but the ref disallows it for handball. Had it gone to 2-1, I think they'd have been twitchy and reckon we could have got something. I couldn't believe it and we end up losing 3-0. Next we went up to Burnley who hadn't won for 19 games and everything they did was spot-on that night and everything we did was useless – it was just one of those games that we'd been destined to lose. It didn't look like my team that night and we were 3-0 down at the break and eventually lost 4-0. TWFH was about to get even worse, though. Next up were Leeds and to be fair to the lads, their response was fantastic even though we lost 2-1 to a last minute goal. So my win nine from 10 had started well, with one win and four defeats from five and we sank to our lowest position in the table all season and I'm feeling the pressure again! Who'd be a manager?

We then end the season by winning our last five games, stacking up the club's best ever finish and set a new club record for most points in a season at Championship level. Peter Halmosi blossomed towards the end of last season and looks like he's going to be a real find for us and I have to say that we probably ended up around about where we should have done, just outside the play-offs – but we could have done so much more. The amount of rubbish decisions that we were on the end of probably cost us about eight points and that would have been enough to get us in the top six. I've never had a season when my team has competed so well in almost all of the games we played so I feel really positive about my first year with the Green Army. The support we've had has been fantastic and they're unbelievable, these people, and I think that, with a little more luck, a bit more belief and the whole city behind us, we can take what I think is the club's rightful place in the Premiership – and won't that ruffle a few feathers? Ollie and the Green Army rubbing shoulders with Man U and Chelsea.

I can't wait.

Well there you are, that's my life in brief, and the one thing I've learned is that my whistle is my family – not my job, not football, and I'm going to endeavour to do my best for them for the rest of my life. Nobody on their death-bed ever says 'I wish I'd spent more time at work'. Human nature demands we place importance on money and we can sometimes very easily get it wrong. I strongly advise anyone reading this to weigh up the balance between what is important and what isn't. Make sure you shift the bar if the balance between work and family life is off-kilter, especially if you have young kids, because you only get one chance to educate your children. Make sure you get it right and make sure you keep your ego in check, because I think nearly all of us are guilty of doing that from time to time, especially us blokes.

So where are we all today? Well, my mum's doing really well. She takes more tablets than Moses climbing the mountain, and I swear I can hear her rattle when she walks, but she's 74, and an absolute star – and she still works at a chemist in Bristol, which is quite handy because she's also their best customer!

My sister Sue and her husband Phil have sold their business, as they'd always planned to do when he reached 50. They are enjoying their granddaughter, Iris, given to them by their daughter Becky and her husband Vaughan, and I don't think I've ever seen two happier people – or a baby spoiled with love quite so much.

As for my little ones, well, they aren't so little anymore. Eve is still doing equine studies and doing very, very well and she's hoping to get her national diploma in horse care. Chloe, who'd been doing the same course decided that wasn't for her and in her own inimitable way said, "Dad, I don't want to shovel horse-shit all my life," so she's off doing other things now and is pursuing art at a college in Exeter and she's got quite a talent, too – very instinctive and natural. Hattie is studying for her GSCEs, totally unsure of what she wants to do, though with the amount of pictures she sends up to her boyfriend, it could be something to do with photography. She constantly asks me if we can move Hornchurch closer to Plymouth and I tell her if she folds the map in half and glues it together, it looks really close.

Will is still in Bristol being 'looked after' by his older cousin Luke, who is doing a fantastic job, and we're incredibly proud of both lads. Wills, Paul Lewton and me are in the process of setting up a building company that William will be a partner in.

Kim loves living in Devon and has started writing again, after being inspired by somebody we met recently, though I can't reveal his name... She's picked up her laptop again and I've never seen her happier when it all starts flowing again.

My brother John is still treading the boards in Surbiton and has just finished a project where he was working with Johnny Depp and Sacha Baron Cohen, which was all very exciting and will hopefully lead to other things for him, and I wish him all the best in that.

Kim's mini-me, her sister Trudi, is now happily married to Dave who is a Formula One racing car designer and Trudi is now a player with a big American company. Kim's mum Wendy is courageously battling breast cancer and it's fantastic to see her dad Terry has overcome his battle with bladder cancer. .

That's about it, really. What about Ollie? Well, I just watched the movie Castaway recently and I'm just waiting to see what the tide brings in for me. You never know what is going to be washed up next, but as long as I keep combing the beach each day and realising what's important and what's not, I think I'll be OK. I may not be the finished article yet, but I'm getting there, I believe.

As for my dad, well, I think about the old bugger all the time, and though I can't actually prove he's seen everything that's happened to my family and me, part of me knows he has. He's watched my career and seen my children growing up and I hope in my heart he is as proud of them as I am, because that's what he taught me all those years ago, that the most important thing in your life is your family.

Now, as the great Robert Shaw once said while portraying Quint in Jaws, "Farewell and adieu to you fair Spanish ladies..."